# BEHIND
# ENEMY LINES
# WITH THE S.A.S.

# BEHIND ENEMY LINES WITH THE S.A.S

*Amédée Maingard,*
*code name 'Sam',*
*SOE agent in France 1943–1944*

## Paul McCue

Pen & Sword
**MILITARY**

First published in Great Britain in 2007 by
Pen & Sword Military
an imprint of
Pen & Sword Books Ltd
47 Church Street
Barnsley
South Yorkshire
S70 2AS

ISBN 978 1844 15618 4

A CIP catalogue record for this book is
available from the British Library

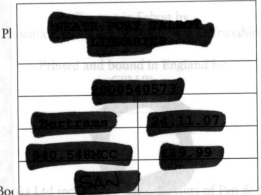

Pen & Sword Books Ltd incorporates the imprints of Pen & Sword Aviation,
Pen & Sword Maritime, Pen & Sword Military, Wharncliffe Local History,
Pen & Sword Select, Pen & Sword Military Classics and Leo Cooper.

For a complete list of Pen & Sword titles please contact
PEN & SWORD BOOKS LIMITED
47 Church Street, Barnsley, South Yorkshire, S70 2AS, England
E-mail: enquiries@pen-and-sword.co.uk
Website: www.pen-and-sword.co.uk

Car tout passe
Comme l'ombre d'un rêve
Qui n'a jamais été


For it all passes by
Like a shadowy dream
That never was


By Lieutenant Maurice Pertschuk (served as Lieutenant Maurice Perkins), SOE 'Prunus' circuit, Gers region, France 1942–3. Arrested April 1943. Executed in Buchenwald concentration camp, Germany, 29 March 1945.

# Contents

# Introduction and Acknowledgements

The impetus to my writing this biography came first and foremost from Alain Antelme, the nephew of a SOE agent executed by the Germans during the war, and a former employee and friend of Amédée Maingard.

Alain's initial approach, from Mauritius, came after I had written of Major Maingard in my earlier book, *SAS Operation Bulbasket*, and with the support of the Maingard family, Alain asked if I would undertake a biography. Although I declined due to other commitments, I subsequently agreed to carry out the UK-based element of the research.

The writer of the book was then to be Tony Kemp, an established author with special forces expertise. But the events of 11 September 2001, and the involvement of special forces in the ensuing conflicts, saw Tony in great demand so that he regretfully had to withdraw from the project. Having by then amassed extensive material from official UK sources (this was still prior to the release of many SOE files into the public domain), I was reluctant to see the project stall and I agreed to take over.

In one respect I was fortunate in that Tony had not yet put pen to paper when he had to pull out, which means that neither he nor I need worry over apportioning blame for errors. Any that exist are unarguably my own. I am grateful, however, to have been able to use early notes and the tapes from two interviews conducted by Tony in Mauritius.

Among the many others who have helped, Sue Spencer deserves very special thanks for taking over the typing at a point when my own limited ability and lack of speed threatened to extend the book's gestation period by at least a decade. In addition, Brenda Ayling proved a master of structure charts, Mick Henson kindly produced the maps and the close scrutiny of Catherine Parsons as proofreader was invaluable.

The patience and support of my wife, Alison, and my daughter, Holly, were as constant as could reasonably be expected and the latter even accompanied her father on a number of research trips. As a result, I appreciate that some will find it unnatural for a six-year-old girl to understand perfectly the concept of sabotage.

My grateful thanks are also extended to:

**Great Britain:** Beaulieu Estate; Freddie Clark; (the late) David Dane; Paul Dawson; David Harrison; Sandra Macniven; Mallaig Heritage Centre; Ron McKeon; Sophie Moore; Malcolm Poole; Denis Rixson; Special Forces Club; Brian Spencer; Duncan Stuart; Kenneth Tattersall; Paul Wate; Michael Wallrock.

**France:** Sandrine Braun; Paul Chantraine; Jean-Louis Cirès; Pearl Cornioley; Louis R. Dalais; Veronique Dalais; Albert Dupont; Roger Ford; Maurice Fuzeau; Pierre Hirsch; Raymond Jovelin; Tony Kemp; Jean-Francois Maurel; Musée d'Eguzon; Maurice Nicault; Philippe Palancher; Roger Picard; Claude Pavard; Christian Richard.

**Mauritius:** Air Mauritius; the late Jean Larcher; Didier Maingard; Jacqueline Maingard; Jan Maingard; (the late) Sir René Maingard; Sir Harry Tirvengadum; Zsuzsanna Szemök.

**Réunion:** James Caratini (Le Collège Bourbon de Saint-Denis); Roxane Le Guen; Florence Leveneur.

**Canada:** Dr Antoine Hirsch; David Poissant; Judge Allyre Louis Sirois.

**United States:** OSS Society; Jenelle Peterson.

I would finally add that I have used the term Mauritius throughout the book, trusting that my French and Franco-Mauritian friends will understand that I did not wish to overcomplicate issues by using the more accurate Île de France for the period 1715–1810. Likewise I have used Réunion, though it was once Île Bourbon.

*Paul McCue*
*Witley, Surrey*

The Stationer circuit extended over 500 kilometres, from Châteauroux in central France to Tarbes near the Spanish border.

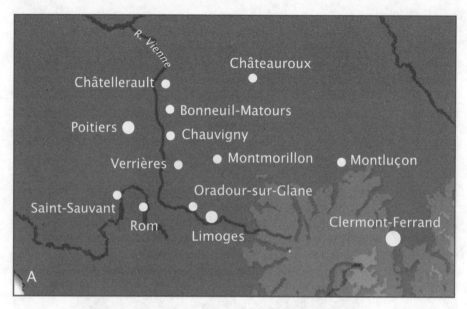

A – the central France sector of the 'Stationer' circuit.

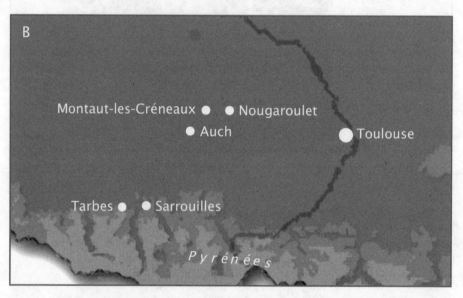

B – the southern sector of 'Stationer'.

# Foreword

Back in 1943, F Section of the Special Operations Executive (SOE) established the 'Stationer' circuit in occupied France. 'Stationer' was headed by 'Hector' (Maurice Southgate), a former school friend of mine, who was parachuted blind in January 1943 together with 'Jacqueline' (Jacqueline Nearne) as courier. The wireless operator, 'Samuel' (Amédée Maingard), was dropped in April 1943 and I, 'Marie' (Pearl Witherington), was parachuted in September of the same year also to act as courier to the circuit.

My thoughts and recollection of 'Samuel' are as clear today as they were all those years ago. Our relationship was always open and warm, and I fully trusted his complete understanding of the dangerous life which was ours, and in particular his – involving as it did his duty as a wireless operator, sending and receiving messages from the same room in Châteauroux for over a year.

'Hector' was recalled to England from October 1943 to January 1944 and while he was gone we received an order from London to 'sabotage the Michelin works in Clermont-Ferrand or we will bomb them!' I got in touch with the Resistance group in Clermont-Ferrand and gave them this ultimatum. After three failures of sabotage an RAF air raid hit the Michelin factory so precisely that no damage was done to the surrounding workmen's houses.

From September 1943 'Samuel' and I worked hand in hand and my admiration for him never failed. He became deputy to 'Hector' in April 1944. On 1 May 1944 I decided that we badly needed a rest and I organized a picnic by a lake at Montluçon. We set off from our circuit HQ while 'Hector' was away to greet the new circuit leader, being dropped by parachute, for the Auvergne region. To our horror and dismay 'Hector' was caught by chance when he arrived back at our HQ where the Gestapo, looking for someone else, had already discovered our secret messages.

It was at this point that I realized the grasp that 'Samuel' had of our sorry state. With great determination he immediately took charge and split our very large circuit into three smaller ones, taking responsibility himself for Châteauroux, Montmorillon, the Vienne and Haute-Vienne, the Charente and even beyond. He assigned Jacques Dufour to the Dordogne and I to the Nord-Indre/Vallée du Cher.

It was due to the maturity of 'Samuel' (although he was only twenty-five years old), his integrity, charisma and foresight, that our original circuit did not collapse and that we were all able to contribute to liberating these French regions.

Pearl Cornioley, née Witherington
Châteauvieux, France

# Chapter One

# 'Is there a house in the wood?'

On the night of 5/6 June 1944 the skies above Britain, the English Channel and the northern coastline of France were witnessing the spectacle and noise of the greatest naval and aerial armadas ever assembled. Yet as the Allied invasion of France was about to unfold, several hundred kilometres to the south of the Normandy beaches, few were disturbed by the deep drone of a lone *quadrimoteur* above the blacked-out countryside of German-occupied central France. The distinctive sound of four powerful aero engines suggested that the aircraft was Allied, but this was no straggler from bombing operations. For the Halifax, a variant of the RAF's standard heavy bomber, came from 161 (Special Duties) Squadron, based at Tempsford aerodrome in Bedfordshire, 50 miles north of London. And 161 Squadron, together with its sister unit at Tempsford, 138 Squadron, served two of Britain's most secret intelligence services: the Special Operations Executive (SOE) and the Secret Intelligence Service (SIS), the latter sometimes better known by its other title of MI6. The job of the two squadrons was to deliver agents and supplies, either by parachute drop or by landing at clandestinely prepared airstrips, behind enemy lines.

In addition to Pilot Officer Tattersall and his crew, the Halifax carried two special forces teams of five men in total, who were to be dropped into the Brenne marshes, some 30 kilometres south-west of Châteauroux in the Indre region. Three of the men constituted one of SOE's inter-allied Jedburgh teams, code-named 'Hugh', the first such team to be dropped into France. Reporting directly back to Special Forces Headquarters in England, 'Hugh' was detailed to make contact by 0900 hours on 6 June, and take orders from an agent code-named 'Samuel', who headed SOE's existing 'Shipwright' network in the Indre region. The mission of 'Hugh' was twofold: firstly, to help arm and train the thousands of Maquis volunteers who would now, with the invasion, be eager to join the Resistance movement; secondly, in the area Châtellerault–Châteauroux, to accompany a reconnaissance team from the 1st Special Air Service (SAS) Regiment and establish a base to receive SAS reinforcements for 'Operation Bulbasket', designed to carry out raids on enemy lines of communication.

The latter task, a late amendment to the role of 'Hugh', was indicative of the eagerness of the different special forces factions in Britain to make a contribution to the invasion of the Continent. As a result, a two-man advance party from

1

1st SAS's B Squadron, Captain John Tonkin and Lieutenant Richard Crisp, comprised the second team flying in the Halifax, having joined the Jedburgh team at a relatively late stage. This was a not entirely welcome surprise for the Jedburgh leader, Captain Bill Crawshay, who felt he already had quite enough to think about and a last-minute change of plan, especially one that might upset operating arrangements in France, was little to his liking. But during final preparations it had become clear that the two SAS officers, like the Jedburgh team, had been carefully briefed at SOE headquarters in London. They, too, were under orders to defer to the judgment of 'Samuel', the experienced man in the field who, they had learned, had been operating clandestinely in France since April 1943. Realizing that the SAS's Captain Tonkin and Lieutenant Crisp were equally at the whim of higher command, Crawshay and his men had made the newcomers welcome.

Aboard the Halifax, the combination of snug sleeping bags and the soporific drone of the engines had lulled all five men to sleep, but at 0120 hours the dispatcher shook the parachutists awake. They finished their coffee and strapped on their bulky leg bags to the quick-release clips below their knees. The two SAS officers, Tonkin and Crisp, were to be the first out, followed by the 'Hugh' team and finally by the supply containers that were carried in the bomb bay of the Halifax. Captain Tonkin edged forward to the jump hole in the floor of the aircraft and, peering out at the moonlit landscape, immediately identified the landing zone from the reconnaissance photographs he had studied back in England. The pilot banked sharply to bring the Halifax in to the dropping point. The engines were throttled back, but as Tonkin prepared to jump, watching for the red light to flash green, the containers were released by mistake and the pilot had to circle and run back in. As the light at last changed to green, the dispatcher shouted 'Go!' and dropped his raised arm. Tonkin looked down, saw open fields, and at just 500 feet he pushed forward out of the hatch.

The night air had only a faint breeze to disturb the silence as the noise of the Halifax receded into the distance, but the five parachutists did not have long to appreciate the experience as wooded fields loomed up below them. The spot where the group landed, Les Cherpes, was close to Moncousinat Farm, some 5 kilometres north-west of the small town of St-Gaultier. Almost immediately after Tonkin landed, a young man ran up, welcoming him enthusiastically in voluble French. Remembering the briefing given at SOE headquarters, Tonkin attempted to exchange the pre-arranged code words, but was not overly surprised when the Frenchman displayed absolutely no sign of comprehension. SOE's briefing had suggested that if the correct answer were not received, Tonkin would be justified in shooting the stranger. But, in addition to his official instructions, Tonkin had been able to snatch some informal advice from an experienced French agent of SOE who was back in London between operations. Tonkin was later to recollect:

Fortunately for everyone, I finally spent some hours in London with a wise old (must have been 40, but I was only 23) Frenchman with long *Résistance* experience in France who was out 'resting'. He gave me much useful advice which I recognised straightaway as being from 'the horse's mouth' and paid good heed to. Amongst a great mass of wisdom was not to assume that the message or passwords will have been received. Until you know who 'friends' really are, hold a gun in your right hand ready to shoot and a bar of chocolate and some cigarettes in your left, both offered as a choice, then try the password, and act on the look in their eyes and not the answer you get.

Judging the young man friendly, Tonkin therefore enlisted his help in starting to clear the field as the Halifax had circled again before running in for a third time to drop more supplies. It would take some time to collect everything and Tonkin was anxious that the Halifax might have aroused the interest of the Luftwaffe and their supporting radar at the airfield near Châteauroux.

Meanwhile, Tonkin's welcomer, Narcisse Girault, had been joined by four others. His father, François Girault, was the farmer of Moncousinat and was accompanied by a farmhand. The two others were members of the 'Shipwright' circuit, SOE's Lieutenant Alex Shaw, code name 'Olive', who was in charge of the reception party, and his locally recruited assistant, Maurice Renard. Shaw, whose real name was Alexandre Schwatschko, was the air landings and drop zones expert for the 'Shipwright' circuit. He often stayed at Moncousinat and was also said to have hidden a radio there. Now, he shared the concerns of Girault *père* and Tonkin over the potential for an immediate reaction from the Luftwaffe at Châteauroux airfield, and he also warned that search parties could be expected in daylight. Everyone pitched in quickly to roll up and hide all the parachutes. They were finished only just in time. Within ten minutes of the drop a German nightfighter swept low over the area several times. In the bright moonlight the fighter was clearly looking for the Halifax bomber and any parachutists, but everything on the ground had been collected and Pilot Officer Tattersall had wasted no time in leaving the area for a safe return to England.

The SAS and Jedburgh teams were taken to Moncousinat Farm where Madame Girault had coffee ready for her visitors. Then, until dawn, they dozed in the hay of the barn. Suddenly, at around 6 o'clock, they heard a car approaching. Given that the enemy used most of the motor vehicles still on French roads, the newcomers grabbed their weapons and peered out from the barn. A large, black Matford car pulled up in the farmyard and the watching men relaxed slightly when they saw it held only one person. A tall, dark-haired young man climbed out carrying a Sten gun and greeted Schwatschko who had come out from the farmhouse. As the stranger turned to face the barn, Tonkin recognized him immediately from photographs at SOE's briefing. To make absolutely certain, but unable to avoid feeling slightly absurd in the circumstances, Tonkin emerged from the barn and asked, 'Est-ce qu'il y a une maison dans le bois?'

'Oui, mais elle n'est pas très bonne,' answered the new arrival.

There was therefore no doubt; the newcomer was Captain Amédée Maingard, code name 'Samuel', or 'Sam', and one of SOE's most successful secret agents.

# Chapter Two

# Family and Childhood

The Jedburgh and SAS officers took 'Sam' to be a Frenchman, but though they were not to know until much later, René Amédée Louis Pierre Maingard de la Ville-ès-Offrans (Amédée or Dédé Maingard for short) was a British subject. And although he had come to the centre of occupied France from Britain, his journey had started in the southern hemisphere, for he had been raised on the beautiful Indian Ocean island of Mauritius, a British colony. Born there at Mont-Roches on 21 October 1918, Dédé nevertheless had strong French roots and the history of the Maingards was one that had more than its fair share of confrontation with the British, dating back hundreds of years.

For the Maingards are an old French Breton family from the diocese of Saint-Malo and the family's history is closely linked to that of the town, its port and La Pointe du Meinga between Saint-Malo and Cancale. It is believed that Guillaume or Yvon, a sea captain, landed in one of the coves at Pointe du Meinga around 1350 and took a version of the name of the headland, Meinga or Mainga, for his own when he decided to settle there. An alternative spelling Maën-gard, in Breton French derived from the Celtic, means a stone or rock which serves as a defence or lookout point, probably also reflecting the name of the headland. The family's later coat of arms, in gold and featuring two angels and an oak tree, has the Latin motto *ut rupes nostra*, again referring to the rock or headland.

Guillaume had five children, from whom five branches of the family rapidly grew and prospered in and around Saint-Malo, and by 1488, in a list of the 150 most important people in Saint-Malo, thirty-five were of Maingard stock. But of the five original branches of the family, only one is believed to have survived to the present day, that of the second son, Alain Maingard.

This branch is Maingard de la Ville-ès-Offrans, named after the family estate, La Ville-ès-Offrans which was not far inland from the Pointe du Meinga.[1] Of this branch, Jacques Maingard, born in Saint-Malo in 1498, became one of the most celebrated names of the time when in 1534 and 1535 he served in two of Jacques Cartier's three expeditions of discovery to Canada.

The de la Ville-ès-Offrans branch of the Maingard family continued this sea-faring tradition out of Saint-Malo for the next 200 years until Josselin-Julien Maingard was responsible for transplanting the branch to the Indian Ocean. Josselin-Julien had displayed a strong adventurous spirit early in life, accom-

4

panying his seafaring father from the tender age of ten. In 1743 he was captain of the armed corsair *Vainqueur*, out of Marseilles, when war broke out against England. He was obliged to cede command to a regular naval officer put aboard, but took part in a successful action off Toulon in 1744 against a blockading English fleet commanded by Admiral Thomas Matthews. The following year, Josselin-Julien returned to Saint-Malo where he captained another corsair to continue plaguing the English, but in 1746 he was taken prisoner and held in England for two months before being released. Returning to Saint-Malo he was appointed first lieutenant of the Compagnie des Indes' merchant sailing ships, but soon returned to naval service as war continued against the English. In December 1746 he became second in command of *Le Lys*, a 1,400 tonnes 64-gun warship which was despatched with a convoy to India. Violent gales scattered the French ships to the extent that the English captured all but one and it was the fortune of *Le Lys* to be the only survivor of the squadron to reach the Indian Ocean. Josselin-Julien thus became the first Maingard to reach Mauritius when his ship anchored off Port-Louis in October 1747.

This same voyage also took in India and Brazil before, in July 1748, Josselin-Julien Maingard again put in to Port-Louis and found rapid improvements under way thanks to an enlightened governor, Bertrand François Mahé de La Bourdonnais, a fellow native of Saint-Malo and appointed Governor in 1735 by the Compagnie des Indes, owners of Mauritius. For although Guillaume Dufresne d'Arsel had taken possession of Mauritius in 1715 in the name of King Louis XV of France (renaming it the Île de France and planting the French royal standard near what is now Port-Louis), the King had handed his new possession over to the Compagnie des Indes in 1719.

Under La Bourdonnais the island's thatched hovels were demolished and in their place had risen forts, barracks, warehouses, hospitals and houses. Roads were being opened throughout the island, a shipbuilding industry had commenced and oxen were imported so that slaves could be used for more skilled tasks. An agricultural programme was started that concentrated on marketable products as well as food for the islanders and the first sugar factory was opened.

Returning home to Saint-Malo when peace was declared by the Treaty of Aix-la-Chapelle in October 1748, Josselin-Julien could not ignore the opportunities that he was sure were on offer in Mauritius. He rejoined the Compagnie des Indes and was successful in being appointed Port Captain for Mauritius, presumably on the strength of his recent visits there. With his new bride Laurence, he sailed from Lorient in December 1750 aboard the *Philibert*. He served the island well and when it was formally ceded back by the bankrupt Compagnie des Indes to Louis XV in 1767, he was made a Capitaine de Brûlot in the French Navy until his retirement in 1772. Reports and letters of the period give testimony to 'son zèle, son activité, son aptitude, sa bravoure'.

In 1800, with British naval might threatening the entire Indian Ocean, the island's settlers asked the Napoleonic government for protection against any potential invaders. The last French governor of Mauritius was therefore appointed by Napoléon Bonaparte in 1803 to bring the colony back to order after 13 years of autonomy and Mauritius (still then the Île de France) became

5

part of the French colony of Indes-Orientales, which included Réunion and the Séchelles. Port-Louis became Port Napoléon and Mahébourg (named after Mahé de La Bourdonnais) became Port Imperial. The job of the governor, General Charles Decaën, was a difficult one. On the one hand he brought some element of protection, but he was also expected to impose France's authority on its wayward possession by setting up a military authority. He allowed the continuation of highly profitable privateering by Mauritius-based ships, but although these were bolstered by three additional ships from France, they would clearly be no match for a determined effort by Britain's mighty Royal Navy. No one understood this better than the man who was responsible for the second line of defence, the island's Port Captain and commander of its detachment of the Royal Corps of Artillery.

The commander of this force was the youngest of Josselin-Julien's six children, Josselin-Jean, who had followed a career as an officer in the Royal Corps of Artillery. As a young lieutenant he had seen service in India with de Suffren's forces against the British, and had eventually returned to Mauritius to follow in his father's footsteps by becoming Port Captain.[2] Josselin-Jean Maingard was therefore destined to be in the front line when, as feared, the British decided they could no longer accept the threat to their vessels plying the sea route from England to British India. Possession of the island became a military imperative and although the British suffered an initial setback when a naval force was soundly beaten off in 1810 in the Grand Port naval battle that took place off the Mauritius coast, this was only to be a temporary respite. The Royal Navy quickly despatched more ships and an invasion force in the same year. When the British fleet arrived offshore, Maingard commanded his artillery gallantly, and was wounded and promoted on the spot by General Decaën. But it was an uneven contest and landings by the British under General Abercrombie could not be prevented. Further fighting was avoided when the French agreed to surrender on the condition that their settlers could keep their land, belongings, status and culture. One of the legacies of this generous agreement is that, even today, French is still more widely spoken than English in Mauritius.

The island's capture completed total control of the Indian Ocean by the British Empire, a power that was to remain virtually unchallenged until the entry of Japan into the Second World War in 1941. Fortunately for the Maingards, however, the British takeover proved relatively benevolent, English became the official language (a move not formally approved until 1832), but the first British governor announced that civil and judicial administration would be unchanged. Only those who refused to take an oath of allegiance to the British Crown were politely given notice to leave Mauritius within a reasonable period of time. Anyone who wished to return to France could do so with all their possessions.

Despite his role in defending the island, and refusing to pledge allegiance to the British, Josselin-Jean Maingard was nevertheless engaged by the new administration to oversee the task of relinquishing ammunition and stores, work which even took him to England. But this duty done, he returned to France to continue to serve in the artillery[3] before being posted back, in the rank of Colonel, to the Indian Ocean to Réunion where he eventually settled. There he became the first director of the island's *lycée*, the Collège Royal de Bourbon, when it was founded in 1819, and he died in 1838. Colonel Josselin-Jean Maingard is still remembered today by a magnificent bronze bust in the courtyard of what is now the Le Collège Bourbon de Saint-Denis in Réunion, and a variety of pineapple on the island is called the Maingard. In the town of Beau Bassin in Mauritius there is also a Colonel Maingard Street, a Maingard sub-library and the Colonel Maingard Government School.[4]

In addition to his other achievements, Colonel Maingard had not neglected the tradition of a large family. Of his nine children, the seventh, Joseph Maingard, himself had six children, the last being Ludovic-Pierre-Jean-Joseph Maingard, born in 1851. By this time, some of those of the family who had left Mauritius returned when it became clear that those of French origin truly did have nothing to fear from the island's new rulers. Under British governorship sugar production had increased, Port-Louis had been transformed into a free port, more roads were built and trade generally flourished. When the last of Ludovic-Pierre-Jean-Joseph's four children, Louis Joseph René Maingard (known as René) was born in 1887, it was therefore into a Mauritius that had easily adapted to its new British rulers, yet had no difficulty in preserving a *'vieille France'* environment in which the Maingard family was an important element. While becoming bi-lingual, the Maingards continued to speak French at home and they also maintained their devout Roman Catholicism.[5] No doubt their prayers included supplications for good harvests, since the family's well-being was almost entirely dependent on the island's main crop, sugar cane.

One Anglo-French enterprise that profited from the sugar cane business was Rogers and Co., founded in 1899 as a private company by Walter Richard Rogers. In the early days, Rogers's activities involved the importing of heavy machinery and equipment for use in sugar factories and the exporting of sugar, and it was this business that René Maingard joined in 1904. By 1917 he had become an associate partner of the company and after the death of Walter Rogers in 1919 he became an equal partner, along with Louis Goupille and the two nephews of Walter Rogers, Eddy and Eric. Together the four businessmen continued to prosper, but in 1929 Mauritius suffered an economic downturn due to the development of sweet beetroot sugar in Europe. Unrest gradually grew among the sugar cane workers until, in 1937, workers went on strike and rebelled against their landlords, demanding better economic conditions and participation in government. The authorities had to use troops to restore law and order, but the writing was on the wall for those far-sighted enough to read it.

In the light of these developments, Rogers and Co. sensibly sought to diversify their business and in the 1920s and 1930s the activities of the company extended to shipping, initially as shipping agents and later as shipowners. In 1932, Rogers and Co. formed the Colonial Steamships Company Ltd. which, through regular services to Rodrigues, played a major role in the development of the island. The partners all consequently became well known and respected members of the business community in Mauritius. René in particular was much sought after to serve numerous trade and other organizations, his appointments included chairmanship of the Mauritius Chamber of Commerce, the Mauritius Hemp Producers'

Syndicate and the Mauritius Turf Club, together with directorships of the Mauritius Commercial Bank and of several industrial and agricultural companies.

All these responsibilities must have entailed a busy life for René's wife, who could have had little day-to-day support at home from her husband. For in addition to the expanding family of Rogers companies, René, like his forebears, had not neglected the expansion of his own family. From 1914 to 1932 Madame Maingard was kept occupied with the births of no less than eleven children, and although one baby boy died, five boys and five girls made for a boisterous household. It was a close-knit, happy family and all the children were close to their parents, but in the traditional way that still then prevailed, René, the first-born boy (after two sisters) was expected to be the next head of the family. This was strengthened by the fact that, at birth, he was seen to bear a facial resemblance to Colonel Maingard, hero of the brief resistance to the British invasion of Mauritius, and so he was promptly nicknamed with the abbreviation Colo. A year later, in 1918, a second boy was born at Mont-Roches. Amédée's name was abbreviated to Dédé and, despite not being destined to be the next paterfamilias, proved to be a very popular boy with his parents, brothers, sisters and friends. His mother complained that he clung to her skirts too much, but once he was at school, Dédé had no difficulty in developing his own character. He started his studies at the Collège St Joseph, an old wooden school run by the Frères des Ecoles Chrétiennes. He was later to recall his enjoyment of activities as diverse as football, stilt-walking and shield-making. The family later moved from Mont-Roches to the rue Barry, Curepipe, where Dédé and his brothers spent many happy hours playing football and tennis on the grass to the rear of the house, staging noisy and boisterous tournaments with friends.

Dédé left behind his younger brothers at the Collège St Joseph when he moved up to senior school to join Colo at the prestigious Royal College in Curepipe. This was a branch of the Royal College in Port-Louis which dated back to 1791 when, as the Collège National or Collège Colonial, it was founded in the capital for the children of the privileged classes. In 1871 an outstation of the Royal College was established in Curepipe to provide local students with an alternative to the long and tiring trip to Port-Louis and the British authorities funded a purpose-built facility in 1914. Again, Dédé was happy there, finding more freedom and enjoying both studies and sport, especially rugby, hockey and tennis. With Colo he reached the doubles final of a local tennis tournament and he also became a proficient horse rider under the tutelage of his uncle, Pierre. With his uncle Emile he learned to love *la chasse* and he enjoyed hunting trips with his father, a pastime long-practised by both his father's and mother's families. Good-natured and full of fun, Dédé would often comically imitate others and enjoyed dressing up in disguise, but he also displayed a gentler side through his hobby of painting birds' eggs (a Chinese art) and his love of singing. Blessed with an attractive singing voice, as a teenager he took singing lessons from Max Moutia, a Mauritian who had been a lyric artist in Paris, and Dédé would regularly meet up with a group of friends to play music and sing.

At the Royal College of Curepipe Dédé proved to be a good and intelligent student and upon leaving, in 1938, he decided he wanted to take up accountancy, a qualification that would serve him well if he were to join the family firm of Rogers and Co., or indeed any other business. Although he had no particular wish to leave the comfort of a large and happy family environment – he had also grown close to Jacqueline Raffray, a young local girl – higher education opportunities in Mauritius were non-existent. The choice for further study was normally to be made in England or France, in that order, and Colo had gone to London in 1936 to study Economics and Finance. He was consequently still there in his final year and would undoubtedly be able to help his younger brother to settle into a new society. Dédé therefore sailed for London in the summer of 1938, even as the clouds of war gathered ominously over distant Europe.

Upon arrival in London, he was helped by Colo, who swiftly arranged a room in the same lodgings at 48 Lexham Gardens in the Earl's Court (W8) district of the capital, already a popular area for those arriving from the far-flung reaches of the British Empire, and handy for the Piccadilly line of the Underground transport system. Before he sailed to return to Mauritius in September 1938, Colo took Dédé for a short trip to Paris to visit their uncle Maxime and aunt Josée, and he helped look for a suitable accountancy firm in London for Dédé to join. Thanks to Colo's efforts, and having passed all five stages of his theoretical chartered accountancy studies, on 15 February 1939 Dédé was formally articled to Messrs Falk, Keeping & Co., Ironmonger Lane, EC2, in the heart of the City financial area, close to the Bank of England. Little else is known of Dédé's first twelve months in England, but a year after his arrival, family letters show that he had settled well, helped by his joining the Mauritian expatriate community in London and picking up the contacts that Colo had already made. He played rugby during the winter with Richmond RFC, and otherwise enjoyed tennis and squash. He was progressing well in his articles with Messrs Falk, Keeping & Co and had managed two holidays on the Continent, consisting of two weeks in Belgium and three weeks in Switzerland. Yet Dédé's world of work and study was about to be irrevocably torn apart.

# Chapter Three

# War

When war broke out on 3 September 1939, Dédé instinctively knew that his duty lay with the armed services, not only because he was a British subject, but also because he was impelled by his strong historical and family attachment to France. Back in Mauritius, Colo[1] and Henri joined the island's local Territorial Force, but the two younger brothers, Roger and Paul, were still too young and at school, though both later served in the British Army. So of all the boys, Dédé alone was geographically well placed to take an immediate active role in the conflict. The only question was which service to choose.

The answer came from close at hand. Among Dédé's London-based friends of Mauritian origin, Jean Larcher, like Dédé, had been studying in London when war was declared, and it was his guardian, Gustave Souchon, who recommended the Queen Victoria's Rifles (QVR), a Territorial Army infantry unit affiliated to the King's Royal Rifle Corps (KRRC), in which he had served during the First World War. Souchon was now representing the Mauritius Chamber of Agriculture in London, but still knew someone in authority in the unit and so, exactly eight weeks after war broke out, Dédé and Jean Larcher called on Colonel Cole at the Colonial Office and, together with another young Mauritian called Joe Rousset, joined the British Army on 29 October 1939, eight days after celebrating Dédé's twenty-first birthday. They were posted to the QVR's camp, then on a hill outside the regimental headquarters in the city of Winchester in Hampshire. There, the sole existing QVR battalion was receiving an influx of volunteers to enable a second battalion to be formed for active service, and it was this new 2nd QVR, part of 23 Armoured Brigade of the 9th Division, that the three young Mauritians joined. Dédé's British Army service number was 6847249 and his medical inspection recorded him as Category A.

Just one week after arriving, the three new recruits applied for commissions, but though they were promised they would undoubtedly become officers, they were told that they would have to wait until six months' service was completed. As they had no reason to disbelieve the advice they began to work hard in their training.

Meanwhile, the Battalion was frequently moving around England. Although the Queen Victoria's Rifles were supposedly mechanized – the 1st Battalion had been equipped with motorcycles since 1938 – the 2nd Battalion seems to have suffered initially from a lack of equipment, since they moved from place to place by bicycle, living all the time under canvas. In June 1940, they were stationed at Ongar in Essex where they were startled to hear a German radio broadcast announce their arrival. Dédé, still a lowly Rifleman (Private), was languishing in the ranks of No. 2 Platoon, 'A' Company, though life was made a little more comfortable by a kind local family, fervent Catholics and admirers of France, who invited him to join them for meals and let him use their bath. The latter was particularly welcome since, in a letter home, Dédé revealed that for some two months he had slept out on open ground, in forests, on hard benches and his muscles and body ached accordingly. With feeling he wrote: 'Non, la vie de soldat n'est pas bien agréable.' He also wrote to his parents praising General Prioux's valiant French troops who were covering the rearguard action of the British Expeditionary Force in France, believing that the entente cordiale had never been stronger and describing how he was heartened by the constant British press articles praising the French troops.[2] He admitted that he had prayed that his unit might be sent to join the other British forces fighting on the Continent for what he termed 'notre beau pays de France', but this was not to be. The 2nd Battalion was indeed put on standby for such a move and the cancellation of leave meant that Dédé could not attend when Jean Larcher married his British girlfriend on 1 June 1940, even though the church was only 200 yards from their billets. Dédé had but a brief glimpse of the bride, Pam, and even Jean Larcher could only be spared two days' leave to spend with his new bride. In the event, however, it was the 1st Battalion that went to France instead, and suffered badly.

By October 1940 Dédé's unit had moved across England to a camp near Hereford, well away from the main battle for survival that was being waged in south-east England under the onslaught of the German Blitz. Instead of being close to the action, Dédé was largely kept occupied by frequent route marches, though he enjoyed the opportunities to play rugby. The weather had already turned cold and he was planning to buy a thick pullover to supplement the small silver brandy flask and its contents that he quietly kept to help his circulation. He was, however, desperate for news from Mauritius, not having received a letter for a month. He had been dutifully sending a letter home each week, describing how, in September, he had applied a second time for a commission with the backing of his company commander, who also recommended him for promotion to lance corporal. This, said the officer, was an essential first step towards an Officer Cadet Training Unit (OCTU). Two weeks later, all seemed to be going well when Dédé was called to a Board, but he then heard nothing further. The lack of any formal result from the Board was only slightly tempered by his gaining the single stripe of a lance corporal, just one rung up the promotion ladder, in early October 1940.

The advent of 1941 therefore found Dédé feeling even more dispirited when he wrote in mid-January (in English) to his father, complaining that batches of candidates had left for OCTU, but that he, Jean Larcher and Joe Rousset were still left waiting in the ranks. His company commander had assured him that his time would come soon, but a week later his patience was wearing ever thinner and he cabled his father for any help that he could arrange or suggest.

Meanwhile the 2nd QVR were again on the move, this time for a longer period, to Northampton where the wearisome bicycles were dispensed with in favour of Bren gun carriers, small, armoured, tracked vehicles, each with a driver and gunner for a Bren gun or anti-tank weapon, and with open-topped accommodation behind for two or three infantrymen. Its Ford V8 engine gave it a useful top speed of 30 miles per hour, but the noise from it made verbal communication among crew and passengers near impossible. This was the vehicle which would supposedly transport Dédé and his friends into action, and the three Mauritians christened their mount 'HMS Mauritius', but the likelihood of such action looked as remote as ever.

Thanks to the length of time that letters took via the sea routes, it was then not until late March 1941 that Dédé's father wrote to a friend in London, Major C. Dumas. A decorated former officer in the British Army, Dumas was then working in the City where he had many contacts in the British 'establishment'. Describing his deep disappointment at Dédé's failure to pass on to an OCTU and asking Dumas to use whatever influence he had, or to provide Dédé with advice, Old René confessed that:

> He has now been in the ranks for the last 20 months, and in spite of recommendations from his superiors, the boy is still a Lance Corporal and I need not emphasize the inconvenience and promiscuity he is subjected to amidst the rank and file.
>
> I quite realise that the Authorities at your end have to be very circumspect, especially where strangers are concerned and I understand that this has been the case with Amédée, who, when asked to show his birth certificate, was discovered therefrom to be a . . . Colonial. As far as I am aware, most Mauritians who have been in England in various capacities, have shown that they were inferior to none from the point of view of physical and intellectual achievements – to say nothing of patriotism – and I fail to see why my son, who, I repeat, has received a sound education should be maintained in an inferior rank simply because he has the misfortune of having been born in the Colonies!

He stressed his own firm support for Britain and the Empire in its struggle against Hitler, and to underline this mentioned that 'My wife herself was recently awarded the MBE for her charitable activities' and that Colo,[3] whom Major Dumas had met in London in 1938, was 'proceeding shortly to join the RAF', spurred on by Dédé's service in the British Army.

The indignation of Old René over Dédé being treated as a 'colonial' would undoubtedly have been all the more acute had he been aware of an irony then brought about by a reorganization of his son's regiment in the British Army. For in March 1941 the 1st and 2nd Battalions, Queen Victoria's Rifles were respectively renamed the 7th and 8th Battalions, King's Royal Rifle Corps (QVR). Dédé and his friends therefore now belonged to the 8th Battalion of the KRRC, the regiment with which the QVR had already long been affiliated, but also one which, ironically, traced its antecedents to the British Army's 60th (Royal American) Regiment of Foot. This regiment had helped finally wrest control of Quebec and Montréal from the French in 1759 and 1760 – control which had its roots in Cartier's expeditions and in which Dédé's ancestors had participated. The old Breton Maingards must have been turning in their graves at the development!

And yet it seemed that even the good offices and influence of Major Dumas were not enough. Though he met Dédé (who described him as 'un vrai chic type') Dumas had not been able to achieve anything by 29 August 1941 when Dédé wrote to his father with the devastating news that, despite his Battalion's CO having recommended him for a commission to the Command Board, he had received the news that he had been graded 'not suitable' to become an officer. It had been the Colonel himself who had sought out Dédé, Larcher and Joe Rousset to tell them the encouraging news that they were again to go before an officers' selection board in Leicester.

The Board, consisting of a War Office colonel and two local majors, asked only three simple questions: do they have the right name? what does your father do? what are you going to do after the war? The interview seemed to have gone well for Dédé, especially since he had been able to read a positive recommendation from the War Office that lay on the table before him. Encouraged, but puzzled by the seemingly simplistic methods of the Board, he and his friends therefore returned to their unit and waited.

When good news arrived three or four weeks later, however, it cheered only one of the hopefuls since the cable ordered Jean Larcher alone to an officers' training unit, destined for the Reconnaissance Corps. Dédé was utterly depressed, feeling it was such an insult to someone such as he who, as a loyal citizen of the British Empire, had given up his studies, and hence perhaps his future, to serve Britain. It was also an insult to the efforts made by Major Dumas, on his behalf by his father, and by the Governor of Mauritius, whose influence had also been called upon. Dédé again wrote home, complaining to his father that for two years now he had worked and trained hard to adapt to life in the ranks, telling himself that it would later stand him in good stead for the greater responsibilities of an officer. But this latest setback was not going to dissuade him from continuing his fight for a commission. He would ask for an interview with the Minister for the Colonies and he would also write to Lady Edith Kemsley, sister of René Mérandon, a prominent Mauritian landowner and former politician known to the Maingards. Now based in London, Lady Kemsley was the wife of the proprietor of *The Times* newspaper. If all this failed, Dédé would ask for a transfer in the ranks, either to Intelligence work or, after speaking to Colo, to the RAF. On a more cheerful and domestic note, however, he mentioned that he, Joe and Jean were making their own jam and thanked his father for his parcel, which had taken three months to arrive.

Yet even as Dédé prepared the next phase of his campaigning, a stroke of luck occurred through Jean Larcher's success in being sent to an OCTU. While there,

13

he saw a request for French speakers to volunteer for special work, he put himself forward for interview and two days prior to his posting to the Reconnaissance Corps he was ordered to London. In a simple interview with an organization called the Inter-Services Research Bureau he soon realized that he was being asked if he was willing to go to France. He immediately accepted and was then asked if he had any friends who might also be interested. Without hesitation, Larcher put forward two names. One was that of Marcel Rousset. A cousin of Joe Rousset, Marcel also had a Mauritian background, but was really much more French than British, having only lived in Mauritius for the first eight years of his life before his parents moved to Paris in 1919. Yet when war broke out Marcel was refused by the French Army on account of his British nationality. Still eager to fight the Germans, he left for England where he worked as a selling agent in Covent Garden before enlisting in the KRRC in December 1939 to join his cousin, Dédé, and Jean Larcher. Somewhat older at thirty years of age, Marcel Rousset had nevertheless struck Larcher as absolutely determined to take an active part in the war and in that respect Rousset was on a par with the other name put forward by Larcher: that of Amédée Maingard.

# Chapter Four

# Special Operations Executive

The Inter-Services Research Bureau (ISRB) that Jean Larcher had agreed to join was, in reality, the Special Operations Executive (SOE), a British secret service founded just two years earlier. Its creation in 1940 was due to the common, if erroneous, belief that the victories achieved by the Germans up to that summer had been won, not just by military might, but also by strong fifth-column elements within the countries that had fallen. Though this belief was largely, indeed almost entirely, wrong, it nevertheless encouraged the British to investigate subversive warfare further. Fired with enthusiasm for the task, it was Prime Minister Winston Churchill himself who had then issued an instruction that would go down in history: 'And now set Europe ablaze.'

But the document that effectively laid out SOE's terms of reference and aims was drafted by a very different character to Churchill. Neville Chamberlain, then the Lord President, but previously prime minister before Churchill, was the British leader who had stumbled into the trap of appeasement in 1938 after so drastically misjudging the intentions of Herr Hitler. Though Chamberlain fell ill and died only a few months after his draft first saw the light of day, it was perhaps fitting that one of the last achievements of this much-criticized man was to help lay the foundations of a service which was to operate at the very opposite end of the spectrum from appeasement – taking the fight to the enemy.

And 1940 was the year when Britain's fight was for its very existence, against a powerful enemy flushed with success. There was therefore no time to be lost in creating this new secret service which reported to Mr (later Sir) Hugh Dalton, the Minister for Economic Warfare. Dalton swiftly recruited Gladwyn Jebb, later Lord Gladwyn, as the organization's chief executive officer, and Sir Frank Nelson, a former MP, as the first head of the sabotage branch of the new body. Together and individually they quickly and confidentially spread the word to a necessary few people in government and the armed services, explaining what SOE was and how it ought to be supported. It was always made clear that Churchill's personal imperium lay behind the new service, whose basic aims were described as: immediate or short-term sabotage; long-term planned sabotage to support Allied military requirements; and the recruitment, training and arming of a secret army, ready to rise on receipt of instructions from headquarters.

Three separate agencies, each possessing some degree of specialist knowledge or ability in the black arts of sabotage, subversion and propaganda, were amalgamated to form SOE. Of the three, MI R was a little-known military intelligence research branch of the War Office; EH (Electra House) was a highly secret propaganda section in the Foreign Office; and Section D (D reputedly standing for Destruction) was an equally inadmissible element within the Secret Intelligence Service (SIS), also known as MI6. SOE was to be so secret that not even Parliament, let alone the British public, were informed of its creation.

SIS, the most senior and established of Britain's secret services, was already charged with work outside the British Isles and was particularly resentful and suspicious of the new, upstart, service. This fuelled a rivalry with SOE throughout much of the war, though relations did improve as time went on. Early distrust was exacerbated, however, when Sir Stewart Menzies, the Director General of SIS, only discovered three weeks after the event that Section D had passed from his control to SOE. Moreover, SIS had good reason for wanting to keep SOE at arm's length. The role of SIS was the gathering of intelligence as quietly and subtly as possible, while SOE's job of creating havoc was almost always certain to provoke a violent enemy response. Menzies continued to take opportunities to undermine the fledgling organization throughout the war and found allies among some of the senior officers of RAF Bomber Command, who resented having to loan aircraft for SOE's 'unethical' clandestine missions and begrudged any aircraft diverted from the overriding aim of bombing Germany.

In February 1942, Dalton was replaced as Minister by Lord Selbourne, a personal friend of Churchill, and three months later Sir Charles Hambro took over as Executive Director, known by the symbol 'CD', when Sir Frank Nelson retired through ill health. Hambro, an old Etonian merchant banker, prominent figure in the City of London, Chairman of the Great Western Railway and late of the Coldstream Guards, had previously served as head of SOE's Scandinavian Section and so was an experienced insider. Below him, Brigadier Colin Gubbins was in command of SOE's Western European operations and was to replace Hambro in September 1943 when the latter resigned over a disagreement with Selbourne over policy.

Brigadier (later Major General) Colin Gubbins, proved a formidable talent. He had previously been responsible for the Auxiliary Units, the stay-behind forces designed to harry the Germans in the event of a successful invasion of the British Isles. From his former command he brought with him several of his most resourceful and able officers who were to give SOE a remarkable backbone of talented staff. He commenced as SOE's Director of Operations and Training from November 1940, shortly after SOE took up residence in London's Baker Street, close to the headquarters of Marks and Spencer, some of whose offices they used. As a military man, he was at first viewed with some suspicion, but he soon proved his grasp of, and commitment to, the unorthodox and this was recognized when he replaced Hambro as CD. In addition to his talent for irregular warfare, Gubbins also seems to have encompassed the art of sidestepping much bureaucracy and administrative requirement. One example of this was that Dédé, together with everyone employed by SOE, including those who never left England, paid no income tax on his salary.

Below Gubbins, Colonel Robin Brook commanded those sections involved in Western Europe, these generally being divided up on a country-by-country basis. With regard to operations in France, however, the picture was much more complicated. F Section, which was commanded by Colonel Maurice Buckmaster, formerly a manager of the Ford Motor Company in pre-war Paris, was informally known as the 'independents'. There was then RF Section, nominally commanded by a British SOE officer, but reporting to de Gaulle who consequently treated the 'independents' of F Section with distrust. Both F and RF Sections operated agents into France from England, but despite their both belonging to SOE, there was no liaison or joint operations in the field. To muddy the waters further, AMF Section also despatched agents from Algiers in North Africa, mainly just to southern France. EU/P, the Polish SOE section, sent at least twenty-eight agents to work with the sizeable Polish expatriot community in France, but they too kept to themselves. There were a dozen or so agents in France from DF, SOE's section that ran several highly successful escape lines for shot-down airmen and the like. And finally, from D-Day onwards, SOE sent 'Jedburghs' to France. Small (normally three-man) inter-Allied teams of advisers, their job was to support and supply the rapidly expanding Resistance forces and to encourage them in rising up against the enemy.

But all this activity took time to develop. SOE's first operation into France had not taken place until March 1941, when RF Section had parachuted six men into southern Brittany in an unsuccessful attempt to attack the crews of a specialist pathfinder squadron of the Luftwaffe. F Section was only slightly behind when they parachuted a radio operator, Georges Begué, into the Châteauroux area of France in May 1941, followed by his group organizer, Philippe de Vomécourt a few days later. From this somewhat cautious start, a steady stream of agents were sent to France to encourage and arm the various factions of French Resistance, but there had then been a worrying number of arrests and setbacks among F Section's circuits. The German counter-intelligence organizations had clearly increased their efforts and efficiency and consequently had begun to achieve success in penetrating SOE's networks. It was therefore against this background of an urgent need for new agents, especially radio operators, that Dédé and Marcel Rousset were ordered to London.

Travelling to London from their battalion camp that was then in Norfolk, they went to Thurloe Street in South Kensington, not far from where Dédé had rented lodgings in 1939. There, Number 10 was a house that had been purchased by Lady Kemsley for the use of Mauritians in the armed forces who were passing through or temporarily staying in London. Meeting up with old friends there, Dédé and Rousset found themselves drawn into an impromptu party which quickly became noisy and merry and went on quite late into the night.

The next morning they presented themselves, as soberly as they could manage, to an anonymous annexe of the War Office, the former Victoria Hotel in Northumberland Avenue. They waited in a reception room until a gentleman appeared in the doorway and greeted them with 'who will be the first?' The two volunteers debated briefly before it was agreed that Dédé should take the lead and he left Rousset, anxiously waiting his own turn. Standard recruitment practice would have seen Dédé commence with a relatively informal and individual interview. The room normally used was dark, bleak and bare, inadequately lit by one naked light bulb and furnished only with the minimum necessities of a table, two hard kitchen chairs and a blackout curtain. SOE's recruiting officers included characters such as Lewis Gielgud, the brother of the famous actor (later Sir) John Gielgud, but Dédé was seen by the senior recruiting officer, Captain Selwyn Jepson, a prolific author of murder mysteries and screenplays and credited with the vision and initiative that saw so many women recruits join SOE. To put the applicant at an initial disadvantage, the interviewing officer would reveal that he already knew some obscure fact or detail about the interviewee, preferably something that would surprise the would-be agent. In the case of Dédé and Marcel this had obviously involved having the pair followed when they arrived in London the previous day, for Jepson coolly commented: 'I see your train arrived ten minutes late at the station yesterday. And didn't you have a noisy party at the house where you were staying? The lights were not out until after two a.m.'

After a few introductory words the interview switched to French, since Jepson had to judge whether Dédé's language skills and knowledge of the country were good enough for him to pass for French. It was also important to make an initial assessment of Dédé's character and his motivation for wanting to be considered for some kind of special duty.

While Dédé's knowledge of France itself was sketchy, his language skills were perfect, with no trace of an accent. He was clearly a stable, well-balanced young man who was looking for more important work and responsibilities, supported by a truly Anglo-French commitment. Here was no impulsive adventurer or risk taker.

At this stage many would-be recruits had little or no idea why they were there and many were still anticipating interpreting or translation work. The two young Mauritians, however, were already in the Army, were therefore bound to secrecy and were demonstrably keen to undertake clandestine warfare. Dédé was therefore asked questions such as: do you want to serve your country better? have you ever flown? how do you feel about parachuting from an aeroplane? and are you courageous enough to be dropped into enemy territory? In fairness to the applicant, the dangers were explicitly described and Dédé was warned that he could expect a slow and painful death if he were caught. It was stressed that it was a volunteer job and Dédé was given the chance to go away and think about it a little more, before making his decision. It was also made clear that if he decided not to carry on, then that decision would be understood, accepted and would not affect his Army career. Still only a lance corporal after nearly three years, Dédé probably reflected that there was almost nothing that could damage his 'career'. One final thing stressed was to keep the matter a secret and to reach his decision alone without discussing it with anyone else. But this last requirement was unnecessary, for Dédé, like Rousset, accepted the offer on the spot.

Having successfully fast-tracked the process (three interviews were the norm), Dédé did not have to return to his battalion, but he still had to undergo the vetting which MI5 (the British secret service that operated on home soil) were responsible for carrying out. This process verified Dédé's loyalty and good character and with this confirmed, a final interview was then able to move on to more detail about the work that might be involved. At this point, the recruit began to understand a little more of the extent of SOE's work, though the actual title of 'SOE' was still rarely, if ever, mentioned or used. Instead, the service was generally referred to only as 'The Racket', 'The Outfit' or 'The Firm' by those who knew of it. The interviewing officer again stressed the potential dangers, together with the sobering advice that there might only be a 50/50 chance of survival, but after his stagnation in the infantry, Dédé was in no mood to be deterred. His decision remained an unequivocal 'yes'.

Officially cleared for training as an agent on 30 May 1942, Dédé formally joined SOE on that date, posted out from the KRRC. For the princely pay of £1 per day while under training he was now 'specially employed', the term used to describe, or rather not describe, the work of SOE's agents. He was given a new service number, P/241290 and whoever started his personal file in SOE's registry was careful to record that Dédé was 'British (entirely French blood)'. Less carefully, he or she began a self-perpetuating error that was to dog Dédé throughout much of his subsequent service. For the name erroneously recorded was MAINGUARD, rather than Maingard, reflecting the British pronunciation of his name. To add to the confusion he reverted from the forenames he had used to date since joining up, i.e. Amédée Hugnin (Hugnin being his mother's maiden name) and reverted to the strictly correct René Amédée Louis Pierre. He thus metamorphosed from Lance Corporal A.H. Maingard of the King's Royal Rifle Corps into Lance Corporal R.A.L.P. Mainguard of the Inter-Services Research Bureau. It was left to Dédé himself to complete the form that gave most of his personal details: he listed his sporting interests as riding, shooting, tennis, rugby and hockey – 'good at all of them', he wrote – and he offered only one other interest, reading. He was also required to detail his knowledge and experience of countries other than England, these being eighteen years' knowledge of Mauritius, two weeks' holiday in Belgium and three weeks' holiday in Switzerland.

After acceptance Dédé would have reported to Norgeby House, a new building which had been destined for the Treasury, but had been requisitioned as F Section's headquarters, ideally located as it was directly across the road from SOE's head office at 64 Baker Street. After administrative formalities at Norgeby House Dédé was then ordered to report to Orchard Court, a tall and imposing block of flats with an entrance hall, thick carpets and uniformed porters, located a short walk away in Portman Square. There, SOE's F Section used a spacious apartment, remembered by many for its black-tiled bathroom, which was often pressed into service for general office use. Also fondly remembered and a highly popular figure was Park, a pre-war messenger for a British bank in Paris who was responsible for reception duties at the flat. It was his job to ensure that agents did not see too much of each other (except where they were in the same team); he achieved this with considerable diplomacy and helped by an impressive memory for agents' code names. The Orchard Court apartment had an atmosphere of simplicity and efficiency, with everyone seeming to work long hours and rank seemingly holding little meaning. Despite its distinctly unmilitary appearance, the apartment, together with the Baker Street offices, constituted a vital element of SOE's worldwide network, from Europe to the Middle and Far East, Africa and Canada.

It was at Orchard Court that Dédé met his future classmates, each being given a code name for the duration of their training. Among them was at least one familiar face, for Jean Larcher was to be with Dédé through some of his instruction. Recruits were of all types, some in uniform, some in civilian clothes, but none particularly looking like would-be secret agents. Their wide variety of backgrounds bore testimony to SOE's willingness to recruit without prejudice. Taxi drivers and shop assistants rubbed shoulders with barristers and public school masters. There were at least two glamorous former racing drivers, a gay music hall entertainer and numerous women who at that time were still a rarity in operational roles in Britain's wartime armed forces. Among the latter were a Chilean actress and an American woman journalist with a wooden leg. Some of the recruits were motivated by loyalty to England, to France or to both, some by a personal hatred of the Germans. The one thing they had in common was that they were all amateurs at this dangerous and secret work, and men and women were offered the rare opportunity to work together as equals because women could pass into occupied territory unnoticed, unlike men of military age.

Dédé now learned that he was to be sent on a preliminary course which would commence his training, but more importantly would also give F Section's staff a further opportunity to size him up. If at the end of it he wanted to pack up and go, then that would still be alright, though it was not mentioned that those who decided to drop out, or were found wanting, were sent off to the north of Scotland. There, at the ISRB Workshops at Inverlair in Inverness-shire, they would work on low-key duties such as the production of operational equipment for SOE and the creation of an assault course for street fighting, complete with moving dummies and targets, which was a forerunner of the facilities still in use today by police and military forces. Thus usefully engaged, they would be held almost completely incommunicado for several months until whatever knowledge they had gained, particularly of the people they had trained with, was deemed no longer valid.

Each small group (typically six to ten, but sometimes up to seventeen or eighteen) of trainee agents had a 'conducting officer' with them at all times. This was sometimes a 'resting' agent, returned from the field, who had relevant experience and was therefore well placed to monitor his charges. In the company of such an officer, Dédé and the other trainees of his group of twelve were next taken to Guildford in Surrey, 40 miles south-west of London. This journey was usually by train and at Guildford station a 30 cwt covered army truck waited. Discouraged from looking out from the truck, the trainees then had to endure a bumpy and twisting drive for anything between one and two hours before they arrived at a large manor house, set in extensive wooded grounds and closely guarded by armed Field Security Police of the British Army's Intelligence Corps. All passes were scrupulously checked at the entrance.

The trainees did not know it, but their journey had been a deliberately circuitous one, encouraging them to believe their destination was something like

30 miles from where the lorry had picked them up at the station. Designed to prevent them knowing exactly where their training establishment was, this was another ploy used against the possibility that they were later found unsuitable. In reality, only a short journey of 10 minutes from Guildford station would have taken them up and out of the town along the Farnham road, which followed the Hog's Back ridge of high ground. Off the main road and downhill in the small hamlet of Wanborough lay the trainees' home for the next three or four weeks, Wanborough Manor.

Requisitioned for use as STS 5, one of SOE's Preliminary Special Training Schools, Wanborough Manor was one of the many large country houses taken over by the British government soon after war broke out. So many were used as Special Training Schools, it was jokingly said that SOE stood for 'Stately 'Omes of England'. Substantial, though not in the grand class of some other SOE properties, the Manor was built in 1527 and had been owned by the Earls of Onslow since the seventeenth century. It boasted an outdoor swimming pool, numerous barns (the largest was built in or shortly after 1388) and stables which were useful for SOE's training and storage needs. The tiny but beautiful thirteenth-century church and graveyard of Saint Bartholomew, mentioned in the Domesday Book and said to be the smallest church in the county, was immediately adjacent to the Manor and available for those trainees, such as Dédé, who were regular worshippers.

Dédé and the other new arrivals were met by the commandant, Major Roger de Wesselow, a very proper and disciplined former officer of the Coldstream Guards and reputedly a personal friend of Sir Charles Hambro. Despite his elite background, however, de Wesselow was perfect for the job, giving the trainees a warm welcome and displaying an easy ability to get on with almost everyone, no matter what their background. He did all he could to make his charges feel at home, although a shortcoming was his own French, described by one agent as 'execrable'.[1] Given the standing order that French would be spoken whenever practical and without fail at all meals, this could have put de Wesselow at a disadvantage, but his considerable charm and good conversation more than compensated. Known as a bon vivant and an admirer of most things French, he was always keen to discuss the merits of continental cuisine and vintage wine in the mess and bar with the trainee agents. The staff were tough, capable instructors, mostly sergeants, assisted by other soldiers and orderlies for day-to-day duties. The Manor's perimeter was constantly patrolled by the Field Security Police and was in an area off-limits to all civilians so that the nascent agents could receive their initial training under the cloak of secrecy. Neither staff nor students were permitted outside the compound unless on exercise and under escort, and leave was only granted in exceptional circumstances. Letters home were still permitted, but were censored. Dédé was not permitted to speculate exactly where he was, or what he was doing and his parents could write to him only via an anonymous PO Box number in London. Even Colo, now in Britain having volunteered for the Royal Air Force, did not see his brother and did not know that he had joined SOE.

A typical day for Dédé at Wanborough began at 6.30 a.m. with a hot drink and biscuit. An hour's physical exercise followed, rewarded by breakfast in the All Ranks' Mess. The full day then consisted of a mixture of lectures by specialists such as intelligence officers, sappers, ordnance experts and detectives from Scotland Yard. Theory was tested by practical exercises in the grounds of the Manor, which included two small quarries, one being used for hand grenade practice and the other as a shooting range suitable for sub-machine guns as well as pistols. Dédé was told how he would be issued with a pistol if and when he was first sent to France, but he now had to forget how to use it in the normal military manner, instead pointing it like a finger from the middle of his body and squeezing off two shots as rapidly as possible in the classic 'double tap' technique. This was in order to deliver, from any position and in any light, even in the dark, maximum stopping power as quickly as possible into the vulnerable part of an enemy's body, the area from his crutch to the top of his head. Two fast shots anywhere into that area should not only stop him, but also break up the nervous system immediately, *killing* the target. If there were no other threat to be dealt with, two more shots would make absolutely certain of finishing the victim off. Dédé also had his first use of the mass-produced Sten gun, supplied in great numbers to the Resistance thanks to its uncomplicated design and cheap cost of manufacture.

There were courses in map reading and sabotage, basic sending and receiving in Morse code, unarmed combat and weapon training. Each subject was first explained by lecturers and then came the practical experience. For instance, Dédé was introduced to plastic explosive and told that the best way of carrying it was to put it in his trouser pockets, where his body warmth would soften it and make it easier to mould onto the object to be destroyed. He discovered that it could be dropped, kicked and heated without anything happening. He learned, too, that detonators, unlike plastic explosive, were very temperamental and had to be handled carefully. Some of them, made of Mercury Fulminate, could not be carried in the hand because even the heat of the body could explode them. It was not unknown for trainees to lose hands or fingers blown off through incautious handling; when in the field many agents carried them inside caps or hats, as this was thought to keep the detonators cooler and they were therefore less likely to go off if the agent bumped into something. It was stressed that it was unwise to run when carrying detonators, because if you tripped and fell it would probably be the last thing you did. In the Manor's grounds Dédé practised setting charges to destroy a short stretch of railway track with, once again, the critical advice never to run away having laid a charge in case he tripped after only a step or two and consequently went up with the target. There were different instructions on blowing bridges, dams or transformers, using plastic explosive or amatol, another explosive which consisted of a mixture of TNT and ammonium nitrate.

Assault courses and more exercises were designed to challenge and improve physical endurance, helped by de Wesselow who, although over fifty, rarely missed setting the pace for the daily run of the trainee agents along the nearby Hog's Back ridge. Despite the Commandant's authoritarian leanings, at least one former agent remembers that the daily run sometimes continued unofficially along the road that led to the local pub. Dependent upon the season, a dip in the open-air swimming pool often rounded off the day before a hot bath and dinner, where officers and sergeants, instructors and staff, mixed freely and enjoyed a good standard of food. Pleasant evenings were often spent in the school's bar where, as in the Mess, there was no rank distinction and everyone seemed kind, welcoming and helpful. The music of Charles Trénet was never far from the gramophone, SOE's favourite tune of the time being 'Je tire ma révérence et m'en vais au hazard sur les routes de France, de France et de Navarre.' Yet even in the bar, the trainees were being closely, if unobtrusively, observed. For the staff were noting not only the trainees' grasp of the material being taught, but also their character traits and actions as well. This included an assessment of behaviour under the influence of alcohol and the conviviality of the bar. The ability to hold one's drink, or an inclination to become indiscreet, were among the details included in de Wesselow's weekly report on the group, backed up by his own regular trips up to London or brief visits by the Orchard Court staff to Wanborough. At the very end of the day, the beds were comfortable, but their dormitory sleeping quarters proved to be yet another testing ground, being bugged to discover whether the students talked in their sleep – and if so, in what language? They would similarly be woken roughly in the middle of the night in order to test whether their first irritable words were in French or English. And if that were not enough, sometimes there were night exercises when a group would have to slip out, lay dummy charges on a railway line some miles away and return to Wanborough, undetected, before dawn.

As part of the Wanborough syllabus, some students undertook a second phase at another school, including Dédé and Jean Larcher who went to STS 2 at Bellasis, another large country house on the crest of Box Hill near Dorking, just 20 miles along the North Downs hills from Wanborough. There they were taught more 'cloak and dagger' work, including additional unarmed combat techniques. They became familiar with the vital points of the body and how to attack them with fist, elbow, foot or whatever came to hand.

The preliminary training was hard and demanding work, backed by the instructors always stressing that lives depended on the use of correct methods in the field, but most trainees thoroughly enjoyed these first elements. At Wanborough, Lance Sergeant Rée reported of Dédé on 18 June 1942: 'He is quiet but not noticeably deep. He is "devout" (R.C.) and has a boyish sense of humour. He gives the impression of being thoroughly reliable.'

His good progress in training was then recognized with the prize that Dédé had long sought, for with effect from 18 July 1942 he at last received an emergency commission as a second lieutenant in the vaguely named General List, relinquishing any link with his former regiment of the KRRC. With this success came £15 to buy his officer's uniform and his joy was compounded when Dédé was notified he had passed the preliminary training stage. He wholeheartedly agreed to continue.

After the reward of a week's leave, the next step was SOE's Group A para-military training schools in and around Arisaig, on the west coast of the county of Inverness-shire in the highlands of Scotland. This element of the training syllabus was also originally planned to last three weeks, but as the war progressed, so did the length of the course until some trainees underwent up to five weeks' instruction.

The Group A establishments, remote from civilization, were the result of one of Brigadier Gubbins's early priorities when he joined SOE: to set up the training schools that would take over after initial assessment and basic instruction. In the early months of 1941 he had quickly achieved his aims. Not too distant from his own family links with the Isle of Mull, he had obtained use of an extensive area in and around Arisaig, which he knew well. This district could only be approached by one road, by a single-track railway or by water. So rugged and desolate was it that it was known as the Highlands of the Highlands and during the Second World War the whole area west of Fort William became a Special Protected Area, off limits to the general public other than the local population who had special passes and could be relied upon not to talk.

The train journey of over 500 miles north from London, via Glasgow and Fort William, was long and arduous. From Fort William, Dédé and Jean Larcher, travelling together, took the Mallaig branch line ever further northwards. But on alighting at Arisaig, Dédé might perhaps have felt an affinity coursing in his blood. For his Breton seafaring ancestors would certainly have approved of how a French ship had brought Charles Edward Stuart – Bonny Prince Charlie – to Arisaig and Scotland in July 1745 to start a rebellion against the occupying English.

For Gubbins, therefore, the area was perfect for his paramilitary schools and he secured the use of ten houses and shooting lodges. Only local residents and those with security passes were allowed into the area. Arisaig House became the centre for SOE's network of training establishments in the area, the other properties being Rhubana Lodge, Meoble Lodge, Swordland, Inverie House, Glaschollie, Garramor House, Camusdarrach, Traigh House and Morar Lodge. Dédé's group used a number of these establishments, but from Arisaig they were assigned to quarters in Meoble Lodge (STS 23) on the south side of Loch Morar, a long, deep, sea loch stretching inland from the coast facing the Isle of Skye. To reach the Lodge, Dédé and Larcher had to continue on to the small coastal town of Mallaig at the end of the railway line. There they embarked in a small boat, one of the modest flotilla operated by SOE from a base at Tarbet on Loch Nevis. This took them along Loch Morar to the isolated hamlet of Meoble where they landed and marched inland for a mile and a half to Meoble Lodge. One of the more remote properties, the Lodge had no road to it and was therefore accessible only by boat or via a testing five-mile cross-country hike from the village of Lochailort. Equally testing was the cuisine, for the food in Scotland was much less appetizing than at Wanborough and matched the spartan countryside. Corned beef was all too common, but the diet was on occasions informally supplemented with venison, salmon and prime beef that fell foul of the trainees' access to weapons and explosives.

Loch Morar, 12 miles long and over a mile wide in places, is the deepest lake in Europe, reaching a depth of over 1,000 feet and is said to be home to Morag, a monster similar to the more famous Nessie of Loch Ness. A sinister reputation is attached to Morag, however, based on the belief that whenever she appears it signals the impending death of a member of the local branch of the MacDonald clan. Much of the loch is wild, mountainous and exceptionally lonely, and as such, was ideally suited to SOE's purposes. The trainees learned to make and throw Molotov cocktail bombs on its shores and they paddled out onto it in canoes to attach limpet mines to steel plates sunk in the water, simulating ship sabotage.

Sabotage techniques on land for both industrial and railway targets were even more crucial, demolition and explosives training being high on SOE's remit. Laying dummy charges and fog signals, rail sabotage was carried out with the cooperation of the West Highland Line, who also arranged for the would-be agents to visit the end of the line at Mallaig where they were given the chance to drive, and become familiar with the construction of, a large steam locomotive. They became more familiar with the different types of explosive, SOE's original plastic explosive being a nitro-glycerine-based substance called 808 which, ironically, was the invention of Alfred Nobel, founder of the Nobel Peace Prize. It had a peculiar smell of almonds, but unless overheated was very flexible and could easily be cut and shaped. By the time Dédé was trained, however, it was being replaced by RDX, a more powerful plastic explosive without the telltale aroma. SOE called it PE, or 'plastique'. To preserve supplies of this valuable explosive, only gelignite was used in training.

A typical sabotage exercise at Arisaig might involve six or so trainees given the task of setting explosives on a railway engine in broad daylight. They would be given the target's map reference, a briefing and were then left to plan and carry out the attack. Two agents might approach the target from one direction, two more from another and the other couple from a third. Courses had to be plotted beforehand so that they could keep out of sight of enemy guards and patrols, roles played with much enthusiasm by the instructors who were always vigilant and ready to advise when things went wrong. The scheme would usually entail a lengthy cross-country approach, during which the saboteurs would follow the lie of the land, using whatever cover there was and keeping out of sight of all high ground where watchers might have been posted. After placing the charge on the engine, equally important was a successful escape.

Techniques that are today the staple diet of special forces around the world were developed and perfected – cross-country map reading by day and night, how to set an ambush or storm a house. The six acres of wild gardens enjoyed by Garramor, just a few minutes walk from the famous white sandy beaches with their breathtaking views of the islands of Eigg, Rum, Muck and Skye, were home to a special shooting range. One of the first of its kind, it had houses whose doors opened and closed while dummy targets suddenly sprang out on pulleys from all sorts of angles, testing the trainees' reflexes and instincts of whether to open fire or not. There they learned to handle arms and ammunition without thinking, practising how to assemble, dismantle and shoot a variety of rifles, pistols, PIATs, Sten and Bren guns, the weapons most often dropped to the Resistance, and how to instruct others in their use. For occasions when a gun was inappropriate, they extended their knowledge of unarmed combat, including, when necessary, that of silent killing. This black art had been perfected by two of SOE's earliest trainers in Scotland: Major Fairbairn, a former Shanghai police officer, and his close colleague Major Sykes, whom Fairbairn had known in Shanghai. Dubbed 'The Heavenly Twins', they were to design the famed Fairbairn-Sykes double-edged commando knife, still in widespread use today throughout the world. Other instructors were usually Army personnel, including many Highlanders.

No distinction was made between the sexes. Men and women trainees alike trekked over the rough country, often in appalling weather, wading through cold, rushing streams and creeping through the heather to hide from the other groups of trainees sent out in patrols to hunt for them. The outdoor, aggressive life proved a severe test of an agent's potential so that up to a third of each course were found lacking and regretfully advised that their training was at an end. For women to undergo this training in preparation for roles as couriers or radio operators was unprecedented and their eventual contribution on active service in the field was not made public until some time after the war had ended, when it was still considered controversial.

No record remains of his performance during paramilitary training, but Dédé passed without any problems and received another week's leave. To an instructor, or an outsider, those men and women trainees whose nerve and stamina had survived the Group A schools were now demonstrably tougher and more self-confident. This strengthened confidence in his own ability would very much be needed for Dédé's next phase of training, short in duration, but as much a test as anything in the entire syllabus – parachute training.

SOE's parachute course involved trainees being lodged in one of two large houses near Manchester: Dunham Massey House (STS 51a) at Altrincham, or Fulshaw Hall (STS 51b) at Wilmslow. Both were conveniently located for access to the nearby RAF aerodrome at Ringway known to SOE as STS 51, and now Manchester Airport. Four or five jumps were required, including one at night and one with a leg bag attached, useful for gaining a second or so's notice of hitting the ground in the dark. It was not unusual for a sizeable majority of each group of trainees to have never flown before and there were isolated instances of agents flatly refusing to take the course. Only if their other ability and promise outweighed this refusal did they continue and receive the option of a seaborne or aircraft landing.

The course commenced with instruction in the grounds of the training school. Dédé learned, from an aircraft fuselage mock-up, how to jump from a hatch in the floor of the aircraft and how to roll and land safely. He and his group were then taken to RAF Ringway where they watched other trainee parachutists and familiarized themselves with the layout of their dropping aircraft. This was the twin-engined Whitley, an obsolete bomber which had been used by the RAF's special duties squadrons for dropping SOE agents in the organization's early days. It had a round hole in the floor of the fuselage; the trainees sat on the edge until the order to jump was given when he or she would then jump up and step rigidly forward into the void. The parachute opened automatically by static line and the elated trainee would then try to heed the barrage of advice being shouted from the ground by an instructor equipped with a loudhailer.

The instructors were vastly experienced, with a macabre disregard for the occasional accidents that occurred. Parachuting was, they declared, 'the only wonderful sensation that the opposite sex can't give you' and they were fond of quipping, 'If your parachute doesn't open, report to the stores and you'll get another.' With such encouragement, Dédé's Whitley took off and climbed to an altitude of around 1,000 feet, heading towards the drop zone of either Tatton Park or Dunham Massey. The instructor announced three minutes to the jump and the dispatcher moved to the open hatch in the fuselage floor. The instructor was to be the first to go and positioned himself, seated on the edge of the hatch with his feet hanging down into space. Dédé and his fellow trainees lined up in pairs behind him. The dispatcher shouted 'Action Stations!' quickly followed by a downward sweep of his arm and the cry 'Number One, GO!' The instructor disappeared as the dispatcher continued, 'Number Two, GO!' and the trainees followed in their turn. Falling, Dédé had only seconds before a sharp tug on his shoulders announced that the static line had done its work and jerked open the parachute. There was little time to admire the scenery as the ground suddenly seemed to rush up towards him and he put his training into practice, bending his knees and rolling on landing. He stood up, unscathed and rolled up his parachute. Two or three more daylight jumps would have followed, culminating, if conditions allowed, in a night jump from a tethered balloon, an experience which many found more unnerving than their first jump from an aircraft.

The course completed, Dédé was issued with the prized parachute wings for his uniform and sent back to London where, at SOE headquarters, progress to date was reviewed and, in preparation for the next stage of training, he underwent assessment as to whether he was to become an organizer, radio operator or sabotage specialist. From his parachute training, Dédé had received another report from Lance Sergeant Rée who wrote on 7 August 1942 from STS 51: 'He has remained the most unapproachable member of the party. He is modest, although proud, and dislikes revealing his emotions or private opinions. This oyster-like quality serves as an excellent check to security lapses. He is very reliable.'

After their preliminary and paramilitary training was over, most trainee agents were then sent on to SOE's Group B schools, known as the 'Finishing Schools'. For Dédé, however, there was a different route, for in the latter half of 1942 SOE were desperate for radio operators, following a disastrous run of arrests in France. A shortage of trained W/T personnel was a permanent problem for F Section, since the wastage rate of operators was high, thanks to the ability of the Germans to locate and catch them. Having demonstrated a good grasp of the basics so far, and backed by his previous military experience, Dédé was consequently earmarked for specialist training as a radio operator, colloquially known in SOE as 'pianists'. Leaving Jean Larcher, he therefore joined a new group of trainees and was sent to the wireless training school (STS 52) at Thame Park in Oxfordshire, another stately home hidden from view 4 miles off the London to Oxford road and some 14 miles from the famous university town.

Set in over a thousand acres of some of the oldest enclosed parkland in England, Thame Park had a long and remarkable history. The main element of the house was Georgian, though the oldest part dated from the thirteenth century and was once part of a Cistercian abbey, still possessing arched cloisters. And similarly to Wanborough Manor, it came equipped with its own place of worship, for within the grounds close to the house was a disused chapel, built by the Cistercian monks and used for post-Reformation Roman Catholic worship in the early seventeenth century. The chapel had been renovated in 1836, but no service had been held there since 1916 when Thame Park was used as a camp for many thousands of young men on their way to the First World War. Dédé would, no doubt, have approved of and visited this historic refuge of his own faith.

Up until 1942, SOE was dependent upon SIS (MI 6) for communications with its agents abroad, but this changed with the opening of two signals stations not far from Thame Park, at Grendon Underwood and Poundon in Buckingham-shire, and the development of codes and ciphers solely for SOE use. Hand in hand with this went Thame Park's training programme which was anything from six to twelve weeks in duration, dependent upon the trainee's previous experience in radio work, though several breaks were involved. The house offered a fine library, sing-songs by the piano and table tennis. There was also the opportunity to go to the cinema and to dances, a marked relaxation after the earlier stages of training. Several different country sections of SOE trained there simultaneously, but they were kept strictly segregated.

No such segregation helped the male trainees face an additional challenge – the highly capable young women of the quaintly named First Aid Nursing Yeomanry, the FANYs. Many of these well-groomed and smartly uniformed women came from well-to-do or even titled families and SOE had initially used them in relatively menial roles such as housekeepers, cooks and typists. But as the war progressed and their numbers expanded, the FANYs became more representative of society as a whole and were used for a variety of more serious jobs such as code clerks and wireless operators, eventually carrying out most of the clandestine radio traffic to and from agents in the field. Thame Park was reputed to have had the best-looking FANYs, who were not only attractive and good company, but were also used to test how easily a trainee could be distracted.

The days at Thame Park were, however, crammed with continuous instruc-tion in codes and the operation of short-wave radio transmitter/receivers, capable of reaching up to 500 miles and with a frequency range of 3.5 to 16 megacycles per second. The set weighed in at a hefty 30 lb or so, but fitted neatly into an innocuous 2-foot-long suitcase. A vital addition that Dédé would have carried separately were the crystals that were fitted to the set and set the wavelength for transmissions, but a great challenge was that the transceiver needed 70 feet of aerial to function properly.

Dédé learned that in an urban environment it would take the Germans around thirty minutes to discover where the transceiver was being used. Where possible, operators were recommended to work in isolated areas and were under strict instructions to transmit short, concise messages, at irregular intervals, at various wavelengths and from different places. In theory the circuit organizer would be responsible for coding and decoding his own messages, while the W/T operator was only responsible for transmitting or receiving them. In practice, however, it was recognized and accepted that the W/T operator often undertook coding as well.

Ideally, the same location ought not to be used on two consecutive occasions, but this meant that either the operator had to move his set from house to house, or have several sets permanently sited in the different locations. The former option was highly dangerous, since if stopped at a checkpoint, an operator would stand no chance of explaining away the transceiver set in his small suitcase. The alternative, however, involved the operator having to be supplied with several sets and this took some time to achieve. Keeping transmissions as brief as possible was in order to give the least possible chance of detection to the Germans' radio interception service, the Funk-Horchdienst.[2] If a lengthy message were necessary, it had to be sent on two or more schedules ('skeds') of which each operator normally had three or four a week. A schedule was the time slot when the home station back in England would be listening on the operator's frequency.

Power could come from two sources. Batteries had the disadvantage of needing recharging, but enabled use of a set in the countryside where mains power might not be available. The electric mains were more reliable, but since electricity consumption would be metered, agents had to learn how to tap the mains before the meter. If practicable, it was also recommended that a guard should keep watch outside.

It was stressed that it could be dangerous for an operator to be seen with his organizer, and that it was best to communicate with him by 'cut-outs', intermediaries whose only job was to act as couriers, carrying messages from one agent to another. This also helped with other security rules, for Dédé was warned of the danger of over-enthusiasm and instructed that he should not attempt to find out more about the circuit than he was told, not know more than one or two members and not undertake other subversive activity.

If the worst came to the worst and he were arrested, Dédé gathered that he could not expect to be executed immediately, but that instead he would be 'persuaded' to reveal his W/T plan so that his set could be operated back to England, either by himself under duress, or by German personnel. To guard against such an eventuality, he had to pre-arrange 'security checks' before he left, words or phrases he could omit from messages in order to alert the home station if all were not well. Unfortunately, agents were prone to forget to include their security checks, to the extent that on occasions SOE reminded and chastized agents for forgetting the checks. This had disastrous consequences in a number of instances where the Germans had captured agents and sets, and were consequently alerted, by SOE's naivety, to their omission of the checks. The comeback on the captured operator could be fatal.

Long-range transmissions were normally practised by two exercises, each a week long, from somewhere in Scotland or the north of England, where Dédé would have had to find lodgings and, without attracting the local authorities, transmit messages every day back to Thame where they were scrutinized carefully for accuracy. The local civil and military police were sometimes tipped off and given details that enabled them to look for and if possible follow and arrest trainees carrying out these exercises.

In the middle of his course at Thame Park, Dédé spent two weeks slotting back into the standard training regime by joining a Group B Finishing School for the security training that was probably the most important part of an agent's tuition. In effect a graduate course in survival in an occupied country, this component of SOE's syllabus was designed to overlay Dédé's newly developed and overt confidence with the covert skills that he would need in France to be able to pass unnoticed and not draw attention to himself.

Originally, trainee wireless operators had received security training during their stay at Thame Park, sometimes at nearby Grendon Underwood. But after many early losses of operators in France, something more was clearly needed and so Dédé was among those wireless operator trainees who, from the spring of 1942 onwards, were sent on far more extensive security training at one of the finishing schools at Beaulieu, in the Hampshire New Forest. Though a full two weeks were spent there, wireless operators nevertheless remained most at risk of all agents and at one time their average survival rate in France was calculated at only three months. Even after security training they were prone to becoming careless when their enforced isolation in the field drove them to become sloppy and take risks. In addition, the Germans knew that a wireless operator, while being technically vulnerable to detection, could also prove to be the key to uncovering an entire circuit. They knew that the operator would at least be in touch with the circuit organizer and probably, as the circuit's 'post-box', with several others.

So, in addition to having to continue daily wireless practice, Dédé was thrown into a compressed version of Beaulieu's syllabus, divided into five sections and each with its own department responsible for delivering the instructions. These were:

Department A – agent techniques, clandestine life and organization, personal security, communications methods and the use of sub-agents.

Department B – exercises to test the instruction from Department A.

Department C – enemy forces, including the Vichy French as well as the Germans.

Department D – clandestine propaganda, both factual and fictitious.

Department E – use of secret codes, ciphers and inks.

The course at Beaulieu was located on the ancestral estate of the Lords Montagu in the New Forest, where the new agents were housed in houses and cottages in the grounds. Even with rigid security backed by barbed wire, and temporary wartime building additions, it was a beautiful place, and many agents later remembered Beaulieu as an enchanted setting, despite the intense concentration and hard work that was demanded of them. It was certainly a pleasant experience compared to the harsh conditions previously encountered in the Highlands of Scotland.

On arrival, agents were allocated to one of a series of twelve houses, of differing sizes but mostly built on the estate by Lord Montague for his friends in the early 1900s. The training staff lived in one of these, a large house named The Rings (STS 31), and were commanded by Colonel Frank Spooner. His lecturers and instructors were as varied and eclectic a group as the agents themselves, and included many talented individuals later to gain fame, or infamy. Hardy Amies, later the Queen's couturier, was one, and Kim Philby, eventually to find notoriety when discovered to be a Soviet double agent, was another before he transferred to SIS. A number of former Scotland Yard officers now found themselves instructing alongside erstwhile adversaries, and all were supported by a sprinkling of agents already returned from France, who could speak from experience in the field.

The houses were generally in good order and comfortable, secluded and with sizeable grounds. Dédé's SOE file does not specify which of the schools he attended at Beaulieu, but F Section normally used The Vineyards (STS 35) for its wireless operators and it is there that Dédé most likely spent his two weeks. Sited on the side of a hill, The Vineyards lay close to the road which ran down into the village of Beaulieu and was run by Captain William 'Nobby' Clark, an expert instructor in survival techniques, living off the land and fieldcraft. A large man with a ruddy complexion, he had risen through the ranks of the Regular Army and had served in the First World War, before becoming a gamekeeper on the royal estate at Sandringham in Norfolk.

Jean Larcher was already at Beaulieu in another training group when Dédé arrived, but there was precious little time to catch up on news. The training staff arrived daily at The Vineyards and began the task of teaching Dédé how to live under a false identity and under enemy occupation. First of all he had to become familiar with the wide range and the myriad of uniforms and ranks of the enemy's military and intelligence forces who he could expect to encounter in France, especially those who might be looking for him. These forces included not just the Germans, but also the Vichy French who operated numerous armed police and paramilitary organizations. A country gendarme would rarely pose any great threat and, indeed, could often be relied upon to help or take part in the Resistance. But the Milice, a volunteer paramilitary organization of French fascists, were always dangerous and frequently operated alongside the Germans. Their agents and informers, local French people with an eye to gaining advantage from the occupier, were always in a very small and generally despised minority. Yet they represented one of the greatest threats to an agent, given their local knowledge and their ability to detect subtler differences in language and behaviour than the Germans.

Dédé learned the critical art of taking on a false identity, by making up a name, fabricating a life to support the new name and even adopting a disguise. The customs of the country would be new even to those who had grown up in France. Very few would be familiar with the ration books used when making purchases, when and how to show their identity papers when challenged, how to pass through a snap control point at a railway station. Dédé might be required to produce, in addition to his identity card, a work permit, a ration card, a tobacco card, a permit if in a coastal or frontier zone, as well as demobilization papers and a medical certificate establishing his exemption from forced labour in Germany. Each forgery of these papers in the possession of an agent had to be the up-to-date official form, correctly signed and stamped.

Expert interrogators then questioned him to see what holes might be found in his story. Any mistake would be pointed out, and the trainee reminded that a similar slip in France would undoubtedly lead to torture and death. It was stressed that survival depended on remembering the details. If captured, Dédé would be expected to stay silent, no matter how harsh the interrogation, for forty-eight hours. This would give some time to warn all the people who had been in contact with him to move house and cover their tracks. Officers from the Intelligence Corps normally undertook the interrogation sessions, lasting up to five hours, getting as close to the real thing as possible without involving actual physical torture. Dédé would have been threatened, screamed at, pushed around, kept standing under bright lights and questioned repeatedly without respite. He would also have received unsettling instruction on exactly how vicious and unscrupulous the German secret police forces were expected to be. SOE knew that their agents, even though members of the British armed forces, and perhaps even in uniform, would receive little mercy if captured, and would fall outside the protection of the Geneva Convention and the normal arrangements for POWs.

From 'Nobby' Clark, Dédé also learned how to survive in the open. With his love of *la chasse*, Dédé must have have been a willing student and he would also have learned how to poach birds and fish, and how to build shelters of branches and leaves, along with a wealth of countryside lore from the royal retainer. From other instructors equally well versed in their specific areas of expertise, Dédé was trained in writing messages in invisible inks and how to search people properly, being warned that some collaborators did not carry written messages on paper but on their bodies. He learned how to make contacts in the field, set up safe houses and mail drops, and to pass messages surreptitiously in public places.

In the event that he was ever suspected by the enemy, he became adept at spotting and shaking off a pursuer when being followed. Another course showed him how to locate and prepare suitable landing and drop zones for the reception of arms and other agents. In one of the smaller houses, set in Beaulieu's woods, he gained knowledge of some particularly useful methods of opening handcuffs, picking locks and breaking safes. Although the instructors were in uniform, some were known to have questionable peacetime backgrounds.

He was taught the drill for entering a public establishment such as a restaurant or bar. Firstly, he should take a good look around outside, just in case there were Gestapo, other Germans or French Milice about. On entering, it was preferable to choose a table facing the door, or the foyer, so that he could see what was going on, and who came and went. It was also advisable to sit with one's back against the wall, both for a better view of the room and so that one could not be watched or surprised from behind. Possible escape routes had to be identified as quickly as possible; options should include windows, the waiters' entrance to the kitchens, the toilets etc. Identity cards and other similar documentation was to

32

be carried at all times in case of spot checks – without them, Dédé was told, he would only draw attention to himself and he might have to accompany a policeman, or someone worse, to his house or hotel to pick the documentation up. That would only serve to give away more information, namely the place where he was staying. It was important, too, to have ready a simple excuse for being in a particular place at a particular time, so that he could explain where he was going, and why.

Lectures included detailed briefings on the different political groupings among the French. The trainees were taught how to organize, nurture, arm and supply a Resistance group. While controversial and often attracting criticism, SOE's policy was to ignore politics in general and to simply support whoever had the most potential for harming the enemy. In France, this meant that agents often had a sensitive role to play between Communist and Gaullist Resistance groups who had very different long-term objectives.

The training was tested by exercises, termed 'schemes'. The 36-hour scheme was often in one of the nearby coastal towns or cities of Southampton, Bournemouth or Portsmouth and involved the agent having to carry out some act of sabotage or intelligence gathering in a closely guarded area. An overnight stay was involved and the local police and Field Security units, on alert, had to be avoided. If they weren't, the exercise would also involve arrest and interrogation, and the trainee had to rely on his or her cover story or escape. Only as a last resort could they telephone a special number in order to be bailed out by the SOE staff, and Dédé's personal papers confirm that he underwent such mock interrogation.

The '96-hour scheme' came at the very end of the course, was much more complex, and involved travelling to and from a more distant city in England. Sometimes alone, sometimes in a small group of two or three, agents were given a specific, often criminal, task such as planting explosives in a factory or on a railway line, or reconnoitring a military facility. Normally, several contacts had to be made and a variety of targets reconnoitred or attacked.

And so Beaulieu and Thame Park, taking care not to dilute the aggression and confidence developed at Arisaig, subtly imbued Dédé with the self-control and caution that was also critical for his survival. It was confirmed that he had passed all his instruction and was now ready for the final preparations that would allow him to depart for France.

Chapter Five

# To France

Once all training was completed, another spell of leave was granted before Dédé reported back to the anonymous apartment in Orchard Court. He did so with the three pips of a Captain on his shoulders – ironically, in view of his long struggle to gain a commission, the first few months of 1943 had brought swift promotion. In January, he was elevated from Lieutenant to acting Captain, and exactly two months later this was confirmed as his temporary (hostilities only) rank, doubtless with an eye to the respect that SOE would wish him to command while in France.

It was now Orchard Court's job to provide Captain Maingard with the final preparation for his mission and it was at this point that Dédé met Pilot Officer (later Squadron Leader) Maurice Southgate. Code-named 'Hector', Southgate was later to be described by Colonel Buckmaster as a 'gifted and intelligent leader, entirely devoted to the cause', rated as one of SOE's greats. Southgate was already briefed and ready to be dropped, along with a courier, into France to lead a new circuit, code-named 'Stationer'. Dédé was to follow as Southgate's wireless operator and another courier was also expected to be included.

Southgate was of English parents, but had been born in France in 1914 and schooled there. He had qualified as a draughtsman, but first pursued a career as a furniture designer, and later as a successful interior designer. He had joined the RAF on the outbreak of war and served with the British Expeditionary Force in France until the country's collapse. Evacuated from St Nazaire aboard the ill-fated *Lancastria*, he was lucky to survive when the ship was dive-bombed and set alight. Over 3,000 of the 5,000 aboard drowned, but Southgate lived to tell the tale by swimming for several hours in the burning oil.

On reaching England, he discovered that a close friend, John Starr, together with his brother George, was already going through SOE's training regime. Another friend, who had been in the year ahead of him at school in Paris, was Pearl Witherington. Pearl had also managed to escape from France where she had been working at the British Embassy in Paris. In London she joined the Women's Auxiliary Air Force (WAAF) and worked at the Air Ministry where she one day bumped into Southgate. Hearing of his wish to return to France, she used her contacts in the Air Ministry to have him recommended to SOE, and he soon followed the Starr brothers through training. Meeting his future radio operator for the first time, Southgate was pleased with what he saw and immediately hit it off with Dédé. While this helped, it was nevertheless stressed that direct contact between the two men in France was to be kept to a minimum, it being the job of couriers to deliver messages between them. Southgate, known for his strict observance of security procedures, would not brook any jeopardizing of this procedure and soon after meeting Dédé he left for France, being parachuted in on 25 January 1943 in the company of a courier, Jacqueline Nearne. Fortunately they did not have to start from scratch, for 'Stationer' was to be developed from the earlier 'Tinker' circuit built up by Captain (later Major) Ben Cowburn, another SOE agent. Cowburn had gone to France in the autumn of 1941 and had operated across a large area of central and southern France, from Châteauroux in the Indre region where he was first dropped, to Tarbes and Pau in the Hautes-Pyrénées, a vast area almost 600 kilometres from north to south.

The foundations for Southgate's new organization were two Frenchmen locally recruited by Cowburn at the two extremes of 'Tinker'. Auguste Chantraine, code-named 'Octave', was to be made head of the northern sector of 'Stationer' in the Indre region, using existing groups of twenty or so good, tried and tested men in the towns and villages of Vierzon, Bourges, Villefranche-sur-Cher, Eguzon, Argenton-sur-Creuse and Dun-le-Poëlier. All were communist groups, taking their orders from the local commanders of the FTP, the Francs-Tireurs et Partisans, the armed wing of the Parti Communiste Français (PCF). Despite this and thanks to Chantraine's efforts, they had all demonstrated a willingness to work with, and even take orders from, the British. In the southern sector, Charles Rechenmann, code-named 'Julien', led a large group of former prisoners of war of the Germans. Located in and around Tarbes in the Hautes-Pyrénées, these men had no political leanings at all and, perhaps as a result, were considered particularly sound and trustworthy by London.

All this information was imparted to Dédé in the somewhat incongruous surroundings of the plush apartment used by SOE on the third floor of Orchard Court. This consisted of some six rooms, very much in contrast to the bare room in which he had first been interviewed. His cover story and assumed identity were all important. If a different profession had been involved, this might have involved several weeks' basic job training, but since Dédé was to become Guy Marguery, a self-employed accountant who worked from home, he was able to call on his interrupted studies for good cover. He received final instruction in the tiniest of details that SOE continually collected to allow him to be as unobtrusive as possible. This included any recent changes in documents needed and the conditions of daily life, including the enemy's latest regulations about travel, curfew and work. Much of this information came from refugees or escapers from France, from messages radioed back and more recently from those agents returning from a first tour of duty in the field.

For Dédé, such up-to-the-minute details were even more important as he was not a native Frenchman and had never lived there. Coming as he did from a

British colony, something as simple as looking the wrong way before crossing the street could prove his downfall.

His civilian 'French' clothes came from a small company in London run by a Jewish refugee from Austria, originally contracted by SOE to collect second-hand continental clothes and personal effects such as wallets, watches and suitcases from synagogues and refugee centres. As such original items became scarce, the company had then expanded into making clothes to order and to their own continental fashion designs. Dédé would therefore have been sent to the company's discreet workshop near Oxford Circus for fittings by a team of tailors and seamstresses. He was to have good suits, with the labels of French tailors sown in, and cut in the markedly-different continental style. Even the smallest incorrect details, such as the way labels were stitched, could on inspection betray an agent and he had to memorize the name of the town and shop where he was supposed to have bought the suits. Anything that was newly made had to be 'worn in' so that Dédé would not look expensively dressed and so arouse suspicion of black-marketeering when he arrived in France. He was also issued with French pants, vests, socks, shoes and ties, and had the pick of items such as pocket knife, fountain pen and pencils. In short, everything he needed he got.

A full medical check-up included an inspection for dental work that had not been performed in the continental manner. Any tell-tale British-style fillings, for example, meant a rather painful visit to an inconspicuous French dentist in Maddox Street. A haircut, given by a French barber, completed the picture and then Dédé was photographed for his identity card, expertly forged along with his other documents at SOE's own directly-staffed establishment.

A complete radio operator's plan came next, containing schedules, call signs etc., and it was impressed upon Dédé how critical this plan was, and his adherence to it. He also had to select a code based on a poem that he could remember by heart. To it were added security checks, which Dédé would only omit if he were captured and made to transmit under duress. It was a far from perfect or secure system, having been inherited from SIS, and SOE's brilliant young code maker, Leo Marks, was working feverishly to introduce a replacement system. It was Marks who gave agents their final briefing on codes before they left for the field, but his new system (WOKS) was adopted by SOE some two months too late for Dédé.[1] Marks would therefore have made a final check on Dédé's ability, based on a fresh poem code (the one used in training had to be replaced), pointing out any errors. Poem codes were still popular with many, as they involved no incriminating evidence, relying as they did on memory. This, of course, overlooked the fact that the Germans could torture the code from an agent.

At some point, Dédé also had a brief interview with the head of F Section. A tall man, with a gentle manner, Colonel Maurice Buckmaster was thought by some to have been a little naïve for a secret service chief, and to have lacked the ruthlessness that one might have expected. But no one ever questioned his dedication to the job; he was acutely aware of the importance and value of his agents and he cared about them deeply. He made a habit of presenting agents, as they were about to depart for the field, with a personal gift such as gold cufflinks or

36

a gold cigarette case. These naturally had no British markings, but would remind the agent he or she was not forgotten back at headquarters. More practically, the gift could also be sold if an agent were short of money. From notes made on Dédé's personal file maintained by SOE headquarters, Buckmaster seemed to like and admire his young Mauritian volunteer.

Lastly, Dédé would have had a sobering interview about his will, next of kin and contacts in the event of his death. This was usually conducted by a forceful woman in the uniform of the WAAFs, Vera Atkins. Nominally F Section's Intelligence Officer and personal assistant to Buckmaster, Atkins was considered by many to be the real power in F Section. Like Buckmaster, she was indefatigable and was always immaculate, with not a hair out of place. Her presence was found formidable by many and intimidating by some, and she could cow even the most ebullient agent with a caustic remark and an icy glare. But she made a point of personally seeing as many as possible of the agents who left for France, making arrangements for letters to be sent to relatives while they were out of touch, taking charge of personal possessions left behind and briefing them on what to expect once they landed. Atkins was also renowned, and occasionally later blessed, for the bits and pieces of daily French life that she collected, from only she knew where, to help equip agents. These included photos of supposed friends and relatives, apparently genuine receipts from French shops, letters with seemingly valid postal franks from other cities, Métro tickets, etc. Even if they were never inspected, these small additions strengthened the impression that F Section knew their job.

With the briefing completed, Dédé was at last ready to become one of what Buckmaster was later to describe as F Section's 'unofficial ambassadors of the free world'. If feasible, agents were permitted home leave, but with strict instructions to say nothing to friends or relatives about the work for which they were now ready. Dédé, having no home in Britain, might well have been lodged in a 'holding house' instead, probably in London and therefore within relatively easy reach of his departure airfield.

For although some were landed by boat on deserted stretches of the French coast, Dédé was to be among the 90 per cent of agents who were delivered to France by air. Flights were normally limited to only the five or six nights either side of a full moon, when visibility was good enough for accurate navigation and identification of landing grounds and drop zones. That was the theory. In practice, and especially in the winter months, poor weather conditions often jeopardized these 'moon periods' and in reality there were often only a very few nights each month suitable for operations.

If the insertion were to be via a landing ground, the ubiquitous Westland Lysander was usually the aircraft used by the RAF's Special Duties squadrons. Despite its small size, the single-engined Lysander could carry one agent comfortably, two at a pinch and very occasionally three at a very tight squeeze. Its immensely strong and forgiving undercarriage, together with a remarkable short take-off and landing ability, made it ideal for the rough and ready airstrips of the *résistants* – if all went smoothly, agents could be set down and picked up in just three minutes on the ground. One drawback was the Lysander's restricted range, but this was overcome by an additional fuel tank and use of the Fighter Command airfield at Tangmere, near Chichester, on the south coast of England, as a forward operating base. This avoided the need to use up precious fuel, since the Special Duties squadrons' home base was RAF Tempsford in Bedfordshire, 120 miles from the south coast. Twin-engined Lockheed Hudsons had greater range and were also available for landings, but required a much longer airstrip and so were reserved for operations where groups of personnel had to be delivered or brought out.

The alternative to a landing by Lysander or Hudson was to parachute in, as taught at Ringway during training. Drops were generally from just 500 or 600 feet, with the aircraft flying at a relatively sedate 100–120 miles an hour, and were flown from Tempsford using the Special Duties squadrons' longer-range aircraft, which were converted four-engined bombers such as the Handley Page Halifax and, later, the Short Stirling.

A parachute drop was to be the method used for Dédé and as his departure for France at last approached, he found himself in the company of another agent, Harry Rée, also on his first operation and destined for the 'Headmaster' circuit in Clermont-Ferrand, which already had links with Southgate's 'Stationer' circuit. An engaging, but complex character, Rée was Manchester-born, and well educated at Shrewsbury School and St John's College, Cambridge, where he had shared Dédé's passion for rugby. He had chosen to teach modern languages as a career and was a schoolmaster in Kent when war broke out. Holding pacifist views, he had first volunteered for minesweepers in the Royal Navy, but when France fell he realized he must play a more active role. He joined the Royal Artillery as a lowly gunner, but soon applied to join his brother in the Field Security Service of the Intelligence Corps,[2] serving in the unit whose job it was to help SOE in planning and delivering exercises for its agents under training. He even played the part of a Gestapo officer on occasions, interrogating trainee agents who were captured during their sabotage exercises. He quickly decided, however, that the role of poacher, rather than gamekeeper, would be of greater interest and he therefore applied to SOE and was accepted for agent training.

Rée followed much the same training path as Dédé, though initially his language skills came under scrutiny. He rated his German 'fair' and his French 'good', but the latter had caused concern during his training where he was described as 'fluent, but not correct'. He had improved through mixing with his French-speaking fellow trainees and had shone in response to the physical demands of the training. Hard working and intellectually quick to learn, he proved to be extremely popular with recruits and instructors alike, though the latter were worried by Rée's own self-questioning as to whether he would ultimately be up to the job. They need not have worried, for he was to prove to be one of SOE's most efficient and courageous operatives.

While Dédé had undergone his own additional training to specialize as a radio operator, Rée was singled out to become a sabotage instructor. He therefore took the industrial sabotage course at STS 17 at Hatfield in Hertfordshire before being finally ready to be sent to France in this specialist role. Code-named 'César', he was to act as second in command to Captain Brian Rafferty's 'Headmaster' circuit in the Bourbonnais region. 'Headmaster' was a three-man team that had parachuted into France in September 1942, but its organizer, Major Charles Hudson, was arrested shortly after arrival and Rafferty's job of taking over was made more difficult when his radio operator, Captain George Donovan Jones, suffered a bad bicycle accident not long afterwards and permanently lost the sight of one eye. Jones managed to continue some of his work, but 'Headmaster' nevertheless needed support and Southgate kept in regular touch by visits and the efforts of Jacqueline Nearne as courier. 'Stationer' and 'Headmaster' overlapped in the city of Clermont-Ferrand where the enemy-controlled Michelin works, manufacturing tyres and caterpillar tracks for the German Army, had been designated as an important sabotage target. The necessary expertise to launch an attack was not, however, available and to remedy this no less than three abortive attempts had been made to drop Rée in the moon periods of February and March 1943. Each time the aircraft had been unable to find the drop zone (DZ), while on the third attempt the Halifax had been coned in the searchlights and hit by anti-aircraft fire. One engine out of action had meant a slow and tension-filled return to Tempsford, but Rée was not dispirited. Hitting it off immediately when he joined up with Dédé, Rée was champing at the bit to reach France, but again he had to wait until the next moon, decent weather and the availability of aircraft coincided.

The April moon period of 1943 was a hectic one for F Section after the poor weather of previous months. Like Rée, Dédé had suffered a number of abortive attempts to drop and he was one of several agents now eagerly awaited in France, badly needed radio operators being in the greatest demand. This was his best chance, before the moon period ended on the 25th. The two agents were driven up from London to spend a final day or so enjoying the good food and wine provided by a staff of FANYs at one of SOE's holding houses within easy reach of RAF Tempsford, such as Gaynes Hall or Hassells Hall. The latter, an imposing Georgian mansion just 2 miles from the aerodrome, was frequently used by F Section to while away the agents' final, nervous, hours before being dropped. All the while they waited the two men went over the details of the life of the person they were to become, so that date of birth, names of family members, schools attended, military service, job history etc. would all be automatically quoted when they were questioned in France.

Finally, on the evening of 12 April 1943, some two to three hours before their aircraft was due to take off, the short trip was made to the airfield from the holding house. Close to the village of Everton, in Bedfordshire, Tempsford airfield was a wartime creation, having only been built in 1941, and was reputed to be one of the worst-affected aerodromes in the country for fog and flooding. Bordered and overlooked by the main London to Edinburgh railway line, it was an odd choice of site for clandestine undertakings and some of the RAF's most secret operations. Nevertheless, the airfield had become the base of the RAF's Special Duties or 'Moon' squadrons, 138 and 161 Squadrons. Their crews had an esprit de corps special even for the RAF, knowing that they faced death every time they flew, but priding themselves on the safe delivery and collection of their mysterious charges. Together, the two squadrons served both SOE and SIS, and in early 1943 were operating Halifax aircraft, easily capable of reaching even the furthest dropping points in southern France.

The short final drive to Tempsford for Dédé and Rée, accompanied by their Air Liaison Officer, was in a large car with drawn blinds at its windows so that, as the FANY driver entered the airfield through the station's main technical site, curious eyes could not see the shadowy occupants. The car continued on past the RAF's offices and as dusk was falling it swung onto the concrete perimeter track, which encircled the runways. A short distance further and it turned inwards from the perimeter and pulled up in front of a cluster of Nissen huts and old farm buildings, seemingly marooned on the wide open expanse of the airfield.

The buildings were the last vestiges of Gibraltar Farm which had otherwise made way for the aerodrome's construction in 1941 and which lay astride the line of an ancient road built by Rome's legions many centuries before. In the privacy afforded by its relatively isolated position, the agents and military personnel handled by SOE and SIS could make final preparations for their operations in the farm's 150-year-old barn before boarding their waiting aircraft.

At Gibraltar Farm Dédé and Rée were checked one last time for any tell-tale evidence that might soon compromise them – such as an overlooked English coin or the stub of a theatre ticket. Their escort from F Section's Air Liaison staff, who had accompanied them to the holding premises and had shown them their drop-ping points on a map, now helped them to sort out their equipment. He also offered Dédé and Rée their two sets of pills: one was Benzadrine, designed to keep them awake for at least another three hours when exhausted; the other was the 'L' (for Lethal) tablet, in a little rubber cover, which was a suicide pill of potassium cyanide. A last option if an agent despaired of all hope in the face of torture or execution, the 'L' tablet took some time to act if swallowed, but if bitten death came within fifteen seconds. Many agents either refused their 'L' pill or threw it away on landing.

They were then kitted out with their personal equipment, including money belts, a .45 Colt revolver, commando knife and an entrenching tool, the latter in order to bury parachutes on landing. They both wore ordinary lounge suits, but over the top of everything went thick camouflaged overalls. Encumbered already by this bulky jump suit, they then had their parachutes strapped on, the harnesses being tightened so much that they could not stand upright. Hunched up in this manner the two men were finally ready and were driven out to a dispersal point where a Halifax of 138 Squadron's 'C' Flight waited, a solid dark mass against the expanse of the blacked-out airfield. As they pulled up alongside, Dédé and Rée could see that the aircraft's bomb racks were already laden with the containers that contained not only arms and ammunition, but their own suit-cases, tinned food, cigarettes and chocolate, clothes and wireless sets.

All RAF personnel at Tempsford were under strict security instructions not to show too much interest in their agents or their loads – in marked contrast to their American counterparts in the USAAF's Special Duties 'Carpetbagger' squadrons, where crews often asked agents to sign the aircraft's autograph book. On one occasion a SAS team being landed by 'Carpetbagger' C-47 into a clandestine airstrip in central France were startled to find themselves accompanied by an

American official photographer, complete with large flash for pictures on the ground. The RAF took the job much more seriously, one former pilot of 161 Squadron, for instance, recalling that he was only expected to note 'Duty carried out' or 'Duty not carried out'.

Irrespective of security considerations, mutual respect between aircrews and agents was high. On this occasion, Flight Lieutenant Gryglewicz and his crew, all Polish,[3] were waiting outside Halifax 'C for Charlie' to greet the two 'Joes', as both the RAF and SOE informally termed the agents. No names were exchanged, just handshakes all round and wishes of 'good luck' and 'happy landings'. Dédé and Rée were then lifted, pulled and pushed into the aircraft's fuselage where mattresses had been laid out for them. The dispatcher fussed over them like a mother hen, handing each a pack of sandwiches and a flask of coffee laced with brandy, and helping to make them as comfortable as circumstances permitted. They were also given sleeping bags and advised to sleep if possible.

One by one the four powerful engines were coaxed into life and the Halifax eased out onto the perimeter track. Slowly, it made its way to the end of the runway in use, the crew making last-minute checks and adjustments. At the runway the lumbering former bomber turned into the wind and momentarily halted. Inside the fuselage the lights were switched off and the airframe shuddered as the engines were run up against the brakes. Final checks completed, the pilot again eased the throttles forward and the aircraft roared down the runway. At 9.20 p.m. 'C for Charlie'[4] lifted off from Tempsford's runway on 'Physician 19/Stationer 1/Scientist 14', one of six operations that night by 138 Squadron, and headed south for occupied France with its cargo of containers, packages and two secret agents.

A fine night had already set in and before he settled down on his mattress, Dédé peered out at the ground far below, surprised to see so many lights showing in a country that prided itself on the thoroughness of its black-out precautions. Conversation proved near impossible over the roar of the engines, so Dédé and Rée settled down, sipped from their thermos and, as suggested, tried to sleep. After two hours or so the dispatcher shouted that they were crossing the French coast and the Halifax dropped to low level, rocking and pitching more and picking up the Garonne river which was to help guide them towards their goal. As over England, lights could be seen here and there, sometimes clearly signalling a friendly 'V for Victory' in Morse code.

Now fully alert, Dédé and Rée ran through the drill that would soon take place. There were two lights, one red, one green, close to the exit hole in the floor of the aircraft. When the pilot spotted the drop zone he would illuminate the red light and the dispatcher would then warn the agents and connect their parachutes to the static line inside the fuselage. As packages and containers were also to be dropped with the two parachutists, the practice would be to drop the agents on the first run, and the supplies on the second. Most supplies were dropped in containers or panniers, sometimes with small packages. Panniers were used for dropping less fragile items such as clothing and sleeping bags, but they would occasionally burst open on landing, scattering the contents. Containers were long cylindrical drums divided internally into cells. To simplify matters they were

41

delivered pre-packed with code letters on the outside denoting their contents and would normally hold a mixture of clothing, rations, ammunition, weapons, 'comforts' such as rum and cigarettes, medical kit, tents and sleeping bags.

Suddenly, the Halifax jolted and juddered as its engines were throttled back. Dédé and Rée looked at one another and agreed they must be getting close, but at that moment the dispatcher came down the fuselage from the front of the aircraft, where an intense conversation had been going on. The news was disappointing: the pilot and navigator believed they had found the DZ, but there were no lights from the ground or any other sign of a reception committee. Despite this setback, the RAF's orders were to drop the two men 'blind' if necessary, i.e. without a reception, which was what the dispatcher now told the two agents, shouting the pilot's wishes for good luck and a safe landing. A red light suddenly glowed, showing that they were running in for the drop, and the dispatcher, opening the hatch door in the floor of the fuselage, called 'Action stations!'

Dédé and Rée struggled clumsily to their feet and looked at each other, not without emotion. The dispatcher hooked them both onto the static line and signalled them forward to the exit hole. Together, they peered out at the moonlit landscape as the pilot banked the Halifax for the final run in to the DZ. Dédé, who was to be first out, eased himself down into a sitting position, feet dangling over the edge of the hole, and braced himself against the cold, inrushing air. Rée squatted opposite him, each man facing inwards with their back to the wings in mid-fuselage. The note of the engines dropped again, but as the jump light flashed green the dispatcher's 'Go!' was initially not heard by Dédé and there were a few moments of confusion until the dispatcher confirmed the order. In retrospect, it would have been better for the pilot to have turned and made another run-in. But the dispatcher again urged Dédé to jump, so he pushed himself forward into space and, keeping his body as upright as he could, disappeared from view.

Below, a reception committee commanded by Southgate awaited the two new arrivals, but a parachute drop and its attendant reception could be a complex affair. When an aircraft's engines were heard, the decision had to be made as to whether it sounded like the expected aircraft. If so, a pattern of torches would be shone, or flares lit on the DZ in an inverted L-shape, while a previously agreed code letter was repeatedly flashed in Morse. From the RAF's point of view, the exercise was somewhat more complex. The aircraft needed to fly at a specific height and the pilot and dispatcher had to take careful account of wind direction and strength. Even a slightly inaccurate drop could cause great problems, a one-second delay meaning a difference of about 100 yards, without taking into account any wind. Personnel or supplies could therefore easily be scattered over a wide area and it was no simple matter for a small reception party to carry containers weighing up to 500 lb each through woods and across ploughed fields in the dark, in a hurry and in silence. Flying slow and low, at night and over unfamiliar enemy-held territory, might sound like a recipe for disaster, but the RAF never shirked the task night after night, often in highly unfavourable weather conditions and always at the risk of meeting a prowling nightfighter.

Southgate, with his courier Jacqueline Nearne, had dropped over eleven weeks earlier, on a DZ in the south used by SOE's 'Wheelwright' circuit led by Southgate's old friend, George Starr ('Hilaire'). A spate of arrests on landing grounds further north had made Southgate wary of DZ's nearer to his planned centre of operations, which was initially to be at Clermont-Ferrand and then Châteauroux. He had therefore chosen one well to the south near Tarbes, a town some 90 kilometres from the Spanish border, where SOE already had local contacts and helpers upon whom Southgate could rely.

Southgate had spent his first two and a half months picking up the threads of the 'Tinker' network, but knew he would need his own radio contact with England as quickly as possible. As soon as he had satisfied himself of the reliability of Charles Rechenmann's southern group, he therefore had a message radioed back to London, arranging for Dédé and Rée to be dropped on the night of 12/13 April 1943.

On the evening of the 12th, the BBC twice broadcast the coded messages 'Bien le bonjour de Valérien' to confirm that Dédé and Rée would be dropped that night. The BBC's transmissions were at 7.30 p.m. and 9.00 p.m., the earlier broadcast being a warning that an operation was planned for that night and the later broadcast, just twenty minutes before the Halifax took off from Tempsford, confirming the drop by repeating the message.

Elated by the news, Southgate, Rechenmann and a helper named Jacques Hirsch, together with a local doctor and a couple of other men from the Resistance, set out for the DZ they had chosen on the plateau of Sarrouilles, a sparsely-populated farming area some 6 kilometres due east of the town of Tarbes. It was the first time that a *parachutage* had been made to Rechenmann's group, and the first to this DZ on the plateau, but all had seemed well when, on cue, they recognized the distinctive sound of a low-flying four-engined aircraft coming towards them. Still unseen, the Halifax could be heard circling, so the reception party quickly swung into action with lights and the required Morse code letter. But excited anticipation turned to bafflement as, suddenly, the Halifax audibly opened up its throttles and turned for home, leaving Southgate and his companions staring upwards in puzzlement. In the distance, however, they caught a glimpse of a number of parachutes drifting earthwards and they set off in hot pursuit.[5]

Only about 3 kilometres away, but frustratingly far from the waiting reception committee, the umbilical chord of the static line snapped taut and Dédé's parachute jerked open. From just 500 feet, however, there were only about forty-five seconds to enjoy the gentle swaying before the ground was already rushing up. A quick glance behind showed the three other parachutes in line astern. Otherwise all that he could see on the rapid descent was the full moon's reflection on the snow-covered peaks of the Pyrenees, some 30 kilometres to the south, and a few pale lights which might have been farm buildings. Dogs barked somewhere nearby as the drone of the Halifax receded, but otherwise there was no sign of life. As clouds scudded across the moon, Dédé fleetingly made out that he was descending over a large wood. He tried to manoeuvre away, but crashed into the upper branches of a large tree on the edge of the wood, his parachute becoming entangled and suspending him helplessly over a narrow paved road.

Being rather heavily laden, he was loathe to take the risk of dropping the last few feet, but he was able to swing himself sideways and take a firm hold of the tree's trunk. Thus stabilized, he operated the quick release clasp on his chest, slipped from the parachute harness and leapt the last ten feet or so to the ground, fortunately without injury.

Occasional clouds were still obscuring the moonlight, but he could just make out a landscape of wooded farmland, crossed by a line of tall electricity pylons. Much more obvious was the tell-tale parachute firmly lodged in the treetop, but Dédé realized he had no chance of retrieving it. Drawing his revolver, he therefore cautiously moved off along the hedgerow in the hope of finding Rée and their packages. After only a short distance he heard a low, urgent, call of 'Sam!' and found a much-relieved Rée who had managed to avoid the trees, but had been dragged across a field.

Yet even as they greeted each other they suddenly heard voices in the distance. Crouching behind a hedge they waited, hoping that the voices came from their reception party, but after three-quarters of an hour no one had approached and the night was again silent. Guessing therefore that the voices had come from the disturbed occupants of a nearby farm, Dédé and Rée agreed that they must carry on and use their own initiative.

The lack of a reception committee posed two problems: they had no idea of exactly where they were; and there was no one to help with the heavy containers which carried the arms, ammunition and explosives. To make matters worse, one of the containers had landed high up on a pylon and Dédé and Rée alone had no hope of recovering it. But of much more pressing concern were the seven suitcases dropped with them on two separate parachutes and whose contents included two radio transmitters, money, clothing and their immediate rations. These would have to be found.

In the distance, at the edge of the field, they could see a blacker shape that might have been a house. Dédé and Rée therefore approached it cautiously, only to discover that it was a large, deserted barn, showing no signs of use. But fortunately, it was here that they found the first bundle of equipment, lying beneath its parachute against the wall of the barn. It had split open and part of the contents had spilled out, but all was safe and the other parachute was likewise retrieved shortly after. Normally it would have been of the utmost importance to hide all indication of the drop, by burying the parachutes and hiding the discarded containers, but in this instance, with Dédé's parachute still irretrievably entangled in the treetops, and another parachute and container draped over a pylon, there was little point. Any enemy search party would have no difficulty in finding the evidence. This meant there was the possibility that the local people might fall under suspicion, but there was no alternative in the circumstances.

Nor was there much time remaining, for with dawn not too distant, decisions had to be made. There were seven suitcases in total, two of which contained vital radio transmitters. This was far more than Dédé and Rée could hope to carry, so four cases were chosen, containing money, clothes and one of the radio sets. The two men then set off in order to distance themselves as much as possible from their landing site and the tell-tale parachutes. Heading in the opposite direction to the source of the voices heard earlier, they passed through a wood before reaching a deserted tarmac road. They followed this for a fair distance, then over another field at the far side of which lay a stream. Remembering their training, they considered wading along it for two or three hundred metres in order to hide their scent from any tracker dogs that might soon be following. But the suitcases were already taking their toll and after only an hour's march they realized that their load was still too heavy for any prolonged trek such as they might be facing. They therefore buried one of the cases with the radio set, together with some of the contents of two more, leaving the money and enough clothing for a few days in the one remaining, but still heavy, case. This they took turns at carrying until, with dawn now beginning to break, the two men agreed to find a spot to lie up and rest.

In the half-light they could make out a copse on a small hill which seemed to promise decent cover and a good observation point. They set off towards it, but as they did so workers began to appear in the fields and so Dédé and Rée had to revert to stealth, keeping behind hedgerows and any other cover to reach their chosen spot. Having gained the shelter of the trees, they made a thorough survey of the copse before electing to base themselves close to a thick hedge which would provide a good hiding place in the event of danger. Rée, from his Boy Scout training, gathered branches and twigs to make two reasonably comfortable beds and, though they had no rations, he produced and shared part of a bar of chocolate before they both lay down and quickly fell into an exhausted sleep.

They awoke suddenly in daylight and to the sound of voices. Fearing that the Germans had found the containers and parachutes, and were already on their trail, Dédé and Rée slipped into the dense hedge they had earmarked earlier and peered out. Happily, the source of the noise proved not to be a German search party, but a group of brushwood cutters coming their way across the fields. They passed and worked close by for an hour or so before returning the way they had come.

Emerging from their hiding place, but remaining in the cover of the trees, the two agents gazed out over the tranquil countryside. France, the land of Dédé's ancestors, looked beautiful. Green, undulating fields and hills were set against a backdrop of the majestic, snow-peaked Pyrenees in the distance, and Dédé was thinking of the words of a popular song, 'Montagnes Pyrénées, vous êtes mes amours, rien n'est plus beau que ma patrie', when his reverie was harshly interrupted by the drone of an approaching aircraft. The noise grew louder until suddenly there it was, flying low past the hill and easily identifiable as a Messerschmitt. With its clearly defined German markings it seemed a brutal violation of the peaceful French countryside. It was the enemy and it brought Dédé back with a jolt as to why he was there. This was no exercise, as in his SOE training, but the real thing. Could the Germans already be aware that two British parachutists had landed?

Towards noon, the workers in the fields left, and Dédé and Rée took the opportunity to make their way cautiously back to the stream they had crossed early that morning, in order to slake their growing thirst. In the evening, a young

45

cowherd shepherded his cattle close by, singing a pro-Vichy song, 'Maréchal, nous voilà, c'est bien toi le sauveur de la France', that made the two agents exchange an ironic smile. After the boy had departed, and silence once again reigned, the two men shared another portion of chocolate bar and settled down for their second night. They slept close together, covered by all the additional clothing they could muster, for the night was cold. Around midnight they were suddenly woken by the barking of dogs nearby. As they listened, the dogs seemed to be coming closer and then they heard voices, though they seemed to be French. Who would be abroad at this hour in such an isolated spot? But as the voices and yapping passed, the two agents realized it had probably only been a group of men after rabbits. They lay back in relief, but the rush of adrenalin meant that the remainder of the night was spoiled for sleep and they dozed only fitfully until Sunday morning dawned.

Reviewing their options the two men agreed that Dédé, who spoke much the better French and who also possessed the advantage of having previously met Southgate, should leave their sanctuary and see if he could find any of the reception party. If he failed, he was to try to find his way to Tarbes where they had the address of two safe houses. Rée was to remain hidden with the wireless set in the bushes, and give Dédé two days at the most to return. If he were not back by then, Rée was to assume he had been captured – or worse.

And so Dédé, donning a mackintosh and sporting a Basque beret, set off alone, still keeping to the treeline where possible until he reached a road. Even on a Sunday morning it seemed relatively busy as he took his time watching from cover and wiping the mud from his shoes. There were few cars but numerous cyclists and pedestrians; eventually, accepting that he had to make an educated guess at which direction, he slipped down onto the road and began walking.

Coming to a junction, he summoned up the courage to ask an elderly lady, in somewhat hesitant French, if he were on the right road for Tarbes. Thankfully he was, and just a short distance later he recognized a spot close to where he and Rée had landed two nights before. This was almost immediately confirmed when, to his astonishment and in a moment of pure farce, Dédé recognized the grey cardigan worn by a girl walking in the opposite direction. Of a distinctive, double-breasted design, it had been knitted for him by his sister Margot shortly before he left Mauritius for England in 1938. Stifling a broad smile and the urge to stop the girl, Dédé realized this meant that at least some of their suitcases had been found, but by local people rather than by the police or the Germans. In the circumstances, there could be no better outcome and Dédé hoped that the lost food, chocolate and cigarettes had likewise gone to deserving homes.

After a while he reached the village of Sarrouilles and, rounding a bend in the road, came face to face with a detachment of German troops – Dédé's first, throat-drying look at the enemy. He instantly recognized their grey, tight-fitting tunics from photographs he had studied in training, though their dull and un-polished boots surprised him. He had assumed that German soldiers would be as smartly turned out as their British Army counterparts. Feeling at least a degree of satisfaction, if not superiority, he decided these soldiers paled decidedly in comparison to the standards he had learned on joining the Queen Victoria's

Rifles, but they were certainly busy and industrious, rushing in and out of houses and shouting orders. Looking away in case his curiosity attracted attention, he continued towards Tarbes.

In the town he negotiated a level crossing and continued along what looked like a main road, leading to a square. He noticed several French gendarmes and what he thought were French military police, men who looked much more tidily dressed in their uniforms than the Germans he had passed earlier. There were several cafés and shops around the square, and it being a pleasant and peaceful Sunday morning, people were sitting at outdoor tables on a terrace. Suddenly becoming conscious of how very hungry he was, he first bought a newspaper at a stall, and then chose a table. Ordering a coffee, he was careful not to ask for a 'café crème' which would have given him away as an outsider, and he settled down, not to actually read his newspaper, but rather to observe a bit of everyday French life from behind it.

Mindful of Rée still waiting in the woods, Dédé finished his coffee and, paying his bill with a handsome tip, asked the waiter for directions to the Hôtel Family in the rue Victor Hugo. There was something in the look of the waiter when he replied that troubled Dédé, but the hotel proved not to be far and now feeling full of confidence, he made his way there, remembering his detailed briefing in London. His contact, one of two given in the town, was Charles Rechenmann, an engineer who had a room on the ground floor, second on the left from the front door.

Reaching the hotel, Dédé noticed several Citroen 15 Traction Avant cars parked outside, and a fair number of people coming and going from the hotel. Only as he reached the entrance did he belatedly realize the reason for this activity. After the episode of his cardigan, and then bumping into the German soldiers, a third surprise now greeted Dédé as, above the door, he read a sign bearing the sinister words GEHEIME STAATSPOLIZEI. Recognizing this as the formal name of the Gestapo, he turned abruptly on his heel and, without speaking to anyone, walked away as nonchalantly as he could.

Shocked that he had somehow been given the address of Gestapo head-quarters, he slipped into Mass at a nearby church to compose his nerves. As he recovered, he reflected that the hotel must have recently been requisitioned by the Germans, a guess that he later confirmed. Indeed, several of the town's hotels had been taken over by the enemy who had to accommodate some 600 troops and other service personnel. The presence of two important works in and around the town, the arsenal and the Hispano-Suiza aircraft engine factory, was one reason for this relatively strong German presence in Tarbes, another being the headquarters in the Hôtel Moderne of General Mayer, commanding the Hautes-Pyrénées area. The dreaded Gestapo/SD, with no sense of irony, had chosen to install themselves in part of the Hôtel Family in early 1943,[6] and were supported by a locally raised unit of the despised Milice that had taken over the Jeanne d'Arc school with a strength of about a hundred.

Emerging from the church, Dédé continued on to the second address given to him at SOE headquarters. Only a few streets away, this was 14 rue Brauhauban, a residential apartment above a shop in the centre of town. According to his instructions, Dédé knocked four times and when the door was opened by a slim, attractive young woman with a welcoming smile, he had the feeling that he was expected. Asking for Miss Pilar Alvarez, whom he knew to be Rechenmann's fiancée, Dédé was rewarded with the confirmation that the young woman was she. He then explained that he had 'come on behalf of your friend Charles Rechenmann' and when he gave the pre-arranged password, he was immediately invited in.

Pilar was clearly as relieved as Dédé that he had made it to her apartment, explaining that she and her fiancé had abandoned all hope of finding him and had even been preparing to leave their homes that same day in case he had been captured by the Germans and forced to talk. She explained that the Germans were searching every single building in Sarouilles and was startled when Dédé replied, 'Well, I did come through that place and I did notice a lot of them looking busy as a beehive.' Pilar could scarcely believe that Dédé had managed to get through the police control points, to which he replied, 'I never saw a single control, I just walked along the road and was never stopped.'

Pilar was convinced that luck had played a large part, saying that the Germans, through rumours, knew that British officers had been parachuted in, but although they had searched the neighbourhood thoroughly, they had as yet not found a single parachute or container. What was also rumoured among the local people was that one of the parachutes had landed in a tree and the tree had had to be felled to spirit away the evidence.

Relieved and feeling less guilty, Dédé confessed that this must have been his parachute and he listened to how Southgate and Rechenmann had been on the DZ, only to see the parachutes of Dédé and Rée drifting away into the distance. They followed as best they could, but it was not until dawn that they discovered Dédé's parachute entangled in the tree. The help of a logger had been enlisted to cut the tree down, but later, realizing that he had possibly been taking part in something dangerous, the man decided to warn his employer. Luckily, the employer was a good patriot and, after Southgate and Rechenmann explained the position, he had the parachute burnt. There the issue might have ended but for the employer's son who, on hearing of the event, rang up the police and announced that a parachute had been found. The father, learning of the action taken by his boy, rang the police again and persuaded them that his son was a fool and only spreading false rumours. That then became the official line, even though it was known that several of the gendarmes had somehow come into possession of English cigarettes and chocolate.

Dédé laughed at the story and then remembered Rée, explaining that he needed to retrieve him from his hiding place as soon as possible as he was down to the last eighth of his chocolate bar. He also explained that Rée did not speak French with a good accent and that it would surely be better for him to practise his French with friends before he was allowed out on his own. Mention of the chocolate bar prompted Pilar to realize that Dédé, too, had not eaten properly for some time. Explaining that Southgate had had to leave for Toulouse, but that Rechenmann would return at lunchtime, Pilar declared there was nothing more for Dédé to do in the meantime but relax and eat. Installing him in a comfortable armchair in her bedroom, she conjured up a tray of ham and eggs that Dédé was to savour as the best he had ever tasted, the more so as it was accompanied by a fine Monbazillac wine that left Dédé in good spirits. But reflecting that he had repeatedly been told in England that food was terribly scarce in France, he gently reprimanded Pilar as he was sure she must have given up the best part of her rations for the week. And what a courageous girl, he thought. Code-named 'Irene', Pilar was originally from Spain, but was then living with her family in Tarbes. She and Charles Rechenmann, recently confirmed by Southgate as leader of the southern group of 'Stationer', became engaged and together they formed the nucleus of a strategically located and active circuit of which London had great hopes. Surely, thought Dédé, the danger that he faced was in no way comparable to that constantly present with Pilar and the others of Rechenmann's group. Here she was, having led a secret life for months, if not years, yet she was still all smiles and with a kind and generous character that did nothing to detract from her attractiveness. She had accepted of her own free will to make her house a *boîte aux lettres*, a contact address known to many who, if arrested, might talk under torture. Dédé reflected that her love of freedom must have been of the highest order for her to be able to live such a nerve-racking life.

Leaving Dédé briefly while she dealt with some clients in the shop below, Pilar then went to fetch Rechenmann, returning an hour later with a dark-haired young man with an open, intelligent, face. Shaking hands and welcoming Dédé warmly, Rechenmann explained that he had many demands in his job as an electrical engineer – even on a Sunday afternoon he had an important business appointment that he could not cancel. Suggesting therefore that Dédé go with him to his new apartment (which he had been compelled to take when the Gestapo took over the Hôtel Family), they thanked Pilar and left the rue Brauhauban. Together, the two young men walked through the town, Dédé feeling the thrill of it all – and it was almost amusing to pass both German and French military and civilian police in the streets.

Charles lived in a pleasant flat in a newly built house not far from the railway station. The owner, an old lady, lived on the ground floor and Charles on the first. When they were indoors, Rechenmann introduced himself more fully and explained in more detail the consequences of the parachute operation. Rechenmann was from Sarreguemines in the Lorraine region, just inside France on the German border. After service as an officer in the French Army, he had been released by the Germans from a POW camp as part of an arrangement whereby Alsace and Lorraine were given preferential treatment within the 'Greater Reich'. His Germanic name and a facility with the German language helped considerably, though in reality he was a great French patriot, eager to take an active part in the Resistance. His cover in Tarbes was sound, for his Lorraine-based employer had sent him there legitimately as their local engineering representative, and he had first come to SOE's attention when he made contact with Captain Ben Cowburn's 'Tinker' circuit. 'Tinker' had laid the foundations for Southgate's and Dédé's 'Stationer' organization and Rechenmann was one of the two initial contacts that Southgate had made and developed on arrival in January, proving every bit as dependable as recommended by Captain Cowburn.

Pilar Alvarez supported him, not only by providing a safe house, but also by acting as a courier, involving a great deal of travel to and fro to maintain Southgate's, and now Dédé's, links with this far-flung outpost of the 'Stationer' circuit's empire.[7]

Rechenmann had doubted whether he would ever find the newly arrived agents, for he knew that London were continuing to send people to the Hôtel Family, but Southgate was still without direct wireless contact with London and was unable to warn them. He explained that the Gestapo, backed up by SS and regular German Army troops, were still searching the neighbourhood and there was therefore no question of going out yet to bring Rée in, especially as Southgate was not due back from Toulouse before late in the afternoon and Charles himself would not be available before the evening. In the interim, another meal was called for.

Lunch consisted of well-cooked chunks of meat, a good mix of vegetables and copious quantities of wine, and when Rechenmann left, recommending that Dédé lock himself in, the young Mauritian was more than ready for a good rest. The bed was especially comfortable after two nights spent under the stars, but sleep would not come. Instead, Dédé ran over recent events in his mind, counted the large sum of money that he had brought and read a magazine to while away the time. Everything was quiet on this lazy Sunday and the war seemed remote when suddenly, late in the afternoon, Dédé heard heavy footsteps coming up the stairs. Instantly alert, he listened as someone came along the corridor and to the door of Rechenmann's apartment. The door was tried, but found locked and as the unknown visitor turned about to return along the corridor, Dédé squinted through the keyhole and recognized the back of Maurice Southgate. In great relief, he unlocked and flung the door open, startling Southgate who swung round in alarm before his face creased into a broad grin as he recognized the fellow agent he had met before leaving England.

There was much back-patting and congratulations. Southgate looked tired and worried, but was cheered by Dédé's arrival. For a good two hours Dédé gave him the news from London, explained who Rée was, what he had come for, and why he had been left in the woods. They studied the documents that Dédé had brought and Southgate took two million francs of the funds that had been strapped to Dédé's body, leaving enough for his radio operator's own needs. They chatted happily together, Southgate revealing how desperate he had become for Dédé's arrival, if only to warn London not to keep sending agents to the Hôtel Family. With Dédé's arrival he would soon be able to work directly with Home Station and not have to overburden the wireless operator of another SOE agent, Captain Francis Cammaerts ('Roger') who covered south-eastern France. Listening to this wholehearted gratitude for his arrival, Dédé realized he could be of real help; that although only a small cog, he had an important part to play. He was especially pleased to feel Southgate's relief at his arrival and already he felt a strong bond, not only with his organizer, but also with Charles Rechenmann and Pilar Alvarez. It was a peculiar feeling, but the common, shared danger somehow made Dédé feel that these people had always been close friends. It was an exhilarating emotion and one that was undiminished by Southgate explaining the details of life as a secret agent, of tedious precautionary measures and of responsibility. Their duty, he stressed, was to be worthy of the many patriots who had agreed to help them and therefore now depended upon them.

The next day, Dédé, Southgate and Rechenmann returned to the Sarrouilles area. Collecting a mightily relieved Rée from where he had been left, the group then spent several hours recovering what contents of the containers and the suit-cases could be found. Much, including the supplies of the container on the pylon, had already been recovered and hidden away by the local Resistance. They then cycled back into Tarbes where Dédé and Rée were concealed in the attic of a safe house.

After three days there, the Germans began searching the town in earnest since the Gendarmerie, after a respectable delay, had had to notify the occupying power of the suspected *parachutage*. The delay was thanks to Jacques Hirsch who, when the Gendarmerie had earlier started their own search on the Sarrouilles plateau, had contacted a friend who quietly explained the situation to the sympathetic Commissaire de la Gendarmerie. The latter suspended enquiries for a couple of days, by which time all the parachutes and the wayward container had been recovered. Not wishing to risk his new arrivals any longer in Tarbes, however, Southgate then took Rée to Clermont-Ferrand,[8] while Dédé was teamed up with Jacqueline Nearne, who was now to act as courier between himself and Southgate. Jacqueline accompanied Dédé first to Montauban and then on via a safe house to Châteauroux where, four days later, Southgate came to brief his new radio operator.

# Chapter Six

# The Circuit

Southgate's circuit, 'Stationer', had only been operating for about two months before Dédé's arrival and was relatively slow to develop as there were initially few contacts other than the two suggested by London, Charles Rechenmann and Auguste Chantraine. Both were able to bring in existing Maquis groups to help build up the organization, but there were a number of constraints and tensions, particularly in the northern area, which Dédé and Southgate discussed when they met up again in Châteauroux.

Communist Resistance had been organized in central France for a long time, as far back as 1940, but this had originally consisted only of the publication of anti-Nazi and anti-Vichy literature. In 1941, however, the communists began armed action, escalating such activity dramatically after the German invasion of the Soviet Union in June of that year. Thus it was that the more experienced and active groups of the Resistance were to be found within the ranks of the main communist organization, the Francs-Tireurs et Partisans (FTP).

A different kind of Resistance was formed under the title of the Armée Secrète (AS), which was largely composed of former officers of the defeated regular French Army, or officers of the Reserve, and followed a more strategic path. Concerned that pinprick sabotage operations would only serve to encourage reprisals against the civilian population, the AS instead concentrated on preparing itself to take part in open action only after an Allied invasion. In November 1942, after the assault on Dieppe and the Allied landings in North Africa, the Germans disbanded the demarcation line, occupied the Vichy zone and disbanded the French Army of the Armistice. This indirectly managed to swell AS ranks, since many officers of the Vichy French Army could not stomach the total occupation of their country and so pledged themselves to the clandestine cause of the AS. Overwhelmingly loyal to de Gaulle and his Free French headquarters in London, the AS was suspicious of the communist FTP's long-term political goals, particularly post-war. Nevertheless, Southgate and Dédé soon found that the Indre region's FTP, encouraged by Auguste Chantraine, were the most willing to carry out active work for the Resistance.

Even so, progress would take time. Some people worked for ideals and some for their future. Clearly, many more people than were currently involved wished to help, but they were as yet too fearful. There tended to be more help from the poorer classes than from the rich, for the former had less to lose, but recruitment had unintentionally been boosted when the Germans managed to score a dramatic 'own goal'. In 1942 Fritz Sauckel, the German Labour Minister, had struck a deal with Pierre Laval, Prime Minister of Vichy France, whereby 50,000 French prisoners of war in Germany would be exchanged for 150,000 'voluntary' skilled workers. Known as the 'Relève', the issue was soon exacerbated by the Germans demanding more and more men after Laval had delivered the promised 150,000 by February 1943. By 31 March 1943 the Germans had drained France of 250,000 more men for what was termed Service du Travail Obligatoire (STO), and then demanded another 400,000.

The potential for resistance to these demands seems to have been overlooked or ignored by the Germans, but was ultimately to prove far more costly to them than a lack of skilled labour. For now, young Frenchmen liable to compulsory service under the Relève quickly changed address, obtained false papers, or, increasingly, disappeared into the countryside to join groups and camps of like-minded *réfractaires*, living outside the law and providing a ready pool of manpower to create bands of Maquis, fighting groups of the Resistance. From the beginning of 1943 the Germans also began to arrest many of the considerable numbers of Republican Spanish refugees in France, in the belief that they posed a potential threat to their troops. Again, the result was that many more men were driven to disappear into the Maquis, often, in the case of the Spanish, with recent combat experience from the Spanish Civil War.

In the spring of 1943, however, the existing Resistance movements had only limited ability or opportunity to address the level of military organization now needed. If taken in hand by a SOE F or RF Section circuit, a Maquis group stood a good chance of being properly trained. But if instead they were controlled by, for example, the communist FTP, then military leadership and arms might be harder to come by. In an effort to improve matters, the Free French intervened from London to create the Mouvements Unis de la Résistance (MUR) from the fusion of three organizations: 'Combat', 'Libération' and 'Franc-Tireur' in early 1943. This was soon followed by the Comité Nationale de Résistance (CNR), a complex organization that aimed to co-ordinate all the various political groups engaged in the Resistance in France.

While all these attempts at co-ordination were still being made by the French, SOE's aim was to ensure that most, if not all, Maquis groups had arms, some level of military training, money if needed, discipline and a command structure in place to be called upon to support the invasion expected in 1944. Against this backdrop, Southgate, Jacqueline Nearne and Dédé had no time to lose, but a vast area to cover. Southgate therefore immediately split the area into two, Chantraine heading the northern sector and Rechenmann the southern. The SOE circuit's base was to be in and around the Châteauroux and Montluçon area in the north. Rechenmann, with a military background himself and the ability to call on former members of the French armed forces, was considered more able to develop his own organization in the long run. He could pass messages to London via Jones, the 'Headmaster' circuit's radio operator in Clermont-Ferrand, and in the interim could still benefit from visits, help and guidance from

'Stationer'. Chantraine, a farmer, local mayor of the village of Tendu and president of the Fedération Paysanne des Landes based in offices in the Rue Diderot, Châteauroux, confirmed that he would continue to receive instructions from the FTP, but was also happy to continue to help the British against their common foe. Chantraine was already experienced in clandestine work and was enthusiastic, but the FTP would need help in preparing for the more military aspects of the Resistance.

Ready to play his own important part in this, Dédé had first spent a couple of days at a safe house after leaving Tarbes for Châteauroux where he was to be based. The house belonged to the family of Jacques Hirsch who immediately welcomed him and made him feel at home. Jacques' younger brother, Pierre, recalls that his first impression of Dédé was that he was 'fairly aristocratic, yet his humility showed'. The newcomer's French seemed to have no regional accent, though Pierre detected an inflection and certain mannerisms of speech which he thought to be the result of Dédé having lived in England. None of them had the slightest notion that the young man before them was not a French national, but from a British colony in the Indian Ocean.

Dédé heard how Southgate had also been sent to this safe house just a couple of days after his reception, with a recommendation from Rechenmann to try to recruit Jacques Hirsch to SOE's cause. Southgate had duly explained that his mission was to harass the Germans and to prepare the way for the Allies – would Jacques help? Hirsch gave a qualified answer. Yes he would, but only if he were satisfied of the necessity for any sabotage in which he might be involved. For the moment, he wanted to preserve his own freedom of action, but agreed that he would look out as many secure contacts as he could and would put Southgate in touch with others who could help him. Southgate was initially satisfied with this arrangement and that same night Jacques had introduced him to an industrialist, Jules Pecheur, of 96 avenue de Lespinet in Toulouse. Pecheur was already carrying out some sabotage work (though Jacques had no idea where the sabotage materials had come from to date) and was a leader of the Armée Sécrète in the Toulouse area. Pecheur also proved invaluable by allowing Southgate to become a representative of the firm of which he was a director, thereby providing excellent cover for travelling around.

A few days after Southgate's arrival, his courier, Jacqueline Nearne, had also reached the Hirsch family home. Then twenty-six years old, Nearne had been born in England, but her Scottish father and French (Spanish-born) mother settled in Boulogne in 1920. Jacqueline had also lived in Nice, giving her not only fluent French, but also an up-to-date knowledge of the country. All three Nearne children – Jacqueline, Eileen and Francis – elected to go to England to continue the fight after the fall of France and all were eventually to serve in SOE.[1] Despite her Scottish father, Jacqueline looked every inch the chic, attractive young Frenchwoman, but when she parachuted into France with Southgate in January 1943, it represented a test of faith by Colonel Buckmaster. Though adored by many who met her, she had not done well during her preliminary training at Wanborough Manor, despite proving to be an excellent shot with a pistol. She found it particularly difficult to adjust to the theory delivered via military-style instruction and the school Commandant was concerned that she did not appear to absorb much from the lectures. Jacqueline herself expressed strong doubts about continuing, but Buckmaster, during one of his visits, persuaded her to continue and concentrate on the practical aspects of the work. She did so, and proved adept at demolitions, but her course report from Beaulieu could not have been worse:

> Mentally slow and not very intelligent. Has a certain amount of determination but is inclined to waver in the face of problems.
>
> A reserved personality and somewhat shy. Little depth of character – in fact, she is a very simple person.
>
> She is lacking in self-confidence, which might be entirely due to inexperience. She might very well develop after long and careful training, but at present she could not be recommended.

To his credit, Colonel Buckmaster kept faith with Jacqueline and, convinced that she would not let him down, he scrawled in the margin of this assessment: 'OK. I think her one of the best we have found.'

Once in the field, she was meant to act as courier for Captain Rafferty's 'Headmaster' circuit as well as for Southgate and 'Stationer', involving constant travel over huge distances. She had a flat in Paris, but otherwise her cover story was that of Josette Norville, a chemist's representative constantly required to travel round the country. This enabled her to move about freely and she was soon put to work shuttling backwards and forwards with messages from Pau, Tarbes, Poitiers, Toulouse, Châteauroux and Paris, helping considerably in the early and secure build-up of the circuit.

Perhaps Jacques Hirsch was swayed by the arrival and evident courage and commitment of this young woman. For just a few days after preferring to keep his options open, he made up his mind that Southgate could be trusted as someone who was working in the best interests of France and who understood the country and its people. He therefore agreed to go to Pau to help make more contacts for Rechenmann's sub-network and from then on to act as an assistant to Southgate. His apartment in Toulouse would continue to serve as a safe house while he himself served as an additional courier, reception committee organizer, letterbox and general dogsbody.

Jacques' decision brought other help, for the entire Hirsch family then likewise volunteered to support the 'Stationer' circuit – Jacques' parents, grandparents, younger brother Pierre and sister Jeanne. This was excellent news, for it brought with it the offer of two more Hirsch family properties that could be used as safe houses.[2] One, in the town of Montluçon, was especially suited as it had separate front and rear exits and, being registered under Madame Hirsch's maiden name, did not attract unwelcome attention. The other property, a substantial château in the small country village of St. Sulpice-les-Champs, northeast of Limoges, was under the name of the grandparents and was the main family home to where the Hirsch parents had fled from Paris. In the capital they were too well known on the father's side as being from a long-established French

Jewish family. They left behind a successful confectionery shop and had started a new life under the name of L'Allemand in St. Sulpice. Despite the obvious dangers of drawing attention to themselves, the Hirschs' house became one of the most important and often-used safe houses of the 'Stationer' circuit, and it was here that the family welcomed Dédé en route to Châteauroux with Jacqueline Nearne.

From this welcome and early evidence of the potential offered by a tight-knit family, Southgate and Dédé became firm adherents to the principle of basing much of their circuit around family groups – *la résistance familiale*. The Hirschs were the first and classic example, spanning three generations, but four other families soon volunteered: the Néraud, Bidet,[3] L'Hospitalier and Rousseau families. This helped with recruiting in the difficult early days, almost all new recruits being members, friends or contacts of these families. Southgate, Dédé and Jacqueline Nearne would normally always prefer to stay with these families or with trusted friends. It was planned to arrange a safe house in every major town in the areas they covered, so that any new arrivals from England would be taken as soon as possible from the ground to a secure haven.

During his first visit to the Hirsch family, Dédé learned more about the thickset young man whom he would come to affectionately call 'le gros Jacques'. When war broke out Jacques Hirsch had been serving as an officer cadet in the French Army at the prestigious Saumur cavalry school and had seen action against the Germans in a famous defence of the Gennes bridge in June 1940. After the fall of France, he remained in the Army, but in 1941 he discovered that his Jewish background was no longer acceptable and he was discharged. Fortunately, this had done nothing to dilute a deep love of France and he had pledged himself to the Resistance cause soon afterwards. His parents had rented an apartment for him in Toulouse, where he studied law after demobilization, and he had made this available as a meeting place and safe house. Dissatisfied with only this limited involvement, he had then tried to leave France, via Spain, for Algiers. His attempt had not succeeded, but in Tarbes, in November 1942, he had come into contact with Pilar Alvarez who introduced him to Rechenmann. Jacques again offered his own apartment, in the rue Ingres in Toulouse, as a safe house, soon became a trusted helper and was still keen to do more.

The coming of the 'Stationer' network therefore provided Jacques with the opportunity to take a more active role. One of the first important tasks he carried out was, however, entirely cerebral. Given that Jacques and the three SOE agents would frequently travel by train, his prodigious memory for facts and figures was put to practical use when he memorized the train timetables that the group needed.

Jacques Hirsch was also nominated by Southgate to become responsible for Dédé's security, including arranging his travel and accommodation when necessary and building up contacts to ensure advance notice of any German direction-finding activities. This was no easy task, for Jacques Hirsch was still working in Toulouse and in the southern sector in support of Rechenmann. In the meantime, therefore, Jacqueline Nearne continued as Dédé's escort and together they continued on to Châteauroux.

There, Southgate caught up with him again and introduced him to the town. One immediate impression was the large number of Germans, the town hosting some two dozen depots, offices and barracks. These included supply, transport, construction, engineer and sanitary units, whose personnel went about their routine military duties and posed little or no danger to Dédé. There was also a sizeable Luftwaffe force based at the two nearby airfields of Déols, north of the town alongside the N20 road, and La Martinerie, 6 kilometres from Déols and south of the D925. Guarded by Luftwaffe troops and protected by an anti-aircraft flak unit, the two sites shared the aircraft of Major Ihlefeld's Jagdgeschwader JG 103 fighter squadron, together with a dreaded Henschel Hs 126 light reconnaissance aircraft. This droned about the region almost daily, looking for, reporting by radio and photographing Resistance activity and dropping leaflets. In addition, Déols was home to a production facility of the Bloch aircraft company.

Of the German Army's fighting troops in the area, the 6th Security Regiment was responsible for Châteauroux, but the greatest threat was to be found in the town's Place du Maréchal Pétain, home to an office of the feared Sicherheitsdienst, or SD, the SS intelligence and police service which was a sister organization to the Gestapo. Led by SS Untersturmführer Metschler, the SD's peak strength was fifteen agents and four French assistants, supported by a network of paid informers. The French helpers were especially despised as their local knowledge was to be feared. Most notorious of these traitors was a former waiter called Pierre Sutter, renowned for his various methods of torture; another particularly brutal man employed by the SD was a German Czech by the name of Schmitt who had come to live in Châteauroux in 1938, and was suspected by some to have been a deep cover agent of the Germans in preparation for the war. The common enemies of both the SD and the Gestapo were judged 'communists, terrorists, foreign agents, Jews, Anglo-Saxons and Bolsheviks'. Much of the SD's effort was therefore directed towards hunting for arms and equipment stores in the countryside, together with the illegal vehicles that the Resistance used to transport them. Their other major responsibility was to search for British agents.

To make matters worse for Dédé, there was not only a history of SOE activity in the town, but also a worrying record of German success against it. On the night of 5/6 May 1941, F Section's very first agent into France, Georges Bégué, had parachuted into the unoccupied zone some 30 kilometres north of Châteauroux. His contact was Max Hymans, the former socialist member of parliament for Châteauroux, who put Bégué in touch with a nascent network of sympathizers in the area, helped by three more agents who quickly followed from England. Bégué recruited a chemist called Renan and a local garage-keeper, Fleuret, in the town itself and they subsequently became F Section's first 'live letter-boxes'. This was a dubious distinction, since in those early days the importance of cut-outs and security in general was undervalued. Fleuret's garage, in particular, rapidly became a general rendezvous and bicycle park where *résistants* and agents met. A large circuit, including Auguste Chantraine and his helpers and another local mayor, Armand Mardon of Dun-le-Poëlier, was built up, but problems had begun almost immediately when the Germans' wireless interception service detected Bégué's transmissions.

Counter-jamming started and direction-finding vans soon joined the search, while the local Vichy police began challenging any strangers in and around the town. Nevertheless, another six agents parachuted in in early September 1941 to a reception committee including Chantraine on his farm at Tendu. Among these six was Captain Ben Cowburn who later recommended Chantraine as a contact for Southgate. Cowburn was fortunate enough to have left the area when only a month later the circuit was disastrously blown and several agents, including Bégué, were arrested along with a number of their French contacts. Chantraine was one of the few who had survived this catastrophe and, undeterred, had continued his work with the FTP. He was again lucky to survive the arrest of seven people in his area a year later in October 1942, and he remained as keen as ever to take an active role. Ignoring the obvious dangers that he faced, he offered his office premises in Châteauroux as Southgate's main post box.

On his arrival in the town, Dédé's immediate concern was the setting up of his clandestine life, a task full of daily challenges ranging from obtaining secure lodgings, to gradually learning not to panic when in a shop, station or other establishment that might suddenly fill with Germans. Allied to these first challenges was learning how to avoid, as much as possible, the local and enemy police forces. Only when these elements were mastered could Dédé settle to helping Southgate with the two main aims of a SOE circuit – the co-ordination and encouragement of Resistance forces (often a politically sensitive job); and their military training and supply. The latter was much more straightforward than the former, yet Dédé was to prove highly successful in both.

In Châteauroux, Dédé was helped by Southgate and Jacqueline Nearne, both of whom already knew the town, and he found lodgings at 24 rue de la Gare, conveniently situated between the town centre and the railway station. There he had no difficulty in convincing his landlady, Madame Lebas, that he was an accountant able to work from home for much of his time. Madame was a milliner and although she appeared in no way suspicious, Dédé instinctively felt that she was the sort of person who would be horrified to know what was happening under her roof. He therefore took great care with his radio work, hiding the transceiver in its case at the back of a wardrobe and transmitting only when he was sure he would not be overheard or interrupted. A *boîte aux lettres* for messages to reach him was set up close to Chantraine's offices in the Café du Cygne, rue Diderot, using one of the waitresses, Simone.

Dédé had three schedules a week for transmitting and receiving, each being a 45-minute slot and, despite the advice given during his SOE training, he chose to transmit most of his messages from this same apartment in which he was to stay for ten months. Nor did he have anyone watching out for him while transmitting. At first sight, such arrangements flew in the face of all wisdom, and SOE's losses to date of radio operators in the field had not been unconnected with such seemingly lax arrangements. The drill, as taught in England, recommended operating from a number of sites, each having a W/T set located in it. This conveniently overlooked the fact that there was no electric current in most of the country districts, and certainly none in the woods where the Maquis might have been able to provide some level of protection. To operate away from his town base would therefore have meant Dédé having to spend time going backwards and forwards to town to have his wireless batteries recharged – not always possible owing to the lack of electric current, bombing or sabotage.

Nor was it advisable to travel too often with a wireless set. Couriers could and did manage to hide their written messages through checks and searches, while an organizer, such as Southgate, would have had little or nothing on him to betray his or her true role. But a radio operator, if stopped while travelling with a radio set in its suitcase, was the most obviously guilty of all SOE agents.

A radio operator was also transparently guilty if caught in the act of transmission. It was therefore also approved practice to have someone on guard outside the place where a W/T set was being operated, someone versed in looking for the slow-moving and unmarked vans which housed the detector equipment, and bulky men, often wearing trench coats. The coat could hide a small detector set strapped to the waist and linked to a direction-finding dial carried on the wrist like a watch. But in Châteauroux Dédé had an ace up his sleeve – Chantraine had a contact in the local police who was responsible for liaison with the Germans' direction-finding service. And from 1942 onwards the French police forces had become increasingly willing to help, or at least turn a blind eye to, the Resistance. In some cases the police formed or joined Maquis groups themselves, but the Germans were not slow to recognize this and as they lost confidence in the French police, they took over much of the work themselves, helped by the Milice. Fortunately, although Chantraine's friend was a patriot, he remained trusted by the Germans and so remained in a vital position where he could pass on a warning for Dédé of any potential operations by the Germans. This was an important safety net that was not available in any other town and as such was an encouragement to Dédé to operate his radio as much as possible from Châteauroux.

Dédé's other security arrangements more closely followed the procedures instilled in him by his training in England. His address in the rue de la Gare was known to no more than five people and he had several safe houses, farms etc., to which he could go in case of emergency. He never once used the normal postal system owing to the likelihood of censorship (letters were frequently steamed open, usually clumsily and therefore noticeably) and the risk of being linked with another person. Similarly, he shunned use of the telephone as potentially being open to phone tapping. Telegrams were considered secure and were used frequently without any trouble and only live *boites aux lettres* were used, often in the form of trusted waiters and proprietors of cafés and restaurants. These people had to be totally trustworthy since many of the enemy's informers were women whom the Germans dressed well and employed in cafés. Hence, the members of the 'Stationer' circuit rarely, if ever, used cafés, other than for leaving messages. Though they could be useful as meeting venues, or simply as places to pass the time, the Germans knew this too and cafés were therefore subject to frequent snap checks by the enemy, scrutinizing papers and delving into the reason why one was in the area. Jacques Hirsch, for instance, never went inside one for four years, consequently suffering considerable inconvenience since he had relatively few safe houses and therefore found it difficult to pass the time other than by staying on the streets. Rendezvous and meetings were held in houses instead or at pre-arranged places in the street. For meetings with unknown persons, descriptions were more frequently used than passwords, and they always had a fixed danger signal and time limits for waiting before trying an alternative rendezvous. Southgate had tried a system of putting on gloves or carrying papers, but this never worked. Safety signals in houses were considered equally useless; people usually forgot to use them and valuable meetings were thereby lost.

Dédé's communications with Southgate were originally planned to be via Jacqueline Nearne acting as courier. In the event, however, the two men hit it off so well that, although they did regularly use Jacqueline's services, they also accepted the risk of meeting face to face when time and circumstance permitted. This proved especially important for Dédé who led a solitary existence for long periods. Consequently, either Southgate came to Dédé's lodgings, or vice versa. Their preferred method for passing other messages did, nevertheless, remain by courier, feeling that the use of women aroused less suspicion and that they could more easily explain their reason for travelling, normally under cover of visiting friends or searching for food. Orders and messages sent by courier were either verbal or sometimes written on cigarette paper, in very small uncoded writing.

Another aspect in which the 'Stationer' circuit diverged from SOE standard operating procedures was in respect of contacts with other networks in France. Perceived wisdom was that such contact carried too much risk if agents were arrested. There was therefore no way that Dédé could transmit or receive messages from other operators in the field, and personal contact was normally discouraged. Despite this the 'Stationer' network, with London's apparent agreement, liaised with at least four other circuits that overlapped or bordered its area of operations. In the Indre, contact was recorded at Saint-Gaultier with Captain George Wilkinson of the 'Historian' circuit, and Southgate had a regular meeting on the 25th of each month with Captain Francis Cammaerts ('Roger') of the 'Jockey' network operating to the east around Montélimar. This was always held at the home of Monsieur and Madame Dezandes in Riom, just north of Clermont-Ferrand. The two agents would stay overnight, exchange material and financial help, and pass on any W/T messages as necessary. They had a rule never to discuss personnel or movements. Both Monsieur Dezandes and Southgate were also in touch with another SOE contact, only recorded as 'Felicien' in reports, who also operated in Clermont-Ferrand and the south-west.

The 'Stationer' circuit's most frequent liaison was with the 'Headmaster' team of Captain Rafferty and Captain Donovan Jones in Clermont-Ferrand. Jones had helped with radioed instructions for the blind drop of Southgate and Jacqueline Nearne and it was the latter who had the tiring job of shuttling back and forth between the two circuits. Liaison was nevertheless thought essential as 'Headmaster' had already been active and was directing itself to targets within the remit of 'Stationer'. Just before Dédé's arrival, Southgate had devised and planned an operation whereby a Resistance group broke into a quarry and stole 250 kilos of dynamite. This followed identification of a strategic target in the form of a water tower at Ussel on the main railway line between Brive-la-Gaillard and Clermont-Ferrand. The tower, poorly guarded and vulnerable, supplied water for all the railway engines in the district and when some of the stolen dynamite brought it crashing down on the night of 4/5 April 1943, rail traffic was considerably disrupted for some five weeks. Given its location, this target was almost certainly first identified by the 'Headmaster' circuit. On 3 June 1943, it was a Rafferty-inspired arson attack that saw the Auvergne Resistance destroy some 36,000 used tyres in Clermont-Ferrand's Michelin factory which was under German direction and producing tyres and caterpillar tracks for the enemy. The inferno blazed for forty-eight hours before being brought under control, the stench and pall of smoke serving as a useful reminder to the local population of the growing presence of the Maquis.

Yet less than a week after this success, catastrophe struck 'Headmaster' and also threatened to engulf the 'Stationer' circuit. Rafferty and his helpers met one evening in a café in Clermont-Ferrand prior to receiving an operational supply drop by the RAF. After a few drinks and in high spirits the group left and as they did so Rafferty is reputed to have said, 'It is a fine moonlight night; we shall have great fun.' An informer overheard him, quickly reported the comment to the Vichy police, and Rafferty was followed and arrested while still on his way to the DZ at Rochefort-Montagne. Jones was picked up soon after and although both were originally treated leniently, they were nevertheless handed over to the Gestapo.[4]

For several days Dédé, Southgate and Jacqueline waited apprehensively in case the captured agents gave away any information about 'Stationer'. But both Rafferty and Jones withstood interrogation without revealing the existence of another SOE circuit in the area and there was no further reaction from the Germans.

When word of this disaster first reached him, Dédé immediately radioed London and, in reply to a request by return from Baker Street, Southgate agreed that 'Stationer' would step into the breach. This included Dédé transmitting all messages for the remaining members of the group and helping Southgate take up the reins of reorganizing the blown circuit's surviving elements and contacts. These included the sabotage group of the strong Auvergne Resistance under its sometimes difficult leader, Emile Coulaudon ('Gaspard') and a group in the Dordogne region, close to Limoges, under the leadership of a young Frenchman named Jacques Dufour, code-named 'Anastasie'. This latter Maquis now started working directly to Southgate and Dédé, but needed considerable training.

Though these groups were closer than Rechenmann in the south-west, they nevertheless added a considerable additional burden to Southgate, Dédé and Jacqueline Nearne. Another courier and an additional radio operator would clearly be needed, but in the meantime Dédé became Dufour's radio link to London for arms and supply drops at a DZ near Limoges, and began to help Southgate with his organizational duties. Jacques Hirsch also now took more responsibility, having started at the end of April when he had chosen a DZ in the Gers region to receive supply drops. This was to become as well used as the one at Chantraine's farm in the northern sector of 'Stationer' and was near the village of Marsan, some 13 kilometres east of Auch. Hirsch had made several secure contacts in this area, in particular Madame Daubeze who, despite the absence of her husband as a prisoner of war in Germany, was managing the dual role of brave Resistance worker, while also looking after her two daughters and her mother. It was therefore on the land of the Daubeze family that Dédé had radioed for the first drop, allocated to Pecheur's AS group in Toulouse and confirmed by the BBC message 'Que j'aime le soleil du Midi', on the night of 1/2 May.

Half of the containers dropped accurately to the reception committee, which Jacques Hirsch led, and although the remainder fell a few kilometres away on the outskirts of the villages of Leboulin and Montaut-les-Créneaux, the operation was nevertheless a success. From this promising start, reception committees were often left to Jacques Hirsch, the normal method being for Dédé to transmit the requirements and chosen DZ. The BBC's French-language *messages personnels* would then confirm the drop with enough time to mobilize helpers and transport.

Jacques Hirsch's reception committees normally consisted of four people to deal with a single-aircraft supply drop, though this proved problematic if the containers were badly dropped and scattered because with so few people it was not possible to recover all the parachutes and supplies. As the number of recruits and helpers grew, so the reception committees grew larger. Jacques Hirsch became the circuit's accepted expert on receptions, and attended whenever possible. He and only one other would know and listen out for the alert message on the BBC – once the message was heard, Jacques would gather together his reception committee and head for the designated field. He did not always warn the owner of the field, as it only increased the risks. When agents were expected, Jacques preferred to have one or two women in the committee as he felt they were better at taking charge of the agents and attending to their immediate needs.

It was Hirsch's wide contacts, however, that brought the first threat to 'Stationer'. On 13 May 1943 one of Pecheur's AS group was arrested and Pecheur himself had to flee as an arrest warrant had been issued by the Vichy authorities. There was a possibility that the arrested man might reveal Jacques's identity and his links to a British network, so Hirsch left his apartment as a precaution, but continued his clandestine work, receiving another drop in May at Bourbon l'Archambault, north-east of Montluçon. In this he was helped by his cousin, Marius Loisel, as they welcomed an agent code-named 'Laurent' and, un-expectedly, a Eureka radio homing beacon. The Eureka, unhindered as it was by cloud or other weather conditions, enabled aircraft to locate accurately a DZ at night and removed dependence upon the moon periods for operations. Dédé had, however, been sent no signal to warn of the arrival of this equipment, there were no instructions with it, and transportation of the installation was extremely diffi-cult and dangerous owing to its bulk and weight. Pending further advice it was taken to Chantraine's farm and stored in his barn's loft. After this puzzling diver-sion, and when it was clear the captured AS man had not talked a month after his arrest, Jacques moved back into his apartment in Toulouse.

The increased responsibilities in respect of the Auvergne and Dordogne regions not only involved Dédé in a great deal more radio work, but also in more travel as Southgate began to use him as an assistant organizer. With this, his risks also increased and Dédé was not entirely comfortable with the false identity with which he had arrived. As a fit and healthy 24 year old he ran the risk of being caught for STO, obligatory forced labour for the Germans. Consequently, another false identity, with all supporting documentation, was created for him by Rechenmann. He was still to be an accountant, but his name was now much closer to his true identity, being Amédée Maigrot, born in Port-Louis, Mauritius.[5] He was shown as being resident in Tarbes, at an address he could not fail to remember – while he had been in Tarbes he had discovered there was a street, close to Pilar Alvarez's apartment, with the same name as his good friend and fellow SOE agent, Jean Larcher. His address therefore became 33 rue Jean Larcher. Most importantly, he was reinvented eight years older than before, and, thanks to a friendly mine owner known to the Hirschs, shown as having a more responsible job as the head accountant with a mining company in Buxières-les-Mines, north-east of Montluçon, that was working under German direction. This would therefore help avoid any questions as to why he had not registered for working for the Germans. Other new documentation included an extra ration card, with the same name and earlier date of birth, but describing Dédé as an export agent living in Nantes. All these papers were entirely false and were therefore not registered with the authorities, but were to serve Dédé well.

The reception of stores, in response to Dédé's messages to England, now began in earnest. Only in SOE's operations in Yugoslavia and, to a lesser extent, in Denmark, were arms able to be delivered by sea, otherwise they had to be dropped by parachute. In England this required thousands of airmen and other personnel supplying and operating the RAF's special duty and transport squadrons, a drain on resources which the RAF's high command had only eventually accepted with ill grace after the personal intervention and explicit orders of Churchill. In the squadrons, however, there was nothing but total commitment to supplying agents and their networks. In addition to Tempsford's two squadrons, the RAF's 38 Group provided the majority of aircraft – normally converted Halifax and Stirling bombers – to drop the containers and packages that held the much-needed supplies, money, explosives and weapons.

As these weapons and explosives continued to arrive, courtesy of the RAF, so the word spread that the Resistance now meant business and had the means to take action. More and more people, through the summer and autumn of 1943, felt that now was the time to play their part and they were encouraged by news of more successes against the enemy. In late June a partial stoppage of three days was achieved by sabotage at the Gnome-et-Rhône factory in Limoges, and at Bersac-sur-Rivalier two separate attacks resulted in the burning of twenty-seven lorries and the destruction of an electricity sub-station. This was the start of a series of actions against power supplies. Around the same time the FTP destroyed two electricity pylons at Dun-le-Poëlier, while in July, the huge and strategically important hydroelectric dam at Eguzon in the Indre was attacked, though results were only described as 'encouraging'. In the south one of Rechenmann's groups brought down several electricity pylons at Pau in July.

To Dédé, this was excellent news, but he yearned to break free of what was still a terribly lonely existence in Châteauroux and to help his organizer more materially. Southgate and London were in agreement, but radio operators continued to be in short supply and there was no one to send in the immediate future. Fortunately, at this point, Southgate was reminded of the offer of Pierre Hirsch, younger brother of Jacques, to help.

Southgate had first met Pierre at the Hirsch house in Saint-Sulpice-les-Champs and even then had been impressed by the young man's keenness to join his brother in working for SOE. He had already been involved in Resistance work by furnishing false identity papers and distributing the clandestine newspapers *Combat* and *Libération*. He was aware of sound security procedures, since he had no knowledge of where these newspapers came from or how they were printed. They were simply given to him, roughly 250 at a time, by a contact, and he in turn gave them to other contacts in bundles of forty for posting and slipping under doors. At this point, Jacques revealed that his brother was already a trained W/T operator (from his service in the French forces early in the war) and he understood codes. With Southgate's and Dédé's agreement, Jacques therefore arranged for his brother to go to the other family house in Montluçon in late July. Dédé left his own base and met Pierre there for eight solid days of instruction on the standard B MkII set. At the end of this training Hirsch made a trial scheduled transmission to England under Dédé's supervision; a few days later he was accepted by SOE in London and was designated to support Dédé and Jacqueline Nearne in particular. Southgate's only concern was that he found Pierre 'frightfully French' and was later to grumble about the need to keep his new 'pianist' supplied with cigarettes and other small perks. But an SOE interrogator who later debriefed Pierre found him to be 'more modest' than his brother and 'a brilliant W/T operator'. Jacques was thought to be the cleverer of the two and was acknowledged to have wider experience, but both the Hirsch brothers were reported as 'clearly sincere, determined and intelligent with a high sense of integrity and family loyalty'.

At last freed from at least some of his W/T duties, Dédé now began to develop his role as assistant to Southgate. Recruitment to the 'Stationer' circuit and its Maquis groups remained a priority, but extreme caution had to be exercised. If someone, perhaps with a specific skill or position of influence, was particularly wanted as a helper for the network, full enquiries would be made about him or her, and then a person other than Dédé or Southgate would carry out the recruitment. Wherever possible, this person would know the individual beforehand and frequent use was made of messages via the BBC for convincing people of the circuit's bona fides. A certain amount of security training would then be given to the new recruit, usually in the form of an informal chat either at home or during a stroll. Locally recruited agents and helpers received money for expenses and, where they had no other means of livelihood, some sort of wage. Arrangements were always made to look after the family or dependants of an agent who had to flee the area or who was arrested. In the case of indiscretion, an agent was either dropped altogether, told to leave the area or country, or, if it was something more serious, orders could be given for the individual to be shot.

Recruiting for the Maquis was always carried out by the heads of the groups themselves. Again, care had to be taken to ensure that paid informants were not recruited, or that otherwise reliable men did not prove garrulous or boastful of their clandestine activity. In the northern sector of 'Stationer' in the Indre, the communists were generally considered to have better security than the Gaullist or Giraudist groups. This also had the drawback of making it harder for SOE to contact and engage them, but Chantraine was particularly helpful in this respect. One example involved introducing Southgate and Dédé to a local communist group leader who had been carrying out a campaign of burning crops and barns in order to deny food supplies to the enemy. Southgate, following SOE's policy of preparing for the future, managed to persuade this FTP leader to desist, arguing that it would only serve to bring down German reprisals and cause suffering for the local people.

An issue that exercised Southgate and Dédé considerably was the funding necessary to maintain the Maquis groups. It was of course the BBC that had appealed to Frenchmen to avoid forced labour by hiding in the Maquis. But these men then had to be clothed and fed if they were not to descend continually on local communities to steal cows, chickens and other edible commodities. There was also the not inconsiderable matter of supporting the families they had left behind and in all this SOE, as the local representatives of the British, were expected to provide. The men of the Maquis were paid either individually or money was given to the group's chief for their upkeep in order to avoid having to steal food, but it often proved difficult to maintain an adequate flow of funds from England.

Technical training in the use of weapons and explosives would be given in the country on farms or in wooded areas, often where the arms were stored in small, dispersed dumps. Guards were posted and usually the leaders would read the instructions and, with the help of pamphlets sent out by SOE from England, would then pass the information on to their men. Sometimes, however, SOE officers would help with weapons and explosives training, this being the case when Dédé and Southgate together trained the Resistance group in Dun-le-Poëlier in sabotage techniques. One unproductive inclination of the French was to use too much explosive when sabotaging a railway line. Standard procedure was to use only two small cartridges, which would bend the rail and almost certainly then derail the train passing over it. Dédé always had to stress this was adequate, since the maquisards would often enthusiastically use four or five cartridges. This would normally produce such a neat and clear cut of the line that a speeding train stood a good chance of passing straight over the break.

And so the strength of the Resistance, carefully and diplomatically nurtured by SOE, increased throughout the middle and latter half of 1943. The number of supply drops increased proportionately, though there were several problems. A number of parachute failures were experienced, thankfully only in respect of containers and not incoming agents, but it was a problem which had worsened throughout the summer. There were also occasions when the aircraft seemed to pay little or no attention to the placing of the signals on the ground, coming in from the wrong direction and dropping stores over a frustratingly wide area. Each container or parcel was supposed to be marked with the total number sent so that supplies were not missed, or fruitless effort was not expended looking for non-existent supplies. But, inexplicably, this marking did not always happen and caused considerable exasperation among the reception committee. Another source of irritation was the practice of sending 'comforts' from England. These might consist of a couple of packets of cigarettes or chocolate for just Southgate and Dédé, but they only served to create a bad impression when there were four or more in the reception committee.

The continuing build-up of arms and explosives prompted more and more action. Thirteen trucks at Limoges and another eleven at Châteauroux, all bound for Germany, were sabotaged, and a note on surviving SOE files also credits the 'Stationer' circuit with having supplied abrasive tablets that loyal French workers introduced to aircraft engine blocks at Marignane airfield, well to the south near Marseille. But perhaps the most dramatic single act of sabotage came when Charles Rechenmann passed on rumours that the Germans were testing some new form of high-altitude aircraft at Tarbes. Via Dédé, London approved an attack and if Southgate's post-war account is to be believed,[6] he elected to undertake the venture himself, though his contemporary report to SOE headquarters on the incident oddly failed to mention his involvement. A plastic explosive charge, encased in rubber tubing, was smuggled on to the airfield and placed in one of the test aircraft's wings. When it next flew, the aircraft was climbing to altitude when it suddenly lost a wing and crashed to the ground.

The late summer and autumn of 1943 also saw an increasing number of railway targets suffering at the hands of 'Stationer' and the groups it armed. Rail traffic between Vierzon and Limoges suffered noticeably from almost constant attention, including abrasives in engine-oil pans and the blowing up of lines, signals, sub-stations and pylons. In August a new patent reaper and binder machine, under German control and said to have been worth five million francs, was destroyed in the station at La Souterraine; four trains leaving there for Germany were reported derailed; and a railway turntable was destroyed at Tulle. Two railway breakdown cranes were destroyed at Brive and at Tulle in September and October respectively.[7]

Further south, power supplies were a speciality, but Charles Rechenmann received an unusual surprise after successfully placing a charge on a transformer serving the Hispano-Suiza factory in Tarbes on 24 August. Returning home to bed, he had the satisfaction of hearing the distant explosion, but as he settled down to sleep a few minutes later he was startled to hear another detonation, and then another. The next day it became clear that three transformers had been destroyed and Rechenmann discovered that, by coincidence, a saboteur from another group had chosen the same target on the same night. Gratified at the extent of the damage, Rechenmann was nevertheless a little put out that his competitor had succeeded with two explosions to his one. In another power supply attack on 12 September, Southgate himself, assisted by two men, took part in cutting the electricity source to the aluminium works at Lannemezan. The molten aluminium solidified in the ovens and needed to be drilled out, resulting in the claim that the works were '50 per cent destroyed'. The Reyrode works were also attacked that month, and the electrical distribution board was put out of commission in the construction workshop of the Tarbes arsenal, resulting in a stoppage of several weeks. In a similar attack, the power plant was blown up at Tulle arsenal, an intercepted Gestapo report confirming that armament production had completely stopped as a result.

The month of August also brought one of the strangest incidents in Dédé's wartime career, after the arrival of another SOE agent, Eliane Plewman. Code-named 'Gaby', Plewman was a good-looking and vivacious young woman of twenty-five who, together with her brother, had joined SOE through personal contacts. She was Anglo-Spanish by nationality, but had been born in Marseille and had spent her early childhood in France. Educated in England and Spain, she worked for the British embassies in Madrid and Lisbon before returning to England and marrying a British army officer. Dropped on the night of 14 August 1943 to a reception notified to Dédé and organized by Chantraine, her orders involved making her way to Clermont-Ferrand and then on to Marseille where she would act as a courier to the 'Monk' circuit. There, her first job was to deliver the 500,000 francs that had been dropped with her in a case attached to a separate parachute. But she jumped off target and missed her reception committee so, burying the money and a number of important documents that she had also brought, Plewman headed for a safe house in Clermont-Ferrand as instructed by London. There she made contact with 'Felicien', another SOE helper known to the 'Stationer', circuit and was shortly afterwards passed on to Jacqueline Nearne at a rendezvous in Clermont-Ferrand. Jacqueline took her to Dédé in Châteauroux, who then passed her on to Southgate. A week after her drop, she returned with Southgate to the spot on a farm where she said she had buried the money and documents, but there was no sign of either. For whatever reason, Plewman showed no great surprise at the loss, which both angered Southgate and aroused his suspicions. Discussing the matter with Dédé, he then discovered that Plewman had told Dédé that she had been twice divorced, while she had told Southgate she was a widow. This only served to add to his suspicions of the new arrival, and to check whether the farmer (the only other likely suspect) had found the parcels and money, Southgate contrived a test. For this he borrowed Charles Rechenmann's second in command, summoned from Tarbes.

Like Rechenmann, this man was from Lorraine on the German border and at one time had been recruited into the Luftwaffe as a pilot. At some point in his military training he had also received instruction in Gestapo methods, but had then escaped from Germany and had eventually made his way to Rechenmann in Tarbes. Using this experience, he and Southgate dressed as Gestapo agents and returned to interrogate the farmer and his family. Terrified though the farmer clearly was, he swore he had no clue as to the cache and Southgate decided he was telling the truth. Plewman therefore remained suspect in Southgate's eyes, but there was nothing he could prove and he had no option but to arrange for her to be passed on to her Marseille area of operations.[8]

Whatever the truth of this curious affair, Dédé never mentioned it in his own operational reports, in contrast to Southgate who recorded the incident at some length. Jacqueline Nearne also reported it in her debrief after returning to England. It could well be that Southgate's suspicions had got out of hand, for there is no denying that Eliane Plewman went on to serve the 'Monk' circuit loyally and bravely, not only as a courier, but also reportedly helping with sabotage. She was arrested in March 1944 when her group was betrayed and infiltrated by the Gestapo. With a group of other SOE women captives, she was sent to Fresnes prison in Paris and then on to Ravensbrück in Germany before being moved to Dachau concentration camp.

In the meantime, the 'Stationer' circuit and its Maquis groups were benefiting from encouraging news of the war's progress. After the invasion of Sicily in July, Allied troops were poised to land on the Italian mainland at the beginning of September. All over France people were at last beginning to hope that it would not be too long before their own country was liberated. Yet just as optimism grew, 'Stationer' suffered one of its most severe blows, and one which especially grieved Dédé.

In Clermont-Ferrand, the Nérauds' family home at 37 rue Blatin had long provided a safe house and meeting place, not just for the members of the 'Stationer' circuit, but also for several other SOE agents. Many were given the Nérauds' address as their first safe house contact in France, including Southgate, Jacqueline Nearne, Major Hudson, Captain G.D. Jones and Captain Starr. Monsieur and Madame Néraud, with their daughter Colette and son Jean, had proved so welcoming and hospitable that up to nine agents had been using their house regularly. Of the 'Stationer' circuit, Jacqueline Nearne enjoyed staying so much that she used it as her main base for five or six months and she frequently met Southgate there. Although the official records do not show it, correspondence after the war revealed that Dédé also went often and became close to the family. Jacqueline Nearne's debriefing after her return to England in April 1944 went so far as to record that, in addition to his apartment in Châteauroux, Dédé had set up early headquarters bases at the Nérauds' house, and later in Toulouse. The 'Headmaster' network had used the house even more frequently before their demise, Rafferty and Jones holding meetings in the house as often as four times a week. All this traffic of strangers must have attracted attention, or perhaps one of those arrested in the roll-up of 'Headmaster' had provided the Germans with information. Whatever the source, suspicion eventually and inevitably fell on the rue Blatin. At 8.30 a.m. on 2 September 1943, the street was suddenly cordoned off and the house raided by the Gestapo. Fortuitously, no agents were staying there at the time, but as ill luck would have it, one of SOE's officers had recently left a suitcase with the Nérauds for safekeeping. On opening it, the Gestapo found 200,000 francs and gold coins. The hapless family could give no explanation and were immediately arrested.

When news reached Dédé and the others it was a great shock. The Nérauds knew so many agents and helpers, and the 'Stationer' circuit, in particular, was in grave danger of being seriously compromised. Once again the team waited anxiously, but no one talked and no further reaction came from the Germans. The heroism of the Nérauds, however, sealed their fate. Young Jean was spared, but Monsieur, Madame and Colette were sent to concentration camps in Germany. Suspected of having harboured British spies, there would be little chance of them re-emerging.

Since brave Colette had also occasionally helped 'Stationer' as a courier, despite having no formal training, her loss was doubly felt. To try to remedy this, however, London was again pressed to send an extra agent and at last agreed, promising that one would be dropped to Chantraine's DZ on the night of 15/16 September. Southgate, newly promoted to Flight Lieutenant, knew who the new arrival would be and so, joining the reception committee himself, he took along with him a young man named Henri Cornioley, who had recently come down from Paris specifically to attach himself to the 'Stationer' network. Henri did so following a message that had come to him from London via neutral Lisbon, and he therefore knew, like Southgate, that the additional courier would be his fiancée, Pearl Witherington, whom he had not seen since 1940.

But Pearl's first attempt to drop was thwarted when Southgate, on arriving at Chantraine's farm near the village of Tendu, heard that there had been unusual activity in the area by the Gendarmerie, who were busy searching for FTP maquisards. Judging it to be unsafe, Southgate quickly dispersed his reception committee and despatched Henri on his bicycle back to Châteauroux to have Dédé urgently radio London to cancel the flight. It was a strenuous journey of over 20 kilometres for Henri, who exhausted himself pedalling as fast as possible to safeguard his fiancée. But when the breathless young man arrived at Dédé's apartment in the rue de la Gare, it was the first time that the two had met and Dédé was naturally suspicious. Cornioley had to answer a number of searching questions before Dédé relented and concluded that the young man posed no threat. Only then could the Frenchman pass on Southgate's request, but Dédé knew it was already too late to warn London and that the flight was surely on its way. This was indeed so and when, a few hours later, the aircraft arrived over-head at Chantraine's farm, no reception lights were lit and the pilot headed back to Tempsford with his impatient passenger.

Meanwhile, there was no point in Cornioley returning to the DZ, so Dédé invited him to stay and join him in going to see a local performance of the opera *La Traviata* in the town. The young Frenchman agreed and he and Dédé had an amusing time at the theatre where the actors knew their parts so badly that the *souffleur* never ceased helping them out. But while later chatting about their backgrounds, an astonishing coincidence emerged. For when Cornioley asked Dédé if he had served in the French armed forces before their capitulation, Dédé replied in the affirmative and described the fictitious service history in the French Army that had been given to him in London. What neither Henri nor Dédé knew was that SOE and Southgate had developed Dédé's cover story by asking Pearl Witherington, then still under training, for details of someone's military service prior to the fall of France. She had given the only record she knew, that of Henri, her fiancé. So, as Dédé recounted his supposed military service, so Cornioley's astonishment grew. They had seemingly served in the same unit, at the same time and in the same places, yet they had never met one another. Eventually under-standing dawned that both men's backgrounds were one and the same.[9]

Fortunately for Cornioley, he did not have to wait too much longer for his fiancée, even though there was a second abortive attempt and it had to be third time lucky for Pearl on the night of 22/23 September. Like Dédé, she was dropped by a 138 Squadron Halifax from RAF Tempsford, but her reception party consisted only of Southgate and Chantraine, since Cornioley was unable to be there. She dropped slightly off target between two ponds, losing her two suitcases on their separate parachute into one of them which meant that she would have to start her new life with no change of underclothes. Despite this setback, she quickly hid her parachute and soon heard whistling from the two-man reception committee of Southgate and Chantraine. Shown into a barn, her bed for the night was a haystack, but she quickly fell asleep and awoke in the morning to find that the haystack was on Chantraine's farm and was reportedly hiding 20 tons of ammunition.[10]

Pearl, a level-headed young woman, had been born in Paris in 1914, the eldest of four daughters of an expatriate English couple. She was working as a shorthand typist to the British Air Attaché in the Paris embassy when the Germans marched into France in 1940 and she made it her first responsibility to take the family to safety in England. They finally made it in July 1941, via Spain and Portugal. In London she joined the Women's Auxiliary Air Force (WAAF) and worked at the Air Ministry where, as already described, her path crossed that of Southgate, whom she had known at school in Paris. Following Southgate into SOE, she had got word via Lisbon to Henri of her plans to return and had persuaded Southgate to recruit Henri in France as soon as possible.

To meet the repeated requests for another agent, Pearl had undergone accelerated tuition which meant she missed out on Arisaig's paramilitary training. She had managed three weeks basic training in weapons, unarmed combat and sabotage at Wanborough, and a good stint of seven weeks at Beaulieu, but proved so inept at Morse code that she feared dismissal. Nevertheless, by September 1943 she was deemed ready to be dropped and was designated to act as an additional courier to Jacqueline Nearne, having specifically asked to work with Southgate's circuit. But despite going to Southgate and Henri, Pearl was later to admit, 'I was terrified.'

Pearl brought with her the W/T set and crystals which would allow Pierre Hirsch to start separate work from the family safe house in Montluçon and the next day Southgate took her by train to Châteauroux where she was at last reunited with Henri who she had not seen for three years. He was the brother of a childhood friend of Pearl's in Paris, but by the time Pearl and her family escaped to England he was a POW. He escaped from imprisonment, settled in Paris and opened up a channel of communication to Pearl through a contact in Portugal. Thereafter, and never thinking for a moment that Pearl would not return, he bided his time until Southgate arrived in France and contacted him to come down to the Indre. Nothing could have prevented him, but now, face to face at last, 'he was shaking like a jelly,' Pearl remembered, while to her it felt as if she had seen him only the night before.

With Pearl's arrival the 'Stationer' circuit numbered about twenty carefully compartmentalized members in total, headed up by the SOE controlling group which now consisted of four: Southgate as organizer, Dédé as W/T operator and assistant organizer, and Jacqueline Nearne and Pearl Witherington as couriers. But the latter's first job was to be one of her most difficult and frustrating.

70

Following the arrest of Rafferty and Jones, contact had weakened with 'Gaspard', the leader of the strong and audacious Auvergne Maquis. London's briefing, based on the belief that she had the required strength of character for the job, had therefore included instructions for Pearl to not only strengthen the link, but also to encourage them in more sabotage against the Michelin works in Clermont-Ferrand. SOE's parent ministry, the Ministry of Economic Warfare, had recently revived their interest in the factory which, close to extensive civilian housing, would be difficult to bomb without collateral damage. Southgate therefore first sent Pearl to Limoges and then on to Riom where she stayed in a safe house in the rue de l'Amiral Gourbeyre, provided by Monsieur and Madame Dezandes. Continuing to Clermont-Ferrand and the Auvergne region, Pearl was able to make contact with the local Resistance, but was embarrassed to discover that SOE's RF Section, typically without any knowledge on the part of F Section, had beaten her to the job. She also suffered personal frustration and anger when she learned that 'Gaspard', while happy to receive arms drops, flatly refused to accept sabotage instruction from, or to work with, a woman. Undeterred, Pearl delivered her blunt message: unless they blew up the Michelin works in Clermont-Ferrand it would be bombed with the potential for great loss of life.

Thanks to this immediate challenge for Pearl, it was not until early October that Dédé had the chance to meet his new courier, when she came to Châteauroux after her abortive mission to the Auvergne and a first return trip to Paris on behalf of Southgate. Pearl's first impression of Dédé was highly favourable. She recalls that, despite his youth (he was then still just short of twenty-five years old, while Pearl was twenty-nine and Southgate a year older), he was a mature and level-headed character. This was backed up by an innate charm that she was to describe as 'vieille France', though she had no clue at the time that Dédé was in reality from Mauritius, and a British subject to boot. There was no accent to his perfect French that she could detect, but one sign of his innate reserve showed over the issue of Pearl's underwear. When Pearl's two suitcases were eventually recovered from the pond a week or so after her arrival, they were taken to Dédé's lodgings and Southgate asked him to dry out the sodden clothes on lines stretched across the apartment. Although Dédé agreed, he nevertheless lived in mortal fear of his landlady discovering the collection of female clothing and concluding that he was entertaining a woman in his room.

# Chapter Seven

# Dédé Takes up the Reins

No sooner had the 'Stationer' circuit settled to operations with the addition of Pearl than Southgate was recalled to London for a rest and rebriefing. It was planned to be only a couple of weeks' absence and he was flown out by a 161 Squadron Lysander on the night of 16/17 October 1943. Departing from a field near Amboise, 100 kilometres to the north-west of Châteauroux on the Loire river, this was Southgate's first journey arranged by Henri Déricourt. One of the most controversial figures in the history of SOE, Déricourt was the Air Movements Officer for dozens of agents and operations and as such was in the critical position of knowing much of the comings and goings of SOE's agents in France.[1]

One of Southgate's reasons for returning to England was to seek a new mission for Pearl, who had struggled to make headway with 'Gaspard', the chauvinistic leader of the Auvergne Resistance. Pearl was nevertheless clearly capable of much more than her courier duties and Southgate wanted to exploit this ability. He was also looking for guidance on how to deal with those Resistance groups that would accept money, assistance and supplies, but would not follow SOE orders and often suffered from lax security. As such problems could endanger the entire circuit, Southgate wanted confirmation that he could choose to steer clear of those groups that he could not control or trust. He also wanted mortars for the Maquis and was keen for Rechenmann to come to England for a couple of months for proper SOE training, including a course covering the S-phone (an ultra-high-frequency radio telephone for ground-to-aircraft communication) and the Eureka homing beacon. He reported that Dédé was having to transmit from various places throughout 'Stationer' territory, with Chantraine's men being responsible for his security, but that he was still bored and felt he could do much more. Southgate's report, which remains today in the SOE archives, reads:

> Samuel [Dédé] is extremely fed up. His work is excellent and his morale is good, but he has far too little to do. The district forces him to work from small places where, after his half hour's work per day, he has absolutely nothing to help pass the time. In his own words he has 'got the blues' and wants to become a paratroop and go into action.

The description of Dédé working from a variety of places is unusual, given that several other accounts and reports suggest that he worked largely from the one base, his lodgings in the rue de la Gare in Châteauroux.

In his report, Southgate went on to describe Jacqueline Nearne as 'magnificent' and described how 'I could not have done half what I have without her.' He also complained that there had still been no clear instructions regarding the Eureka radio beacons that had been dropped. One of these was stored in Chantraine's barn loft, having been sent more than four months before without instructions or forewarning, and London had even subsequently denied having despatched it. However, the fact that Southgate was able to quote the serial number, 1532, proved they were wrong.

But while Southgate wrote his reports, the weather over England worsened and his return was delayed. In his absence, Dédé, Jacqueline and Pearl continued to maintain the tempo of operations, supported by Chantraine's and Rechenmann's groups in the north and south respectively. October brought a marked increase in the willingness of people to carry out Resistance work and saw an attack at Tulle, which resulted in the destruction of a railway breakdown crane.

Both Jacqueline and Pearl were now in frequent and regular contact with Dédé who was at the hub of what was happening. All communication and orders to and from London, and to and from the Resistance, flowed through him, though the two women never knew the full picture, nor even what each was doing.

In Southgate's absence Dédé had to do even more travelling and therefore faced more frustrations and risk. As rail sabotage by the Maquis increased, so too did delays. One frequently used route that was particularly slow was Clermont-Ferrand to Toulouse, the train once being delayed by eighteen hours due to an attack on the line. By having a first-class railway season ticket Dédé avoided having to queue or obtain a *fiche d'admission*, and also gained somewhat in status as a passenger. It offered no additional protection, however, against security checks, as Dédé once found when he was travelling in the first-class compartment of the Toulouse–Boussens–Tarbes train. His courier, Jacqueline Nearne, was travelling with him and was sitting only a few seats away when two or three SD men entered the compartment to carry out identity checks. Nothing special occurred until they came to Dédé, who presented his papers. Somehow they did not look quite genuine to the Germans who started questioning Dédé in their heavily accented French, with their inability to pronounce the letter 'v', that was so irritating to the local people: 'Où êtes-fous né? Où trafaillez-fous? D'où sortez-fous? Où allez-fous?'

Dédé glanced at Jacqueline who looked livid and as the interrogation went on and on, a few comments were made among the passengers, who felt that Dédé was being unduly harassed. But when the SD started all over again, even Dédé lost his temper. Raising his voice in anger he demanded, 'Vous m'en voulez où quoi? Cela fait vingt fois que je réponds à vos questions!' The other passengers also grew angry and the murmur of protest mounted to a level where the SD probably began to fear for their own safety. Suddenly, they handed back Dédé's papers and left the compartment without another word. Drained by the experience, which had lasted at least thirty minutes, Dédé was later to say that he had been saved by 'sheer luck' for he had only just changed his identity yet again, this time with documentation which was properly registered and showed he was older, at thirty-three years of age. The latter helped explain why he had not been called under the Relève, and authenticity was essential now that, with Resistance activity increasing, the Germans were instigating more and more checks at railway stations and on trains. It was Dédé's habit, if he were carrying his incriminating radio set, to try to place his suitcase close to, or even among, those of Germans at railway stations, but the Toulouse–Tarbes–Pau express had eventually to be abandoned because of increased Gestapo and SD checks, even though the much slower local train involved an extra three and a half hours' travel. The bigger stations, such as Toulouse and Limoges, had the most stringent checks. At Limoges there was a regular control, baggage was searched and Dédé was once followed for a day and a half in the city, probably after having been seen with a man who had been arrested. Fortunately, Dédé's training enabled him to spot his shadower and he followed an innocent trail until he was clear.

Similarly, efforts were made to obtain an alternative and more secure identity for Pearl. Jacques Hirsch therefore took her to see Joseph Saint-Martin, a teacher and Secretary of the Town Hall in Montaut-les-Créneaux, a village 10 kilometres to the north-east of Auch. This was in the heart of the Gers region where Jacques Hirsch had developed a reliable network of helpers for his dropping ground. With Saint-Martin's help, Pearl managed to obtain a registered identity card, supported by a real *bulletin de naissance* of a person who had disappeared. As a result, from 12 November 1943, Pearl's identity and cover story changed and she now became Mademoiselle Marie Jeanne Marthe Verges, the Chef de Service Commercial of the cosmetics and beauty products firm of Isabelle Lancray. The firm actually had her on their books and knew her situation; she was to keep this excellent cover, involving a great deal of travel, until she returned to Britain. She plaited her blonde hair in the German manner, read pro-Vichy newspapers when she travelled and otherwise relied on her common sense, fluent French and a relatively up-to-date knowledge of the country, plus a certain 'sensitivity to atmospheres' as she herself described it. Like all SOE agents, Pearl had been issued with a gun, but could never imagine using it to take a life – she was to later judge that discretion and secrecy had been the hardest, saying, 'You can imagine what that was like among the French!'

Monsieur Saint-Martin was also of considerable help with another task in Southgate's absence. Prior to his departure for England, Southgate had asked Jacques Hirsch to position three Eureka wireless beacons for the Royal Air Force. One of these was stored in Auguste Chantraine's loft, pending a location being available in the Corrèze region, while another had been damaged on impact when dropped by parachute. But on or about 15 November 1943, the third Eureka commenced working in the Auch region after Jacques Hirsch, helped by Pearl, again contacted Saint-Martin. The set was to be used not only to guide agent- and supply-dropping aircraft, but was also available to help any Allied aircraft flying over the area, including those heading for targets in northern Italy. The teacher designated two of his students, Charles Fourcade and Célestin Latour, to operate the beacon and together they shared the task of maintaining a night watch from November 1943 to August 1944 without being detected by the Germans.

To the immediate south of the Gers, Charles Rechenmann's network continued to grow and to make attacks on strategic targets in the area. Though it was the most far-flung group from his base in Châteauroux, Dédé and Pierre Hirsch nevertheless continued to transmit messages for the group. In Southgate's absence, Dédé also made sure that personal contact was maintained, not only by Jacqueline's usual courier trips, but also now by Pearl, as well as by personal visits to Tarbes himself. His initial favourable impressions of Rechenmann and Pilar Alvarez had not diminished; here were dedicated people with whom he developed a strong affinity. Back in England, Southgate also reported to Baker Street on Rechenmann's commitment and ability. The Frenchman was spending so much time on SOE work, however, that Southgate had begun to worry about his job, even though Rechenmann's firm had shown considerable understanding to date. He therefore suggested to Colonel Buckmaster that Rechenmann, together with Jacques Hirsch, should be put on SOE's paid staff, and brought out to England for proper training. This was accepted by London and Rechenmann, as the first priority, made his way over 500 kilometres north to a field just outside the village of Soucelles, to the north-east of Angers. There he was picked up on the night of the 16th from an improvised airstrip by a twin-engined Lockheed Hudson of the RAF's 161 Squadron, one of his fellow passengers being François Mitterand, future President of France.

When Rechenmann arrived in England he was immediately debriefed and required to formally report on his activities to date. In doing so he spoke highly of Dédé in particular and described him as 'excellent'. Rechenmann was then formally inducted into SOE, commissioned as a Lieutenant in the British Army and kitted out in uniform. Given a condensed version of SOE's agent training syllabus, he managed to break a leg on the parachute course at Ringway, but nevertheless did well. Promoted to Captain, he was given the go-ahead to return to France as a circuit organizer and was promised his own radio operator as soon as one could be found to accompany him, SOE continuing to lack enough of these vital agents.

Back in France, the Christmas of 1943 proved anything but a time of festivity. On 26 December Dédé and Jacques Hirsch left Montluçon to collect the Eureka set that had been dropped, unrequested, several months before and stored on Chantraine's farm at Tendu in the Indre, but on their way they were given dreadful news. Just before Christmas, the local FTP group had failed in an attempt to release twelve of its members from the prison in Châteauroux and when the Germans retaliated, Chantraine was arrested at home on suspicion of involvement in the affair. It was yet another grievous blow. Over a period of nearly two years Chantraine had personally supervised a large number of para-chute deliveries of stores and personnel, dropped on his own property. He had hidden all newly arrived arms and supplies on his farm and had then been respon-sible for distributing them to the various groups of the circuit. Fortunately, the weapons and the Eureka set were not found before Chantraine's brother was able to spirit them away. But this made no difference to the fate of Chantraine, since the Germans still found enough to condemn him and he was subsequently deported to Germany.

If this shock were not enough, Dédé had to act immediately to avert further disaster. As well as temporarily moving out of his apartment (since Chantraine knew its location) Dédé had to radio London urgently to abort the imminent return of Southgate who was to be dropped on Chantraine's DZ near his farm. Dédé arranged for this plan to be changed and instead ordered Jacques Hirsch to meet Southgate on the DZ at Marsan in the Gers. On 10 January 1944, Dédé therefore joined Jacques Hirsch there for the drop, but it was cancelled yet again.

Neither Dédé nor Jacques Hirsch were able to greet Southgate personally when he eventually did arrive, dropping in a moonless period on a DZ operated by SOE's 'Wheelwright' circuit, commanded by Lieutenant Colonel George Starr. With the help of a S-phone and Eureka for his reception, Southgate made a good landing in the early morning of 28 January 1944. He first went by bus to see Jacques Hirsch and then on to Tarbes, where he had several matters to settle in preparation for Rechenmann's imminent return. He then went to Montluçon to see Dédé and Pearl where Dédé, in addition to describing the tragedy of Chantraine, had to impart even more bad news involving the health of both couriers. After a year in France Jacqueline Nearne was near to exhaustion and badly in need of a rest, even finding it difficult to raise the strength to carry her suitcase when travelling. To make matters worse, Pearl had been stuck in Paris for a couple of weeks, having fallen ill with an attack of neuralgic rheumatism, brought about by long nights in cold trains. She had not been able to find a room of her own, under her new identity, until December and had therefore spent most nights in the first-class compartments of trains travelling between Clermont-Ferrand, Jacques Hirsch's apartment in Toulouse and Châteauroux.

All this supported the point that Southgate had forcibly argued in England, that his circuit was far too big and would have to be reduced or supported by additional circuits. But at least he brought with him the welcome news that more and more SOE personnel had been promised to help. This was something that Dédé already knew, for he had just received the startling news, transmitted from London, instructing 'Stationer' to organize receptions for around twenty agents, commencing from the next moon period in February. London also pledged to send another agent to 'Stationer' for weapon training for the Maquis, and two more to help with finding landing grounds. In the meantime, with no time to be lost and Chantraine's landing ground now no longer available, the onus would fall on Jacques Hirsch and his contacts in the Gers region and around Tarbes.

There was also some good news for Dédé to report to ameliorate the despondency caused by Chantraine's arrest. In December Dédé had sent Pearl to contact Jacques Dufour's 'Anastasie' Maquis group and she had been asked to give sabotage instruction to a party of his saboteurs at Salon-La-Tour, 50 kilometres south-east of Limoges in the Corrèze. Early in the same month the steel works at Les Ancizes-Comps in the Auvergne, 35 kilometres north-west of Clermont-Ferrand, had been sabotaged by arson and the destruction of pumps, resulting in three months' stoppage of production of steel destined for enemy aircraft production. And later in the month 30,000 litres of petrol were captured at Saignes in the Auvergne, 80 kilometres south-west of Clermont-Ferrand. In Clermont-Ferrand itself, a second attack on the vital Michelin factory had burned more tyres, although further planned sabotage of the factory failed due to inexperience and a lack of training. Dédé and Pearl again stressed to London that the failure was solely due to the lack of sabotage instruction. The saboteurs were extremely keen and did some excellent work despite their inexperience, but if they had been properly trained they would certainly have done much better. What could be achieved was shown by another Maquis group on 20 January 1944 when the liquid oxygen works at Massiac in the Auvergne were attacked; the transformers, distributor and two compressors were destroyed. Two days later, transformers and the drawing office were put out of commission at the Chartoir works in Clermont-Ferrand, which were producing aircraft parts for the enemy.

Dédé now received the first of many messages regarding the anticipated influx of agents when London requested reception committees for drops on the two consecutive nights of 10/11 and 11/12 February. For the first, Jacques Hirsch managed the reception of a two-man team from the 'Scientist' circuit, some 6 kilometres to the north of Marsan on another DZ that he had established near the village of Nougaroulet, on the Monfort property. Both newcomers were Mauritians, the team leader being Major Claude de Baissac, brother of Lise, the former Poitiers-based SOE agent who was then back in England. With him was his radio operator, Lieutenant Maurice Larcher, brother to Dédé's friend Jean Larcher. Both quickly moved on to Normandy where good work was done, but Maurice Larcher was to be killed in a shoot-out with the Germans in July 1944.

The night after the arrival of de Baissac and Larcher, Southgate led a reception party on the DZ near Tarbes where Lieutenant (James) Andrew Mayer, Lieutenant Georges Audouard and Lieutenant Pierre Mattei parachuted in. The operation included the use of S-phone equipment by which Southgate was able to talk clearly with the Halifax pilot, Captain Grell, and during this exchange he received a request to identify a landing ground for another incoming circuit, that of 'Bricklayer', led by Major Antelme, yet another Mauritian. Southgate suggested a place near Poitiers where he was expecting two Eurekas to be received by a helper code-named 'Fanfan' three or four days later.[2] While the S-phone worked satisfactorily, there was one drawback which caused unease amongst those on the ground. Reception was so loud and clear that the voice from the orbiting aircraft was heard over something like a quarter of a mile radius – hardly ideal for clandestine operations.

Of the new arrivals, Lieutenant Mayer, code-named 'Franck', was to be Rechenmann's deputy. Southgate had met him previously in England and, impressed, had wanted him to join 'Stationer', but this was not approved. One of three brothers who joined SOE from a background in Mauritius and Madagascar, Mayer had not had an easy time training, with mixed reports, but had nevertheless been confirmed as an agent.

Instead of Mayer, 'Stationer' was allocated Lieutenant Audouard ('Martial') a former *résistant* now returning to France. Together with his father, who ran a safe house in Cannes, he had worked for the Resistance from September 1940, mostly dealing with the reception of personnel arriving by sea. Early in 1943 the younger Audouard had decided to leave France to avoid being called up for work in Germany and had crossed into Spain where he was arrested. After eight months in various Spanish prisons he reached England in October 1943. After training by SOE he was sent to 'Stationer' to act under the orders of Southgate who wanted an extra London-trained agent to help Dufour build up the Maquis near Terrasson.

Lieutenant Mattei ('Gaëtan') was the first of two Lysander experts allocated to 'Stationer'. Trained as agents, these men were normally pilots who had received additional instruction on the requirements of suitable landing grounds for Lysanders and how to pass on the detailed technical information required by London.

After briefing the new arrivals, Southgate left Mayer and Audouard in Tarbes, in the care of 'Fanfan'. All seemed to be well at that time and the newcomers were eager to start. Mattei was immediately sent north on his own, with instructions from Southgate to make contact with Monsieur Gateau, a trusted helper in Poitiers.

On 29 February the circuit's second Lysander expert, Lieutenant Alex Shaw arrived, having travelled overland after arriving in France by submarine. Code-named 'Olive', Shaw's real name was Alexandre Schwatschko and he was one of SOE's more exotic agents. Twenty-four years old, he had been born in Transylvania to a Hungarian mother and a Russian father who fought with the White Russian Army in the country's bitter civil war. Alexandre himself never saw Russia, but took his Russian nationality from his father.

When his mother died at a young age, Schwatschko lived with his father in France. He went to school there and qualified as an engineer, but when a family dispute arose Schwatschko moved out. For some time he lived a life of leisured ease, staying with friends around the country and indulging his passion for sport, especially swimming. Money was no problem since his father was a very wealthy man who still supported his son, despite the quarrel. When war broke out and the Germans invaded, Schwatschko swiftly developed a burning hatred of the invaders of his adopted homeland. He joined the French Air Force and qualified as a pilot, but did not see active service before the Armistice was signed.[3]

Returning to civilian life he had still been able to pursue a playboy-type lifestyle, crossing between the occupied and unoccupied zones with ease, thanks to his money. It was while in Paris, however, that a chance encounter shaped his destiny. To his surprise he came across an acquaintance whom he had met pre-war on the Riviera, but his friend was an Englishman, Dennis Rake, and Rake revealed that he was back in France as a British agent of SOE. Schwatschko was excited at the news for this was exactly the sort of work that would enable him to hit back at *les boches* – could Rake help get him to England? Rake could not, so Schwatschko made his own way to the Spanish border where he had the temporary misfortune to be arrested and interned by the Spanish authorities. While held in a camp, by an odd coincidence he again met Rake, also on his way to England and this friendship helped Schwatschko when he eventually reached England via Gibraltar.[4] Although he was accepted by SOE for training, he was already becoming known for his conceit and boastful nature. He claimed to know Winston Churchill and General Gort, though he did not, and it seems that only his passionate hatred of the Germans, together with his pilot's qualification and the backing of Rake, overcame the many doubts. During his training, STS 7 found him a 'man of action', but STS 23 considered him 'rather selfish and NOT too intelligent'.

Given a new identity as Alexandre Shaw, his dark good looks also gained him an English fiancée in London (surviving records show that SOE did not approve of her), and it was therefore probably with some relief when he was eventually sent to join Southgate and Dédé as one of their two air operations specialists.

Despite his character shortcomings, Schwatschko proved effective once in the field, earning Southgate's approval, but remaining unpopular with several of his clandestine colleagues. Immediately deployed to the Indre and the Vienne to locate new landing grounds, he was given radio support by Pierre Hirsch who, though acknowledging Schwatschko's ability, found it difficult to get on with the flashy, confident, former pilot. In particular, he was concerned that the helpers recruited by Schwatschko seemed to have been obtained only by money, rather than through a love of France or commitment to the Allied cause.

Until Mattei and Schwatschko were able to find new sites, drops continued to the existing sites, the next arrivals landing on the Marsan DZ on the night of 1/2 March 1944. Captain Charles Rechenmann, having finished his SOE training in England, should have been one of these, now briefed to run his own circuit independently of 'Stationer', in the Tarbes to Toulouse area. During his parachute training at Ringway, however, Rechenmann had broken a leg and this meant he was unable to parachute into France. He was instead delivered to a secluded Normandy beach by a Royal Navy motor torpedo boat, while his French-Canadian radio operator, Lieutenant Allyre Louis Sirois ('Gustave') was parachuted in, together with Major Roger Landes, 'Aristide'. The latter was on his second operation in occupied France and was charged with further development of the 'Actor' circuit in and around Bordeaux. Detailed descriptions of the 'Stationer' reception of Sirois and Landes are included in post-war accounts by both men and the event is worth describing in detail.

The drop took place to a reception committee led by Jacques Hirsch, after an abortive attempt the previous night. Among his small group of helpers were two women, the latter greeting Sirois enthusiastically as he landed safely and discarded his parachute. Landes was not so lucky, jarring his back and badly damaging his ankle on landing. He could only move slowly with the support of two helpers and was clearly in considerable pain. The first task, however, was to recover the packages dropped with the two new arrivals. This was not made any easier by the fact that the pilot of the Halifax had been concerned by the gusting wind conditions and had therefore decided to drop his charges from around 1,200 feet, instead of from 700 feet or less, which resulted in the parachutes being spread out over a good kilometre, necessitating an hour's strenuous searching and carrying before all was well. The group then took Sirois and Landes, the latter carried on the back of Jacques Hirsch, to a nearby deserted house where the two women reverted to a more traditional role by lighting a fire and preparing a much-appreciated meal for the new arrivals. To the Canadian Sirois, the presence of wine on the table was a novelty, as was the use of pocket knives with which to eat. Noting this, Jacques Hirsch quickly grew alarmed at Sirois' lack of knowledge of France and current conditions. To make matters worse, his clothes were inappropriate in that he had arrived in a good suit and had silk socks and shirts, yet he was supposed to be an agricultural worker. In addition, his French-Canadian accent would also attract attention. All this had to be thought about, but the first priority was to move on from the immediate area of the drop zone. Landes was still in shock and pain and unable to walk. The only solution was for Jacques Hirsch, being the biggest and strongest of those present, to continue to carry him, fortified by two of the SOE agents' energy pills. Fortunately, Landes was slightly built, but it was nevertheless still a good 5-kilometre trek to the village of Marsan where Landes was left in the care of another courageous helper, Madame Daubeze.

Leaving Landes there, Jacques Hirsch then took Sirois on to another safe house, the farm where the operator of the Eureka transmitter beacon (code-named 'Boot') had hidden the vital equipment inside the chimney. There they rested for a few hours before continuing to catch a train to Toulouse and the safe house operated by Betty Saint-Laudy. Until Rechenmann made his way overland via Paris and then on down to the south of France, Sirois would have to be looked after by 'Stationer' and he therefore remained in Toulouse for almost the entire month of March, gradually becoming familiar with present-day France. Another product of SOE's rush to get as many new radio operators into the field as possible, the young Canadian had received only two weeks' training at Beaulieu's finishing schools and was the first to admit that this was insufficient to become familiarized with a country he had never visited. Dédé, Southgate, Jacqueline Nearne and Jacques Dufour therefore all visited Toulouse, helping to prepare the radio operator for everyday life in occupied France. Sirois, though grateful, was initially somewhat perturbed to discover that Betty Saint-Laudy's house was in the same block as an office of the Gestapo – as she passed it, Betty would often sing a mocking little ditty. Thankfully, the Germans did not understand.

When Rechenmann reached Tarbes in late March, Jacques Hirsch took Sirois to confer with him there, but Rechenmann was about to undertake a recon-naissance trip to Angoulême, in order to sound out reported Resistance forces in the area. While he did this, it was agreed that Sirois would also move north, but that the 'Stationer' circuit would continue to look after and further prepare him. Accordingly, Sirois was then passed on into the safekeeping of the Hirsch parents in Saint-Sulpice-les-Champs for another month. There he again met Jeanne Hirsch, whose courier duties had earlier taken her to Sirois in Toulouse, and Pierre Hirsch, now acting as a radio operator to assist Dédé. Pierre Hirsch was already transmitting from the house and so Sirois kept his own messages for London to a minimum. The Hirsch family continued to instruct him on French everyday life and arranged for another, more secure, false identity and papers. Otherwise, they played bridge or poker, and relaxed in the château's courtyard until, at last, Rechenmann called to collect Sirois. He brought encouraging news from his trip to Angoulême where he had made useful contacts and found several groups ready to be organized and armed. Happy to be called upon at last to take an active role, Sirois left with Rechenmann, though not without regret and profuse thanks for the Hirsch family who had done much to educate him about French life.

While the need to train Sirois had been a diversion, the main task of building up the Resistance had continued unabated. Recruiting was now becoming much easier, but even so, Dédé and Southgate had agreed that if Maquis numbers were to reach the desired levels in time for the expected invasion, risks would need to be taken and security relaxed. As news of Allied successes were reported by the BBC, such as the continued heavy bombing of Germany, much of the French population was now prepared to participate in, or at least co-operate with, the Resistance. A notable exception concerned one of the priority sabotage targets for 'Stationer', the Michelin tyre factory at Clermont-Ferrand.

The works should have been one of the targets for Harry Rée, but he had moved on to the Franche-Comté. There, after an inconclusive bombing raid by the RAF in July 1943, he had persuaded the management of the huge Peugeot factory at Sochaux to agree to sabotage that succeeded in stopping production of armoured vehicle components for the German Army. The plant owner had allowed access to the Resistance in order to carry out the sabotage as the only alternative to further heavy bombing and, undoubtedly, much loss of civilian lives. SOE's success with this target now led to 'Stationer' being asked to try a similar approach with Michelin.

Dédé received the urgent message in Châteauroux and immediately passed it to Jacqueline Nearne to be delivered to Southgate. The latter made an appointment to see one of the factory's service managers and calmly suggested to him that he might like to co-operate in the sabotage of his own works. Unfortunately, the man was indignant and refused to believe Southgate's threats that the alternative would be saturation night bombing by the RAF.

Since the factory's management had effectively called Southgate's bluff, no other choice remained and Dédé was obliged to radio London, urging a bombing raid as soon as possible in order to back up what Southgate had threatened. From SOE headquarters, Colonel Buckmaster pulled all the strings he knew and describes in his book, *They Fought Alone*, how Dédé, Southgate and Jaqueline Nearne waited anxiously for confirmation that their request for action would be answered. There might have been a little fanciful elaboration on Buckmaster's part,[5] but the target was first hit in a night raid on 10/11 March by thirty-three Lancaster heavy bombers of No. 5 Group, RAF Bomber Command.[6] One Lancaster was lost, but this did not deter the RAF who hit the target again on 16/17 March with twenty-one Lancasters, mostly from the Dambusters unit, 617 Squadron. It was finally obliterated by Lancasters and Mosquitos of the RAF in a third attack on the night of 29/30 April 1944.

The latter half of March brought more activity. On 22/23 March a woman wireless operator, Maureen 'Paddy' O'Sullivan ('Simonet') parachuted in to a 'Stationer' reception to join the 'Fireman' circuit which was just being established by Major Percy Mayer and Lieutenant Richard 'Dicko' Mayer in the Haute Creuse region. The Mayers had arrived two weeks earlier on 7/8 March near

Angoulême and were the brothers of Lieutenant Andrew 'Andy' Mayer who had already joined Rechenmann's team. O'Sullivan's arrival was marred by bad weather, but she elected to go ahead with her jump despite thick fog. Landing heavily, she briefly lost consciousness, but recovered in time to surprise her reception party who had no idea they were expecting a woman.

To the south, Rechenmann was now ready to operate independently, thanks to the SOE training he had received while in England and the addition of Andy Mayer and Sirois to help him. His revitalized circuit, with a strength of 250 disciplined and capable men, was renamed 'Rover' and marked its leader's return with another attack on the important Hispano-Suiza works in Tarbes on 25 March. In addition to damage to the electrical transformers, the factory's oil stock was set alight and destroyed, the resultant blaze and dense, oily smoke evidencing the circuit's dramatic return to the action.

1. Colonel Josselin-Jean Maingard, defender of the British invasion of 1810. *(Credit: Maingard collection)*

2. *Right to left:* Dédé, Marcel Rousset and Jean Larcher while serving in the 8th Battalion, King's Royal Rifle Corps. All three were to become SOE agents.

*(Credit: Maingard collection)*

3. Brigadier Colin Gubbins, head of SOE. *(Credit: author's collection)*

4. Colonel Maurice Buckmaster, head of F Section, SOE. *(Credit: author's collection)*

5. Flight Officer Vera Atkins, assistant to Buckmaster in F Section.
*(Credit: author's collection)*

6. Captain Harry Rée, parachuted into France with Dédé in April 1943.
*(Credit: author's collection)*

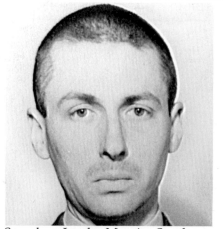

7. Squadron Leader Maurice Southgate, organiser of F Section's 'Stationer' circuit.
*(Credit: author's collection)*

8. Ensign Jacqueline Nearne, courier to the 'Stationer' circuit.
*(Credit: author's collection)*

9. A Mk III SOE radio set, similar to the one issued to Dédé. *(Credit: author's collection)*

10. Dédé's radio codes. *(Credit: Maingard collection)*

| MAINGUARD | | 5/11/42 | LT TURNER |
|---|---|---|---|

| SWITCH (GROUPS OF 5) | |
|---|---|
| ~~----~~ SUPPRESSED | 27 |

| 1ST LETTER, 1ST WORD AFTER 2ND FULLSTOP | SECOND REPETITION OF ~~ADDRESSEES~~ ~~complete form~~. NAME. | 3 WORDS |
|---|---|---|

| EUCALYPTUS | DAY AS WELL AS DATE WILL BE GIVEN. |
|---|---|
| | DATE ONLY. |

K-CH: X-EX: 2-EX

NR 1 2 3 4 5 6 7 8 9 0
    A B C D E F G H I O   B

| | 1 | 2 | 3 | 4 | 5 | |
|---|---|---|---|---|---|---|
| 1 | E | U | C | A | L | DUD LETTER - B |
| 2 | Y | P | T | S | B | A POSTROPHE |
| 3 | D | F | G | H | I | OR DASH — |
| 4 | ~~--~~ K | M | N | O | | ONE WORD |
| 5 | Q | R | V | X | Z | |

11. Parachute training from a Whitley aircraft. *(Credit: author's collection)*

12. The false documentation and maps issued to Dédé. *(Credit: Maingard collection)*

13. The barn at Tempsford (now a memorial site) in which Dédé and Harry Rée were kitted out for their parachute drop into occupied France. *(Credit: author's collection)*

14. A lone Halifax above cloud cover. 138 (Special Duties) Squadron RAF used this type to parachute Dédé into France. *(Credit: author's collection)*

15. 14 rue Brauhauban, the apartment in Tarbes where Dédé was first received by Pilar Alvarez. *(Credit: author's collection)*

16. Captain Charles Rechenmann, caught and executed by the Germans.
*(Credit: author's collection)*

17. Jacques Hirsch.
*(Credit: Maingard collection)*

18. Pierre Hirsch.
*(Credit: Maingard collection)*

19. Jeanne Hirsch.
*(Credit: Maingard collection)*

20. Auguste Chantraine, a courageous Resistance leader in the Indre region and dedicated to working with the 'Stationer' circuit. Caught and executed by the Germans.
*(Credit: P. Chantraine)*

21. Henri Cornioley and Pearl Witherington.
*(Credit: Maingard collection)*

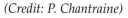

22. A German checkpoint at Pouillé in the Vienne region on the demarcation line between German-occupied and Vichy-controlled France.
*(Credit: Collection Negrault/C. Richard)*

23. Dédé's apartment at 24 rue de la Gare in Châteauroux from where he conducted much of his clandestine radio work.
*(Credit: author's collection)*

24. Railway line attacks were a constant feature of the sabotage promoted by the 'Stationer' circuit.                    (*Credit: author's collection*)

25. The dam at Eguzon, a priority target for 'Stationer'.          (*Credit: author's collection*)

26. A Mosquito fighter-bomber of 464 Sqn RAAF which took part in raids supporting the SAS and Dédé's 'Shipwright' circuit. *(Credit: author's collection)*

27. Some of the troopers of B Squadron, 1st SAS Regiment – 'Operation Bulbasket'. *(Credit: Tonkin collection)*

28. Jacques Dufour, a locally recruited member of the 'Stationer' circuit and later part of 'Salesman'. (*Credit: author's collection*)

29. The impetuous Lt Swatschko, SOE F Section agent sent to join 'Stationer'. (*Credit: author's collection*)

F Section agents received by 'Stationer' and 'Shipright' included:

*(Credits: author's collection)*

30. Eliane Plewman.

31. Denis Rake.

32. Lise de Baissac.

33. Violette Szabo.

34. Nancy Wake.

35. Dédé's specially adapted Matford car, seen here with three SAS troopers and Lt Harper, a shot-down USAAF fighter pilot. *(Credit: Fielding collection)*

36. *Left to right:* Jacques Hirsch, Colonel Blondel, Dédé and Captain Tonkin photographed near to Colonel Chêne's headquarters in late June 1944. *(Credit: Tonkin collection)*

37. Mk IV tanks of Das Reich, the 2nd SS Panzer Division.     *(Credit: author's collection)*

38. Troops of the Indische
   Freiwilligen Legion der
   Waffen SS which caused
   much controversy during its
   retreat through Dédé's area
   of operations in the late
   summer of 1944.
   *(Credit: author's collection)*

39. A narrow escape from enemy fire for one of the maquisards working with Dédé.
*(Credit: Maingard collection)*

40. One of many retreating Germans ambushed by the vengeful French.
*(Credit: Maingard collection)*

41. Men of the 'D2 Bayard' Maquis who served with Dédé's 'Shipwright' circuit.
*(Credit: Paultrot collection/R. Picard)*

42. Headquarters staff of the Vienne FFI pictured at Jouhet in September 1944.
*(Credit: Martin collection/R. Picard)*

43. Colonel Chêne, centre, talking to a visibly drawn and tired Dédé prior to the liberation parade in Poitiers, 5 September 1944. *(Credit: R. Picard)*

44. Major Amédée Maingard DSO at the end of the war. *(Credit: Maingard collection)*

45. Dédé, the successful post-war businessman. *(Credit: A. Antelme)*

46. The first Boeing 707 jet airliner of Air Mauritius.     *(Credit: author's collection)*

47. The bronze bust of Dédé, unveiled in Port-Louis, Mauritius, in 2001. *(Credit: L. Dalais)*

# Chapter Eight

# The Pace Quickens

Rechenmann's return in command of an independent network meant that Dédé, Southgate and their couriers no longer had to travel as extensively as before. The Maquis groups of Couladon and Dufour in the Auvergne and Dordogne respectively could also now expect their own, separate, SOE teams for support. All this would help concentrate 'Stationer' into a more manageable geographical area, doubly helpful since by the spring of 1944 travel by rail was becoming more and more difficult, thanks to the Allied bombing campaign and the rising tide of sabotage. The civilian population was now disinclined to travel unless for absolutely necessary journeys, to the extent that Southgate complained, only partially in jest, that those people left in the trains were either Germans, or SOE agents.

Jacqueline Nearne was already under orders to return to England for a much-needed rest, so henceforth the activities of Dédé, Southgate and Pearl would concentrate on the Indre, and also in the neighbouring Vienne. In the Indre, and despite Chantraine's arrest, two more DZs, code-named 'Carotte' and 'Radis', were now in use and regularly supplying an extra 250 men. This continuing surge in recruitment to the Resistance cause now meant there were some 2,000 men in and around Châteauroux, ready for word of the invasion. A demonstration of their growing ability was given on 1 April 1944, following an Allied air raid on La Martinerie airfield when the attackers had only managed to destroy seven of the twelve aircraft that were on the ground at the time. Mobilizing rapidly, a Maquis sabotage team, equipped with plastic explosives supplied by the arms drops arranged by Dédé, slipped onto the site and succeeded in placing their charges under the cockpit seats of the remaining five aircraft. All subsequently blew up.

Such achievements were critical in winning over the local population, some of whom still regarded the Maquis as little better than armed bandits. Southgate was later to report that 'the farmers in the neighbourhood were always a little shy of us and we could not get their full co-operation, but they were always up to the mark for *ravitaillement*. All the Maquis troops were very well fed.' Small Maquis groups were also now reported as active in the Cher and Loir-et-Cher regions, near Vierzon and Romorantin. This involved not only attacks on German military transport and railway lines, but also the placing of incendiary bombs in any inflammable goods being transported by rail. While their efforts were currently small scale, they were building the expertise and confidence that would be necessary to help tackle, on or after D-Day, the Priority A targets allocated to 'Stationer', among which was the railway at Vierzon.

Yet despite the increase in numbers, Dédé and Southgate noted a worrying dip in morale in April 1944, fuelled by concerns that an invasion might not now be imminent. Their response to this was immediate, for on 4 April Dédé received orders from London that at least sixteen more agents should be expected, all requiring reception parties and more landing grounds. On the night of 5/6 April the 'Labourer' team of Lieutenant Elisée Allard ('Henrique'), Lieutenant Pierre Geelen ('Pierre') and Lieutenant Marcel Leccia ('Baudouin') were dropped on the 'Chat' DZ, between the Château d'Acre and Néret, 15 kilometres east of La Châtre. They were looked after in the house of a local Resistance organizer until they left for Paris on 27 April, after which no more was heard of the team until 4 May when the terrible news was received that all three had been arrested on arrival in Paris. Betrayed by a double agent, they were imprisoned in Paris before transfer, in August 1944, to Buchenwald concentration camp in Germany. They were hanged there on 14 September 1944.

Of the 'Stationer' circuit's two Lysander experts who had recently arrived to help locate new landing grounds, one was already giving cause for concern. Sent immediately to reconnoitre the Poitiers region for suitable sites, Lieutenant Mattei had subsequently reported back to Southgate and Pierre Hirsch in Montluçon with the dispiriting news that he had been unable to find anywhere suitable. Not best pleased, Southgate had sent Mattei back to try again, this time with the address of a *boîte aux lettres* in Poitiers so that he could enlist local help. This was the house of Monsieur and Madame Gateau, loyal helpers of SOE's 'Artist' circuit and Lise de Baissac when she had been based in Poitiers, but no word came from Mattei as to whether he had been successful

While Dédé and Southgate were left to wonder why there was no news from Mattei, the problem was compounded by another SOE agent, Maître Savy ('Régis'), who had arrived in early March with Eileen Nearne, Jacqueline's sister, as his radio operator. He too seemingly wanted to contact and make use of Mattei to locate landing grounds further north. When Savy arrived, Dédé had been in Tarbes liaising with Rechenmann's group before their leader returned from England and he was therefore unable to help out. Consequently, Southgate was so annoyed by this unwelcome additional demand on his time that he complained bitterly to London and wanted to return Savy immediately to England, even ahead of Jacqueline Nearne who was now being looked after by Monsieur and Madame Bidet while she awaited an outbound flight.

One man who was most concerned at Mattei's silence was Pierre Hirsch. Having met Mattei in Montluçon, he was worried that his identity was known to the missing man so, as a precaution, he arranged a new identity in the name of Pierre d'Hamblemont, with the cover of an Inspecteur d'Assurance. This was just as well, for only two days later he received a letter signed by Mattei, asking Hirsch to go and meet him in the main railway station in Poitiers. Southgate smelled trouble and instead sent Pearl to the city to see if she could discreetly find out what was going on. Making her way to the Lycée des Garçons, where Monsieur Gateau worked as its Treasurer, she was fortunate to ask his whereabouts of the concierge who warned her, 'Madame, clear out quickly. I don't know who you are, but I trust you had personal affairs to do with the *Econome*. His house is full of Gestapo and he and his wife have been arrested.'

The arrests had taken place as long ago as 19 February 1944, so guessing that Mattei must have fallen into a trap, Pearl left Poitiers as quickly as possible to report back to Southgate.[1]

Fortunately, there was better news from Mattei's counterpart, Lieutenant Shaw (real name Schwatschko), who had located and brought back into use another landing ground, code-named 'Billiard', 2 kilometres south-south-west of Villers-les-Ormes, to the north-west of Châteauroux. This had been used in 1943 by another circuit and now, on 9/10 April, a Lysander flew in with Major Philippe de Vomécourt on his way to the Loir-et-Cher, Lise de Baissac returning to join her brother in Normandy, and Arnaud de Vogué. Schwatschko organized this landing, his first operation in the field, and after only a few minutes the Lysander was winging its way home with three passengers, two of whom were anxiously awaited in England. For Colonel Buckmaster had not been pleased when a double Lysander operation in early March 1944 had not brought back Jacqueline Nearne, recalled for recuperation as long ago as January. Jacqueline, later described by Southgate as a 'principal and most efficient courier', had worked tirelessly until over-work and strain prompted Buckmaster to order her home to regain her health. Determined to make sure of this second attempt, F Section's commanding officer therefore went down to RAF Tangmere, 161 Squadron's forward operating base on the south coast of England, and personally chalked on the side of the departing Lysander:

*Batting order:*

1. *Jacqueline*
2. *If possible Josette*

*This is an order*

In his book *Specially Employed*, Buckmaster, presumably from memory, seems to confuse the detail of this incident, believing that Southgate was also being recalled, but the essence is correct and he waited anxiously at Tangmere for the return flight. Not only was Buckmaster keen to welcome Jacqueline personally and arrange for her care, he also wanted to smooth the way for the possible arrival of Josette, Southgate's French wife who had continued to live in Paris after the fall of France. In the event, both women were brought back safely, together with Maître Savy of whom Southgate was keen to wash his hands. It was a tension-filled return as Tangmere became fogged in and the Lysander could not land. Low on fuel, Flight Lieutenant Taylor nevertheless continued inland and made a safe landing at RAF Dunsfold, 30 miles to the north. Jacqueline, at last, was back on British soil after fifteen nerve-wracking months of clandestine life. Her return was supposedly only for a rest, but her health had suffered to such an extent that her recovery took many months and operations ceased before she was well enough to return to the field. On her arrival in London, however, she received promotion from Ensign to Lieutenant in the FANY and was quick to confirm the good work that Dédé was doing, an SOE report of the time noting that Jacqueline had 'a very good opinion of SAMUEL, and says that he is very prudent and never goes out'.

In addition to its valuable passengers, the Lysander brought back no less than three reports 'From Hector – Somewhere In the Field', written by Southgate. These were the first detailed reports of progress and activity since Southgate's return in January, and as such were long overdue. Nor did they make for easy reading back in England, for they were somewhat gloomy and pessimistic, not helped perhaps by Southgate having had flu for the past three days and having to compile the reports in a freezing attic.

One pressing issue addressed in the reports was for Southgate to detail his network's expenditure to date of 800,000 francs, a bureaucratic requirement which SOE's Finance Officer seems to have been chasing. Neither Southgate nor Dédé were able to account for every transaction and there was more than a suspicion that London simply did not appreciate the situation in the field. Southgate certainly complained frequently and loudly about the various pressures on him in the months since his return. 'Stationer' had had to organize several receptions, welcome and look after numerous new agents: Schwatschko and Mattei to serve with 'Stationer'; de Baissac, Larcher, Audouard, Mayer, Sirois and Landes to be passed on or temporarily looked after. Southgate had formed a favourable impression of Schwatschko: 'a big fellow, risks anything (a bit too much even) who thank goodness can take care of himself', but had found Mattei difficult to cope with.

In respect of Dédé, referred to by his code name of 'Samuel', Southgate was fulsome in his praise, writing: 'Samuel is sure doing a fine job, I am proud to be his friend.' But in his second report, written at most just a week after the first and confirming Dédé's move from W/T duties, Southgate also painted a worrying picture of Dédé:

The truth is that 'Samuel' is very tired; he is suffering from nervous depression and hardly eats anything. Just as you know him, 'Sam' will not admit that he is ill, and this solution was the only possible one. It is in fact almost a year that he has been living alone in one room, and he is badly in need of fresh air and a more active life. For activity in life, leave it to me, and to please him we shall also give him a gun. He will be my A.D.C. [Aide de Camp] and is just the man that I need in these difficult times.

Southgate also apologized to Buckmaster for having been:

obliged to ask you emphatically to replace 'Samuel' [as radio operator in order for him to operate as an assistant organizer]. Although I knew that your supply of W/T operators was very limited, I did not hesitate for a moment when I remembered your proposal about Samuel during my last visit. Indeed, you proposed making an organiser of him and since then I have thought of making him my *aide de camp*.

Clearly, Dédé had been close to the end of his tether as a lone W/T operator – it suited neither his temperament nor his thirst for action. But Southgate had recognized this as long ago as 1943 when Pierre Hirsch had been locally recruited and trained as a W/T operator by Dédé, to enable the latter to take a more active role as the circuit's second in command. Dédé's ability to take on such a role had obviously been discussed and agreed with Buckmaster when Southgate was back in England from October 1943 to late January 1944. And during Southgate's enforced lengthy absence, Dédé took the major share of running 'Stationer', helped by Pearl and Jacqueline. Perhaps the reason for Dédé's despondency in April 1944 was linked to Southgate's return. At that point Southgate would have picked up the reins again and there was then increasingly heavy radio traffic, arranging more and more supply drops and agent movements. This probably served to tie Dédé back to his wireless set, and consequently reduced his responsibility, at a time when the tempo of activity was clearly increasing. Southgate was as frustrated as Dédé at not being able to use the capable young Mauritian as a lieutenant and in a more active role, though in the meantime Dédé still managed to find the time to arrange a small favour for a family contact, presumably his aunt and uncle now in the Puy de Dôme area, as evidenced by an exchange of internal memoranda at SOE headquarters which remains today on his personal file. Dated 12 April 1944, a request supported by F Section was sent to SOE's finance section for 12,000 francs to be debited from Dédé's account and dropped to him for a relative in France. The advance was approved, but only after a truculent finance officer complained at the exchange rate being suggested by F Section. A much less favourable rate was used, Dédé's account was debited £100, and Finance advised, 'I therefore approve of your informing SHIPWRIGHT [Dédé] that he may use 20,000 of our French Francs, adding that his account has been debited accordingly, without mentioning the sterling amount.' Dédé probably never learned of this penny-pinching, but perhaps, as a trainee accountant, he might even have admired the parsimonious approach.

Around this time Dédé had a particularly unsettling experience one day in his rooms in the rue de la Gare in Châteauroux when he opened the door to a knock and found himself face to face with a number of German officers. Acutely aware of the radio set hidden in the wardrobe behind him, Dédé momentarily feared the worst, but the Germans had not come for any sinister purpose – they had somehow heard of, and were interested in Dédé's hobby of painting birds' eggs. This was the ancient Chinese art which he had learned in Mauritius, and after a brief explanation of the techniques involved the Germans gave their thanks and left.

Another puzzling incident that briefly excited the 'Stationer' circuit merits no mention in any of the remaining wartime SOE files, but was nevertheless later described by Southgate. In one of a series of lurid and almost certainly semi-fictitious accounts published in a British newspaper in 1964, Southgate claimed that he had been involved in a plot to kidnap Adolf Hitler during a trip by the

German leader to the Châteauroux area. In Dédé's remaining personal papers, a handwritten note by him asserts that there never was such a plan to kidnap Hitler, but that there had been a tentative plot to snatch Field Marshal Gerd von Rundstedt, Commander-in-Chief West of the German Army. Ambitious though this may sound, von Rundstedt was certainly known for his lack of personal security, and since his headquarters was almost 300 kilometres from Châteauroux, it is more than likely that an attempt could have been made during one of von Rundstedt's tours of inspection through the Indre. But it is perhaps not surprising that London subsequently vetoed the plan for, despite his position, the aging Field Marshal was just one part of a tangled command structure in France, imposed by Hitler in April 1944, that was assessed as being likely to hinder German response to an invasion. Von Rundstedt, at sixty-eight years of age, had already completed a formal military career that had begun as long ago as 1892. He had been brought out of retirement in 1939 for the war and by 1944, suffering from rheumatism and heart problems, was little inclined to travel much from his headquarters. He was no lover of the Nazis and disliked even communicating with Hitler, though his strict sense of duty kept him from joining the officers' plot against the Führer. Even more importantly he was part of the German High Command that had been targeted by the Allies' brilliant deception plan, 'Operation Fortitude', which had already convinced von Rundstedt that the invasion would not come in Normandy, but in the Pas de Calais area. If, therefore, he had been removed from the scene, the Allies would have run the risk of a more energetic and imaginative commander, such as Rommel, taking over a simplified command structure. Alternatively, a replacement might have proved sceptical of 'Fortitude', with disastrous consequences on D-Day.

The issue of how to release Dédé again for a wider role was at last resolved. In early April a former French Army radio operator, Sergeant René Mathieu ('Aimé') was welcomed by Henri Cornioley on the Souches DZ. Mathieu, who had been seconded to the American OSS,[2] and then loaned to SOE, was an additional W/T operator for 'Stationer' and would release Dédé completely to help Southgate with organizer duties. Yet when Southgate went to meet Mathieu he discovered that he had been sent not just one extra radio operator, but supposedly two, the second being a beautiful young woman agent, Odette Wilen, codename 'Sophie'. Upon talking to Wilen, however, Southgate discovered that she was unhappy that she had suddenly been rushed out to France directly from SOE headquarters without having progressed very far with her training. Southgate therefore left Mathieu for the time being and took Wilen with him by car to Châteauroux and on by train to Montluçon where Dédé then was. That night Dédé put Wilen through a W/T test and quickly confirmed what she herself had said, that she was nowhere near up to the required standard and therefore, having been trained for no other role, was of no use to the 'Stationer' circuit. Both Southgate and Dédé were furious, Southgate firing off a message to London that he had been sent a liability.[3]

Southgate returned to the safe house where he had left Mathieu and arranged to take him to Montluçon with him, but this proved problematic. On catching the train at Vierzon, Southgate decided that it would be safer if he, as the experienced man, took Mathieu's highly danderous codes, money and W/T set. He told Mathieu to follow him at a respectable distance and that they would join up again at Montluçon. But Mathieu somehow contrived to get on the wrong train; Southgate did not realize until he reached Montluçon and discovered that Mathieu had not been on the train with him. In the meantime, Mathieu was in for something of a shock for before he knew what had happened he found himself in Paris, teeming with the enemy. He was, however, astute enough to work out that if he made his way to Montluçon and hung about the station there, either Southgate or Dédé might find him. This he did and three days later spotted Wilen there, being taken by Pearl Witherington to a safe house in Le Blanc, where Henri Cornioley had agreed to hide her until a return to England could be arranged. Mathieu was quickly reunited with Southgate who introduced him to Dédé. This time all was well and Mathieu proved to be a competent operator. At last, Dédé had the opportunity he had longed for. Mathieu was left dealing with all incoming and a good many outgoing messages, while Dédé immediately began to work alongside Southgate, the first priority being to continue organizing all the DZs that would be needed to take delivery of weapons and ammunition for the Maquis in preparation for D-Day.

The issues surrounding supply and arms drops had also been covered in Southgate's written reports sent back to London. Capitaine René Antoine ('Carpi') from the Indre AS, met Dédé and Southgate in April and secured an agreement with the two SOE agents whereby 'Stationer' would supply the Armée Secrète with arms and supplies. In return SOE would be able to use the DZs and landing grounds already researched by the AS, and receive help from them in looking after anyone parachuted in. Two more sites, 'Choux' and 'Rave', were thereby added to the expanding network, but Southgate described several parachute operations as 'exceedingly difficult' owing to the increasing presence of *postes de guet* manned by Germans, and the demarcation line which ran along the whole of the north of the circuit. It was still completely impossible to have daylight operations, or to light fires in moonless periods, as a result of which drops not infrequently proved problematic. 'Stationer' suffered from unopened parachutes on containers, lost containers and difficulties with the RAF making runs from the wrong direction, seemingly not heeding the reception committee's lights. Many requests, frustratingly, went unheeded by London. Bren guns were never sent, nor were the supplies of cod liver oil and Bemax which Southgate requested for Dédé and Jacques Hirsch, both of whom he described as 'extremely thin and undernourished'. Despite all the difficulties with *parachutages*, however, 'Stationer' had not missed a single delivery, nor lost a single gun to the enemy from January 1943 to April 1944. Moreover, only one DZ was ever compromised, when an agent parachuted to a reception and said he had been accompanied by just one other supply parachute. This was eventually found, but in fact there had been two other parachutes; the second one was discovered by local workers three weeks later and handed over to the police. The container held no less than three radio sets – with little doubt as to their intended use, the DZ was then watched and became too dangerous to use.

Another of the tasks for which Dédé was particularly needed was to help

Southgate with the co-ordination of the Maquis groups directly answerable to 'Stationer'. These now totalled five, each of only ten or so men, but all were engaged in sabotage activity against rail targets and electricity pylons. These groups needed not only to be supplied with arms, but also paid so that they could buy food and their own clothing, though they were later provided with army boots from England. One drawback to this structure of command was security. Southgate and Dédé had always tried to ensure maximum security by largely dealing with the local Resistance groups through 'cut-outs', such as Rechenmann and Chantraine, who were then responsible for passing on instructions to their own team leaders. Nevertheless, it was estimated that at any one time, some thirty to forty people were aware of the existence of the two SOE agents, a number which Southgate considered too large and over which he worried. This concern was exacerbated by the twin distractions of Odette Wilen's unpreparedness and a growing belief that Lieutenant Audouard was not following his orders – all of which seemed to be affecting Southgate's health. He was falling behind in meeting the many demands made upon him and Dédé recognized that his leader was clearly very tired and worn out. For a secret agent, as both Southgate and Dédé both knew only too well, this could be as dangerous an enemy as any.

The problems caused by Audouard followed Southgate giving him orders to join up with Jacques Dufour to help organize and train the Maquis in and around the town of Terrasson in the Dordogne. This group had been formed by Monsieur Delord, owner of a clothing depot in the town, but when Southgate visited, he had been very disappointed in Delord's lack of authority and the general indiscipline of his men, despite the efforts of Audouard and Dufour.

Southgate had then gone on to another Maquis near Châteauneuf, south-east of Limoges, and in contrast was very pleased to see how well trained and disciplined this group was. He therefore thought it would be more productive to send Audouard from Terrasson to teach them the use of booby traps and modern weapons, which had just arrived in the field, including bazookas and 2in mortars. Audouard eventually reached this Maquis at Châteauneuf, but in the meantime two of the Maquis from Terrasson were killed by the French Milice in the town. The Terrasson Maquis wanted to avenge their two men and raided the local Milice HQ. Returning from the attack, they also met a German staff car with what was reported to be a general and two colonels in it, whom they shot to pieces. This obviously did not please the German headquarters in Limoges who sent a reprisal squad to Terrasson, where they burnt many houses to the ground, including Delord's clothing depot. The Maquis tried to prevent them and a pitched battle was fought against the Germans, who had the benefit of 75mm guns. During this operation Dufour went to Southgate at Montluçon and urgently asked him to send Audouard back to Terrasson to help reorganize the Maquis. Southgate agreed and ordered Audouard accordingly, only to learn later that the order had been ignored and Audouard had not gone anywhere near Terrasson. The enemy were reported to have lost eighty dead, but in addition to several Maquis being killed during the fighting, the Germans took revenge afterwards by taking and shooting forty hostages and burning many houses. Dufour managed to extricate the remaining maquisards to a safe area some 30 kilometres away, disposing of another eight Germans in the process, but himself only narrowly escaping one further encounter with the enemy.

Southgate and Dédé were furious at these events, not just because of the in-discipline of the Maquis in trying to fight an open battle against superior forces, but also because of Audouard's recalcitrance. The latter was discovered to be having an affair with a woman thought to be suspect, the wife of a local doctor. But despite several warnings, Audouard refused to break off the risky liaison and the situation was now giving great cause for concern. Southgate happened to see him, by chance, in a hotel with his lover and challenged him. Again Audouard declined to give the woman up, refused to leave the hotel as ordered and said he would do as he pleased. Southgate himself left, but later spotted Audouard also leaving town that night by train. After this incident and the disobeying of orders over the Terrasson affair, the final straw was broken when it was learned that Audouard had not attended a supply drop and the RAF aircraft involved had returned to England with its cargo, having made the long and hazardous flight for nothing. Southgate and Dédé were incensed that others' lives had been need-lessly put at risk, and with Dédé's backing, Southgate came to a grave decision. Audouard was too big a risk, he was disobeying orders in the field and was putting dozens of people in great danger. He must be executed. Dédé and Jacques Hirsch were briefed accordingly, a suitable assassin was identified and given his orders and when a radio message came through from London ordering Audouard out of France, Southgate replied in one of his written reports flown out by Lysander that it was too late. Fortunately for Audouard, however, he had not shown up at the rendezvous in Limoges where his demise had been planned and he was later put temporarily beyond the reach of SOE and the Resistance when he was arrested in Ruffec, with his mistress, in late April.

Despite the disruption caused by Audouard, April 1944 saw a huge increase in supply operations for the 'Stationer' circuit (as shown in the table below) since the first two drops a year earlier.

Table 1:   Supplies dropped to 'Stationer' groups, April 1943 to April 1944

| 1943 | Operations | Containers | Packages |
|------|------------|------------|----------|
| April | 2 | 4 | 2 |
| May | 2 | 10 | 2 |
| June | 0 | 0 | 0 |
| July | 2 | 15 | 3 |
| August | 5 | 30 | 9 |
| September | 2 | 30 | 5 |
| October | 2 | 21 | 5 |
| November | 1 | 3 | 1 |
| December | 0 | 0 | 0 |

| 1944 | Operations | Containers | Packages |
|---|---|---|---|
| January | 1 | 15 | 6 |
| February | 2 | 1 | 9 |
| March | 7 | 85 | 12 |
| April | 18 | 252 | 103 |
| Totals | 44 | 466 | 157 |

If this increase in activity were not enough, another pressing demand at the same time was an operation to smuggle out of France the wife of a Free French general serving with de Gaulle's headquarters in London. Madame Cochet was collected from Paris and taken to Châteauroux in late April. From there, Southgate delivered her to a safe house in Argenton-sur-Creuse, organized by Schwatschko who was to arrange her departure in a double Lysander operation from what is now Le Fay airfield, some 7 kilometres south-south-east of Issoudun. There was a wait of a couple of days, but the General's wife successfully departed on the night of 30 April/1 May, accompanied by two returning SOE agents, Captain Philippe Liewer and his courier, Violette Szabo, and another report from Southgate, written over the two previous weeks. Three passengers, for other circuits, were brought in.

After leaving Argenton, Southgate had returned to Châteauroux with Jacques Hirsch on 29 April and slept there, wishing to introduce Hirsch to René Antoine ('Carpi'), the military representative of the Indre AS, the following morning, which was a Sunday. At about 8 o'clock in the morning, however, Dédé arrived and collapsed on the floor after a 45-kilometre cycle ride, warning Southgate not to go and see Antoine as he had been arrested in Châteauroux just two days before on the 28th. The decision was made to clear out of the town and all three men therefore caught the train to Montluçon, arriving at the Hirsch house there at 11.15 that same evening.

The next morning, Monday, 1 May, Southgate and Dédé went to see Mathieu in the house of the L'Hospitalier family, at 16 rue de Rimard. Dédé had recently used this safe house for transmissions and it was now the base from where Mathieu was transmitting. Soon after they reached the house, however, René Coulaudon ('Gaspard') of the Auvergne Resistance, arrived by car and asked Southgate to go with him to meet two more SOE newcomers, Major John Farmer ('Licensee') and Ensign Nancy Wake ('Witch'), who had arrived by parachute the previous night near Villefranche d'Allier, 25 kilometres north-east of Montluçon. Southgate had been expected to be at their reception himself, but had to delegate the task due to pressure of work, only to learn that the two agents had information and funds for him and consequently still required a meeting. He was therefore taken by car to meet them for lunch, leaving Montluçon at 10.00 a.m., having asked Dédé to look through the two dozen or so messages that had arrived in the week since Southgate had last visited Mathieu.

Southgate's lunch meeting was to remain fixed in his memory for ever. On arrival at the Maquis camp where Farmer and Wake were being kept, he was

F.F.I. COMMAND STRUCTURE IN THE VIENNE REGION – AS SET OUT BY COLONEL CHÊNE ('COLONEL BERNARD') IN JULY 1944

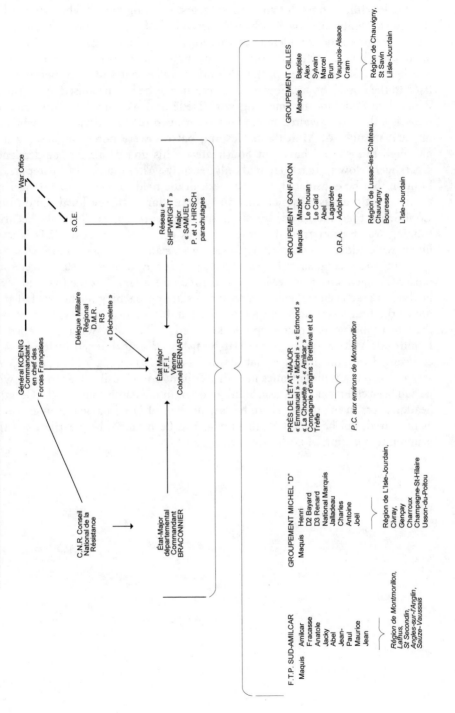

greeted by the sight of Wake, already well on the way to becoming one of SOE's most colourful, resourceful and brave agents, washing herself while stripped to the waist. Unabashed by Southgate's arrival, or by an admiring audience of Resistance men, she completed her ablutions before joining her two fellow SOE agents for lunch. After the required exchange of information and money, Southgate was then driven back to Montluçon at about 4.00 p.m. Before going back to the Hirsch house, however, he returned as he had promised to the rue de Rimard to conclude his meeting with Dédé and Mathieu, and to read the messages that still awaited him. He was dropped off in a back street when an unusual number of Milice and Gestapo patrols were noted in the area and although this should have put Southgate on his guard, his fatigue-deadened senses were slow to react. He had only recently written in one of his reports to London that he considered the first week in the field to be the most dangerous as an agent was usually nervous and unfamiliar with the local conditions. Confidence then increased, but after six months or so, much of the security training was forgotten or dispensed with as complacency set in. If fatigue or illness were added to complacency, disaster was almost certain to follow.

Southgate, recognizing these dangers, had survived in the field longer than most SOE agents. But on 1 May he was tired and weary. For the first time ever he did not take even elementary precautions in approaching the house, failed to notice the four suspicious-looking civilians and a *traction avant* Citröen car in the street, and went straight up and knocked at the door. When it opened he found half a dozen guns pointed at him. Seized and dragged inside he was confronted with the messages that Mathieu had been keeping for him, three W/T sets and about a million francs in cash. Without any plausible reason as to why he had been calling at the house, Southgate was immediately taken to the Gestapo headquarters in the town. There he saw no sign of Dédé having been captured as he feared, but he joined Mathieu who had been taken there earlier, and the brutal interrogation of both men then began.[4]

# Chapter Nine

# A Narrow Escape

The fact that Dédé was not caught by the trap set for Mathieu and Southgate was thanks to the arrival at 16 rue de Rimard of Pearl Witherington, accompanied by Henri Cornioley, Robert L'Hospitalier and his wife Pierrette. The day was brilliantly sunny and Pearl, concerned by how hard Dédé had been working and how fatigued he looked, declared that a picnic was needed to raise spirits.

It had indeed been an exhausting month for Dédé and Southgate. In addition to a deluge of agents arriving, April's total of eighteen drops had delivered no less than 252 containers and 103 packages. All this had involved considerable organization and intensive radio traffic, but although Dédé had completed his task of going through the radio messages by lunchtime on 1 May, he initially declined Pearl's offer, saying he wanted to stay and catch up on his sleep. To his great good fortune, Pearl persisted and eventually managed to cajole him into saying 'yes'. It was therefore a party of five who, after lunch, cycled out of Montluçon to spend their Sunday afternoon by the local lake, Montluçon Plage. Back in the town, Robert L'Hospitalier's mother and elderly grandmother, Madame Deriot, remained in the house along with Mathieu and the messages awaiting Southgate's return.

Shortly after the picnic party had left, Mathieu was in the act of transmitting to London when the door was suddenly forced open and the Gestapo burst in. Witnesses were later to state that the Germans' car had gone straight to the house without the usual cruising back and forth that gave away a Direction Finding vehicle. For this reason, Jacques Hirsch was certain that the raid was as a result of information received and suspected it might have come from a number of arrests made the preceding weekend among the Armée Secrète.[1] Whatever their source, the Germans were elated by their find and, confident that there were more fish to be caught, they staked out the house and the surrounding streets.

Before this net caught Southgate, however, the Germans had a little difficulty with Madame Deriot who was ill and awaiting a visit from the family doctor. By chance, the doctor arrived hard on the heels of the Germans, only to find his patient being arrested, along with her daughter and Mathieu. He was allowed to treat the old lady briefly before she was taken away, but he then realized that he must warn others that the Germans were waiting in the house. Fortunately, he knew enough to go straight to Monsieur Bidet, father-in-law to Robert

L'Hospitalier. Bidet sent word to Jacques Hirsch, who was still in the town and then pedalled rapidly out towards Montluçon Plage. Behind him, Jacques Hirsch quickly sent news of the arrests to all the other members of the circuit. He also called together a number of helpers and posted them as lookouts at the railway station and in the streets approaching the rue de Rimard, hoping to intercept anyone heading there. He was particularly concerned that this might include Southgate, though he was unaware that the latter was being driven back into town. Unluckily, it seems likely that the lookouts only took up position after Southgate had already passed and been arrested; it was therefore then only a matter of warning or intercepting Dédé and the other four members of the picnic party.

Fortunately, Monsieur Bidet had succeeded in finding the group by the lakeside. He looked white as a sheet when he arrived at around 6.00 p.m. and poured out the dramatic news that the Gestapo were at the L'Hospitaliers' house. Appalled, Dédé leapt to his feet and exclaimed, 'We must warn Hector.' He and Robert L'Hospitalier jumped onto their cycles and pedalled furiously back into Montluçon, but it was clearly too late. The Germans were already in a state of high alert and were beginning to close off routes out of the town. Suddenly, it was no longer a matter of trying to warn Southgate – the imperative now was to avoid capture themselves, especially as Pearl, Henri and Pierrette had followed them back into town. Dédé had no hesitation in taking charge and made the quick decision that they should all scatter out of Montluçon and spread the vital news of Southgate's arrest as quickly as possible. He knew that Southgate was likely to be tortured, but would, according to his SOE training, try not to give away any vital information for at least forty-eight hours. Dédé therefore made his way back to Châteauroux alone and then continued on to warn the contacts that 'Stationer' had made more recently in the Vienne region.

Robert and Pierrette L'Hospitalier also left Montluçon and carried the alert first to Limoges and then to the northern Indre. Jacques Hirsch departed immediately for Cosne d'Allier to warn Major Farmer and Nancy Wake before returning to Montluçon the next day to collect Pearl Witherington and Henri Cornioley. This was a brave act, given that German troops and French Milice were doing their best to cordon off the entire town, but Jacques nevertheless arranged for a friend to drive him, Pearl and Henri out of town through the side streets. Reaching Saint Gaultier without incident, they met up there with Pierre Hirsch and Lieutenant Schwatschko in a safe house. On behalf of Dédé, Pierre dashed off a message to London with the bad news. Jacques Hirsch, Pearl and Henri then continued to La Châtre where Odette Wilen was still in hiding pending her return to England. She was warned to stay put and not attract any attention to herself until she was contacted again. Pearl and Henri finally moved on to Dun-le-Poëlier in the northern Indre where, as instructed by Dédé, they set up a new headquarters (in the gatehouse of the Château des Souches) for that region while Jacques Hirsch left for Châteauroux to find new lodgings for himself and a suitable place to meet Dédé. He immediately dropped his false identity under the name of L'Allemand and instead adopted the cover of an insurance agent for agricultural workers. His caution proved justified when he received a tip-off that his arrest had been ordered. On 3 May his house was raided by the Gestapo and though it was found to be empty it was put under surveillance for two months.

After the arrest of Southgate and Mathieu, Dédé moved his operations to another location in Châteauroux, using an apartment in the rue de la République provided by Mademoiselle Guillon, another of the circuit's helpers. This was just in time for, as expected, the captured Southgate began revealing a version of the facts, with some real addresses thrown in, to buy himself time from the brutal attentions of his captors. The Germans even went so far as to drive him back to the region, conducting a tour of the locations that Southgate gave. And yet, despite the Germans ransacking and searching Dédé's small apartment in the rue de la Gare after Southgate's arrest, they missed one vital piece of equipment. For even though it represented a considerable risk, Dédé went back to his room a couple of weeks afterwards and found, still hidden in the bottom of his wardrobe, the all-important wireless transmitter. How the Germans missed finding it will never be known.

Meanwhile, on receipt of Pierre Hirsch's radio message reporting Southgate's arrest, SOE headquarters considered whether they should send another organizer, but Dédé lost no time in confirming that he felt entirely capable of taking over. A post-war report which survives in Britain's National Archives, states: 'So great was our confidence in Maingard that we did not send a replacement', and Dédé lived up to expectations by quickly reconstituting the 'Stationer' circuit, now renamed 'Shipwright', after his own SOE codename. He subdivided the vast 'Stationer' territory into three sectors, retaining personal responsibility for part of the Indre and the northern half of the Haute-Vienne. The northern Indre, which included the important railway targets at Vierzon, devolved to Pearl Witherington, now to be responsible for a separate circuit named 'Wrestler', with her fiancé, Henri Cornioley, as her second in command. To the south, Major Liewer, who had arrived with Violette Szabo, another of SOE's most famous and courageous agents, as his radio operator, was to create a new circuit, code-named 'Salesman' in the remainder of the Haute-Vienne and part of the Dordogne region, taking up responsibility for the troubled Terrason Maquis group with which Dufour had tried to work.[2]

To Jacques Hirsch went the task of establishing contact with Paul Mirguet ('Surcouf'), who was named head of the Indre FFI in May 1944, reporting to the Délégué Militaire Régional (DMR), Eugène Déchelette ('Ellipse'). Hirsch confirmed that the 'Shipwright' network would arm the Indre AS following a new series of parachute drops, code-named 'Fleuve'. In addition, on Dédé's instructions, Jacques Hirsch went to Montmorillon in the Vienne to make contact with the town's sous-préfet, Monsieur Villeneuve, who was a key figure in the local Resistance and who needed help to supervise a series of parachute drops. But as Hirsch left, more disastrous news rocked Dédé's network.

To the south, the new 'Rover' circuit was shattered when Lieutenant Mayer, Rechenmann's second in command, was arrested on 10 May 1944 and Rechenmann himself was apprehended on the 15th or 16th, while in a café in Angoulême. Both Lieutenant Sirois and Pilar Alvarez were lucky to escape the

Germans who were now definitely looking for them. Pilar Alvarez fled to the countryside, and though her brother and sister were arrested, they were freed from prison in June by the FFI not long after D-Day. They were too late, however, to help Rechenmann. He and Mayer had been transferred first to the notorious Fresnes Prison in Paris and then sent to join other captured SOE agents in Buchenwald concentration camp in Germany.

Closer to home, the Hirsch parents had taken the precaution of leaving the house in Saint-Sulpice-Les-Champs, having spread a rumour that Mme Hirsch had gone to a private lunatic asylum at St. Briest. But on 13 May the Hirsch grandparents were arrested in their house, the Germans pointing to photographs of their grandsons and boasting 'that is Jacques, "Arthur", and that is Pierre, "Popaul" – both noted terrorists.' Where the Germans had obtained their information was open to conjecture, but it was disturbingly accurate. The L'Hospitaliers were the next to be arrested, followed on 27 May by Monsieur and Madame Rousseau in Paris. Monsieur Rousseau was later released, but from this time onwards the Germans had Dédé, Jacques and Pierre Hirsch, Pilar Alvarez and Sirois named on their 'Wanted' list, proof that the enemy certainly did have detailed information on their quarry. If further proof were needed, the wave of arrests continued in early June when Armand Mardon ('Le Vigneron'), the Gaulliste leader of the Nord-Indre Resistance and mayor of Dun-le-Poëlier, was arrested by the Gestapo on the 1st·. His communist deputy, Alex, managed to escape, but lacked the initiative to take over so Dédé asked Pearl to assume direct command of the Maquis groups. To help her, Dédé recruited a new radio operator, Adrien Berge, a local man from Mardon's group, operating under the code name 'Tutur'. In the same period Monsieur and Madame Bidet were arrested and subsequently deported to Germany.

Dédé could have had no worse start to his new role of network organizer. Of the tightly knit *Résistance familiale* on which 'Stationer' had been founded, the Hirsch, Rousseau, L'Hospitalier and Bidet families had all suffered badly. Neither Dédé nor the Hirsch brothers believed that these arrests were from information given to the Gestapo by Southgate, since some of the raids took place on the same day as Southgate's own capture and on the following days. They were sure that he would have resisted torture for at least three to four days, but they had no firm explanation as to why so many arrests were made.

# Chapter Ten

# Out of the Shadows

The continuing arrests throughout May and into June maintained the constant presence of danger, but Dédé and his team could not afford to become demoralized or diverted from their frantic preparations to arm the Resistance in time for the invasion. In May, even the record achievements of April were bettered, with 19 drops of supplies and arms, a total of 296 containers and 85 packages. But in June, another huge step forward was taken when 50 drops were arranged, bringing 1,137 containers and 376 packages.

In respect of sabotage operations, of the Priority A targets which had originally been designated for attack on the eve of D-Day, it had already been accepted that both the dam at Eguzon and the airfield at La Martinerie, near Châteauroux, were better attacked from the air. Both were isolated from residential housing and there was therefore little risk of collateral damage or civilian casualties from bombing. Railway targets remained, especially at Vierzon, and up to May it had been estimated that in addition to cut lines, over a hundred locomotives had been put out of action. Together with the sabotage of telephone and electricity supplies, and the destruction of key road and river bridges, all action had the one concerted aim of delaying any German reinforcements which would be moving northwards once the invasion commenced.

At the same time as receiving arms drops, Dédé was still welcoming, temporarily housing and then sending on their way the numerous agents landed or dropped, and he could not afford to miss the nightly BBC messages in case the invasion alert was broadcast.[1] From the increase in the length of these broadcasts, something was obviously in the offing and the evening of 5 June 1944 was clearly special as the longest-ever stream of coded messages was transmitted by the BBC. But nothing was heard of the pre-arranged call to arms for Dédé's 'Shipwright' circuit, only a message confirming the drop, previously postponed, of a two-man reconnaissance team from the Special Air Service Regiment, consisting of Captain Tonkin and Lieutenant Crisp, and a three-man SOE Jedburgh team, code-named 'Hugh'.

Normally consisting of one British or American officer, an officer of the country of destination, and a radio operator of any nationality, Jedburghs were inter-Allied teams that were to carry out ninety-three operations in France between the invasion and liberation. The majority had two British members, and there were many teams with two Americans, but 'Hugh' was a French-dominated Jedburgh, in that while it had a British senior officer, Captain Crawshay ('Crown'), it had two representatives from the Free French Secret Service, the Bureau Central de Renseignements et d'Action (BCRA), Capitaine Legrand ('Franck') and Lieutenant Mersiol ('Yonne'). To welcome these newcomers, Lieutenant Schwatschko organized the reception party, while Dédé arranged to join them the following morning, knowing that they would be bringing two additional radio sets for him.

Expecting nothing out of the ordinary on the historic morning of 6 June 1944, Dédé had driven alone to Moncousinat Farm to greet the Jedburgh and SAS parties and to take delivery of the radio sets.[2] But Captain Tonkin of the SAS handed Dédé a letter of introduction from General Koenig of the Forces Françaises de l'Intérieure (FFI), the Free French forces in London, and told him that the invasion should by now be well under way. Dédé was astonished at the news. Somehow, the BBC message designed to alert him to the invasion had not been transmitted and for a few minutes even Tonkin began to wonder if D-Day had again been postponed, despite having witnessed the invasion fleet on its way. But among the documentation brought from England, Dédé also received new orders from Colonel Buckmaster at SOE Headquarters. These confirmed the invasion and ordered Dédé to leave the Indre region to the 'Hugh' Jedburgh team and his own SOE assistants, Pearl and Schwatschko. Dédé was to move into the adjacent Vienne *département* in order to work with and support the headquarters of the local FFI commanders there. For now, after D-Day, the struggle would no longer be clandestine, but would be out in the open. The Gestapo and SD, while still presenting threats, were no longer the main enemy – now it was the German Army.

The attachment of Dédé to work so closely with the FFI reflected recent political developments back in London, dating from just a few days before. On 3 June 1944, General de Gaulle's Committee of National Liberation had made the bold move of declaring itself the provisional government of France. The timing could not have been bettered, for Churchill then had no option but to let de Gaulle, hitherto kept in the dark, know that the invasion was imminent. Unsurprisingly, the French leader had reacted furiously, complaining bitterly that he had not been told before of the invasion plans. But the British and American governments were equally put out by his surprise declaration of a provisional government. As a result, neither Britain nor the United States would formally recognize the French provisional government until October 1944, long after most of France, including Paris, was liberated. In the meantime, however, SOE took a more pragmatic view, accepted de Gaulle's declaration and worked to it in the field.[3]

At 0730 hours, after the welcoming preliminaries were over, Dédé drove the SAS and Jedburgh officers a few kilometres to the north-east, close to Neuillay-les-Bois, where he introduced the Jedburgh team to Colonel Mirguet. After serving in the French Navy from 1939 to 1940, Mirguet had come to Le Blanc in 1941 to set up a refrigeration plant for a food company. From the following year he had joined the Resistance and had obstructed the enemy until he took over as the Indre's head of the FFI in June 1944. A resolute leader, Mirguet soon showed himself determined not to be swayed by any of the petty jealousies of his different Resistance groups. He had the sole aim of creating a united, strong France and was to be described by the 'Hugh' team as 'completely selfless' in the pursuit of this ideal. Recognizing that they could therefore dismiss any concerns over jealousies within the Resistance movement, Dédé and Tonkin joined in the discussions, planning on how best the Jedburgh team and the SAS could support and complement the activity already being organized by SOE and the FFI.

Dédé, following his fresh orders from Buckmaster and General Koenig, confirmed that he was to leave the Indre to his helpers and the 'Hugh' team, and would move on to the Maquis groups in the Vienne. The SAS would accompany him there and take primary responsibility for disrupting the 'Lot 2' railway line in the area Châtellerault–Poitiers–Angoulême; the 'Lot 1' line south of Châteauroux; and the line connecting the two, which ran via Montmorillon. As he had been instructed, Captain Tonkin emphasized the importance of petrol and railways as prime targets, and while Dédé was already well aware of this, he appreciated that it helped to have a British special forces officer, in uniform, highlighting the task. It was also decided that the arrival of the SAS should be actively and openly broadcast. The countryside was relatively open, and there were so many villages, that this decision was the only practical one and while relatively risky, it might serve to attract useful target intelligence from the local people.

These talks were still taking place when, late in the afternoon, word reached Colonel Mirguet of enemy forces in the area. Apparently the Germans had reached the DZ at Les Cherpes only two hours after Dédé and the others had left the area, and had combed the area unsuccessfully for evidence of a drop. They had then moved on to the Giraults' farm in the early afternoon, but despite giving it a thorough search, everything was safely buried. As a result of this enemy activity, however, Dédé advised against staying in the area, so that night they moved some 40 kilometres south-east, further into the Indre region, to a farm just south of Neuvy-Saint-Sépulcre. It was there, on the morning of 7 June, that the SAS received a radio message through the Jedburgh team's radio confirming that an advance party of Tonkin's SAS troops would be dropped that night. In the last hours of daylight Dédé and Tonkin therefore organized a number of *gazogène* (gas burning) vehicles and shortly before midnight set off for the DZ, some 12 kilometres away, to the north of Bouesse. At 1.51 a.m. on 8 June, a Stirling (like the Halifax, a four-engined bomber adapted to the task) from RAF Fairford arrived over the DZ, immediately spotted the signal lights of the ground party and dropped an 11-second stick of Lieutenant Stephens, eight troopers and nine containers from 600 feet. All landed safely and were picked up without incident, along with nearly five tons of stores in panniers, though the party's Eureka radio transmitting beacon was not found. Its loss was to cause problems for the SAS, but in the short term the enthusiasm of the reinforcements more than made up for the setback.

During the day of the 8th, a move closer to Le Blanc was made in order to attend a meeting of the leadership of the Indre FFI, where tactics, targets and responsibilities continued to be discussed. It was agreed that it would be inadvisable to divide the efforts of the SAS on the railway lines 'Lot 1' and 'Lot 2', since the distance between the two was considerable and would require the SAS force to be divided for considerable periods of time. The FFI were confident that they alone could ensure that the Limoges to Vierzon line ('Lot 1') could be kept permanently cut by the Maquis in the Haute-Vienne, Creuse and Indre regions. This line was already a great favourite with the Maquis – on the night of 6/7 June they had proudly reported having cut it in no less than fifty-seven places. The 'Hugh' Jedburgh team was therefore to remain in the Indre, carrying out Maquis training and operating north of Châteauroux where they agreed to help keep the northern sector of the 'Lot 1' railway line cut. Since the RAF had destroyed all the bridges over the Loire and the Germans consequently had to use the tunnel under the river at Saumur, it was also an important task of the Jedburgh team to keep the railway lines cut leading to the tunnel.

In contrast, the Bordeaux to Tours 'Lot 2' line was strategically far more important, yet more easily guarded by the Germans. The countryside around it was unsuitable for harbouring large Maquis groups and it was therefore felt that small raiding parties of SAS, directed at this line, would be the best use of resources. Tonkin accepted the logic of this reasoning and agreed that his SAS group, with Dédé's help and advice, should operate around Poitiers, some 60 kilometres to the west of Le Blanc. It would concentrate on the specific targets of the Paris to Bordeaux and the Bordeaux–Limoges–Vierzon railways. Other priorities would be the roads from Poitiers to Angoulême, Perigueux, Niort and Limoges; and the disruption of any move towards the invasion area by German military units. The latter would especially include the 2nd SS Das Reich (Armoured) Division now reported approaching from the south and heading towards Normandy.

It was clear that an understanding on such issues would also have to be reached with neighbouring Maquis groups in the Vienne. Leaving the 'Hugh' Jedburgh team near Le Blanc, Dédé therefore arranged for a number of *gazogène* cars to take the SAS party on to the south-west on the night of 8/9 June. They were accompanied by a protection team from the Indre-Est FFI and Colonel Mirguet himself, who wished to confer with his fellow commander in the Vienne region, Commandant Roger Félix Chêne ('Cyclamen').

A 41-year-old former career soldier, Chêne had originally been commissioned in the Chasseurs Alpins and had then served in Libya and Syria. After the Armistice in 1940 he had tried to escape from France to join the Free French, but had been arrested and imprisoned. Upon release he had become an inspector of oilseed in Montmorillon and in April 1943 had been appointed head of the Vienne-Sud sector of the Armée Secrète. This sector was centred on Montmorillon, but the town had become unsafe for him at the beginning of June when the Gestapo had arrested the town's Sous-Préfet Monsieur Villeneuve, on the 2nd and had only just missed Chêne thanks to him not being at home when the Germans raided his house. He had consequently sent his family away to safety and set up an established headquarters at Sazat Farm, only 3 kilometres south of Montmorillon, but in an isolated and sparsely populated area where the approach of any enemy forces, or strangers, would be easily spotted. Another reason that Sazat had been chosen was that it was close by a DZ near to the farm of Le Leché, a little to the south-east. Recognizable without difficulty from the air owing to a nearby lake, Le Leché had already been used for arms drops, including one delivery in early May which had been hidden on the farm and had then helped to further equip the Maquis fighting groups that Chêne was now forming.

Chêne was already proving to be a brilliant Resistance leader and despite his formal military training he proved highly adept at guerrilla and unorthodox warfare. Perhaps most importantly, he also possessed the diplomatic skill to gain the respect of, and lead, the different Resistance factions post-D-Day – in particular the communists. Given the rank of Commandant, he had assembled at Sazat the Resistance leaders who were to form his headquarters: Pierre Martin ('Emmanuel'), Camille Pêcher ('Edmond'), Bouckenheimer ('Léon'), Louis Antigny ('Lulu') and Camille Olivet ('La Chouette').

Chêne's diplomatic skills had been particularly crucial in winning over Olivet, a former aircraft engineer and communist who had volunteered for the Republican cause in the Spanish Civil War, where he had helped to organize medical services. On his return to France he had settled in Montmorillon and had been an early *résistant* in the Vienne-Sud, organizing the local Front National in conjunction with Abel Pinaud ('Fracasse'), a local teacher. Now, in accepting Chêne's leadership and won over by his new commander's diplomacy and ability, Olivet was instrumental in fusing his FN/FTP groups to Chêne's own former AS organization.

Among Olivet's men was a small Maquis group which had arrived in the Montmorillon area in early 1944, having previously operated in the Haute-Vienne. With a strength of about thirty men they were not particularly well armed, but under their leader Roger Artaud ('Amilcar') they were determined and committed, and Artaud ensured their presence and availability for action was made known to the FN's political leadership of Olivet and Pinaud. For security, the Maquis had split into two groups, one based on a farm near Lathus-Saint-Rémy, and the other a few kilometres away at Plaisance, both to the south of Montmorillon. Supplies, however, were difficult, and were almost entirely dependent upon the goodwill and support of local farmers. In early April 1944, this had led to a shoot-out with the local Gendarmerie, when the Maquis had attacked a guard post for weapons and clothing, an incident that left one maquisard and one gendarme dead. The latter death provoked considerable reaction, not just from the local police, but also from the GMR (the Garde Mobile Républicaine, a paramilitary Vichy police force) from Limoges, who mounted a number of raids and searches in the area resulting in several arrests. This was certainly not what the AS needed and Chêne had moved quickly to find out who this group were, to calm their enthusiasm and also perhaps to help them with weapons and supplies, and thereby avoid the need for costly encounters. By the end of April, the link to Olivet was known and a meeting was arranged in a room at the Café de la Paix in Montmorillon between Chêne and Pierre Martin for the AS, and Olivet and Artaud for the FN/FTP. Thanks to Chêne's tact and sensitivity, an understanding was quickly reached. A departmental directorate, headed by Chêne, was created with assistance from Sous-Préfet Villeneuve and Pierre Martin for the AS, and Olivet and Pinaud for the FN. Arms for the

'Amilcar' and any other FTP Maquis were to be provided from the next possible parachute drop and it was agreed that Artaud would, at least temporarily, take his own Maquis further south, away from the dropping zones. Stability returned and the understanding between AS and FN/FTP was firmly cemented.

It was therefore a diverse group at Sazat that Dédé, Mirguet and the SAS contingent now joined, but while there was still some suspicion and enmity, all were united in the aim of pushing the hated German occupiers out of their beloved France. Another planning conference quickly made a number of strategic decisions. Having taken the opportunity to meet Chêne in person and agree tactics, Mirguet was to return to the Indre and lead his own Maquis groups. The Indre would be supported by two Jedburgh teams, the existing 'Hugh' and the soon-to-arrive 'Hamish',[4] who would each cover one of three sectors in the Indre. Pearl Witherington would now stand alone with her own 'Wrestler' circuit and would be responsible for the remaining northern sector, not dealing directly with Colonel Mirguet, but with Commandant Francis, nominated to lead the northern Indre Maquis groups.

Dédé would then divide the remainder of the old 'Stationer' circuit into two. The southern part, together with Dédé's able lieutenant, Jacques Dufour, would become another separate circuit, 'Salesman', commanded by Major Philippe Liewer who had returned to France on his fourth mission on the night of 7/8 June 1944. Liewer was dropped by USAAF B-24 Liberator to a reception organized by Dédé near Sussac, 40 kilometres south-east of Limoges. Accompanied by three other team members, including his courier, the beautiful Violette Szabo, Liewer's job was to join and take over from Dufour, and in particular to organize the wayward 'Bistrot' Maquis after the earlier failure of Lieutenant Audouard.

Meanwhile, Dédé would stay in the Haute-Vienne region with his own 'Shipwright' network, working alongside Chêne's headquarters. Now openly wearing his uniform and rank as a British officer, his task was not only to continue arming and training the Maquis groups, but to act as liaison officer as well with the SAS forces (both present and expected) and any other Jedburgh teams. He would also be responsible for SOE's interests in the neighbouring Deux-Sèvres and Charente regions where little, if anything, was presently known of the organization and supply of the Maquis. Dédé was left in no doubt as to the demands of his new job when Chêne privately outlined the political intrigue that he was now encountering through encompassing the Haute-Vienne The region's local AS commander, Colonel Blondel, was rapidly developing a sour relationship with Olivet at Chêne's headquarters and the latter expressed the hope that he could count on Dédé's co-operation in the difficult task of holding it all together against the common foe. Even at this early stage in their work, Dédé and Chêne developed a close rapport, the latter recalling the first morning that Dédé arrived at the château headquarters where Chêne was briefly lying low, having only just eluded a German force. He later recalled:

I cannot tell you how delighted I was to see Major Sam that morning in the gatekeeper's lodge of the château where I had hidden, with the Germans at my heels. He was in uniform and to us he was the personification of the long-awaited invasion. I remember that the young daughter of our host stroked, with almost religious awe, the khaki cloth of his uniform, as if he were a mysterious being from another world.

That night, the SAS party camped in woods near to Sazat and helped Dédé collect a previously arranged resupply drop for the Resistance. They were joined by Albert Dupont, a young Lieutenant from Chêne's FFI headquarters who could speak decent English and was therefore now temporarily attached to the SAS to act as interpreter. At the same time Jacques Hirsch, now known by the new code name 'François', arrived to join Dédé at Sazat and two days later his brother Pierre, now 'Pierrot', also arrived after being urgently summoned by Dédé.

Since Southgate's arrest on 1 May 1944, Pierre Hirsch had divided his time as a W/T operator between Dédé and Lieutenant Schwatschko. He had already begun to work extensively with Schwatschko, despite finding him extremely difficult to get on with and believing at one time that Schwatschko had even requested permission from London to get rid of him.[5] Certainly, Pierre Hirsch disapproved of Schwatschko's methods in finding landing strips – these consisted of Schwatschko presenting himself as an agricultural agent and requesting permission from the local authorities to scrutinize various pieces of land. He would then go to the place and inspect it; if it were suitable he would ask Pierre Hirsch to radio its details and location to London. If the ground were accepted by SOE and the RAF, Schwatschko approached the local farmer to whom it belonged, announced that he was a British officer, and made the farmer an offer of 200,000 francs. Both Pierre and Jacques Hirsch thoroughly disliked this practice of employing people for money and had more than once pointed out the potential danger of people occasionally having to wait some time to be paid. In practice, no arrests resulted through Schwatschko's methods of work and his techniques on the landing strips were acknowledged to be excellent. He only employed two people for a reception – himself and one other – and he could turn a plane around within no more than five minutes. He ultimately found ten landing strips for Lysander operations, all of which the RAF accepted, but he too, like Dédé, was keen to do more personally to take the fight to the enemy.

With Dédé's blessing Schwatschko therefore undertook to reconnoitre one of the circuit's priority targets, the great hydroelectric power dam near the small town of Eguzon in the Indre, some 60 kilometres to the south of Châteauroux. The dam had been one of the 'Stationer' circuit's Priority A targets for destruction by sabotage in preparation for D-Day, and Southgate had made three reconnaissance visits in all, once during the day using his cover as representative of a *gazogène* firm, and twice at night. It had, however, proved so well guarded by some 250 German troops and twenty-five French guards that Southgate and Dédé had agreed that bombing was a better option. Though London had accepted this view, the matter was then further complicated by the enemy siting strong flak and barrage balloon defences to protect the target. In addition, while all agreed that the dam provided much-needed power for the German war machine, it was also a crucial source of power for the local population. With one eye to the future, the French had therefore pleaded for the dam to remain intact, and it was instead agreed that the Resistance would constantly sabotage the flow of electricity leaving the dam by blowing up transformer stations, pylons and power lines. A start on this had been made in early December 1943 when pylons had been attacked with 'encouraging results'.

Consequently, on 6 June 1944, Schwatschko sent Pierre Hirsch off to establish contact with a particular Maquis group while he himself went to report on the continuing efforts to disrupt the dam's power output. It is believed that on the night of 7/8 June 1944 Schwatschko was on his way to a rendezvous on the RN713 road where he was to receive not only plans on how to sabotage the high-tension electricity lines which fed the telecommunications post in Eguzon, but also information on the enemy flak defences around the dam. Another French source suggests, however, that he was merely on his way to a supply drop by the RAF. Whatever the purpose of his journey, he was in a car driven by an officer of the Armée Sécrète, Jean Traversat, who had been given strict instructions to avoid the town centre of Eguzon, where the Germans accommodated their guard garrison for the dam. But it proved to be a dark night, Traversat took a wrong turn and before they could react the two men realised they were in the town square. German sentries in front of the Hôtel de France, where the German troops were lodged, ordered the car to stop.

It would seem that Dédé's young assistant had been confident of bluffing his way out since he spoke good German and had false papers, which showed he was helping the Gestapo. But the sentries were undecided and while Traversat waited apprehensively in the car under guard, one German led Schwatschko into the hotel for further questioning by his superior. One can only guess at what happened next for, suddenly, a muffled shot was heard from inside the hotel. Outside, and not waiting to find out what had happened, Traversat leapt from the parked car and before the remaining sentry could bring his weapon to bear, he fled across the street and disappeared into the narrow streets behind the church.

To this day no one knows exactly what occurred in the hotel, but it is likely that Schwatschko had not yet been properly searched and still had his pistol with him. What is certain is that Schwatschko shot and killed one of the enemy in the hotel. Local French sources believe this to have been a Feldwebel who was probably the NCO in charge of the sentry who had escorted the SOE agent into the hotel, the shooting taking place in or outside the NCO's room on the hotel's first floor. Schwatschko's action was certainly very much in keeping with the reputation for hot-headedness he had developed during training, and which had not endeared Pierre Hirsch, his radio operator, to him. It was also typical given how much he hated the Germans. But the shot served to alert everyone in the hotel and Schwatschko knew of only one way out of the hotel, the same way he had been escorted in. Dashing down a long corridor he ignored the numbered rooms, which were likely to house Germans, but hammered upon the door of one marked PRIVATE. It was opened by Monsieur Détroit, the hotel's owner, who had been in bed with his wife, his child being asleep in another bed in the apartment. Quickly, Schwatschko described what had happened and Détroit

106

immediately grasped the danger. The hotelier ushered his wife and child out of the apartment, telling them to leave the hotel and go to parents in the village while he stayed with Schwatschko and locked the door.

The hotel was now in uproar, the Germans shouting, bursting into room after room, and loosing off shots in all directions. In desperation, Schwatschko tried to conceal himself in the chimney, but it proved too narrow. From the window he could see more Germans milling about below, negating that means of escape. Inevitably, they eventually arrived at Détroit's door and, finding it locked, pounded upon it, demanding to be let in. Détroit played for time, calling that he had to get dressed but the Germans were in no mood to wait and shouted that they would break the door down if Détroit did not open up at once. The hotel proprietor and Schwatschko looked at each other, lost for other options. Abruptly, the matter was decided for them by a long burst of machine-gun fire from the hotel restaurant below. Coming up through the floor of the apartment, the bullets hit Schwatschko and wounded him badly in the foot. According to the testimony of Détroit, the young SOE officer knew he had run out of luck, but he was determined he would not be taken alive. He lay on the sofa, raised his pistol to his head and pulled the trigger.[6]

When news of Schwatschko's death reached him, Dédé had immediately sent a message to Pierre Hirsch on the 8th, recalling him from the Maquis to which he had gone and ordering him back to join Dédé at Sazat. Reunited there, the Hirsch brothers would now man Dédé's SOE base. Jacques would act as Dédé's liaison officer with the various Maquis groups and took over as Dédé's driver, chauffeuring his distinctive Matford car. Pierre became responsible for operating the SOE radio in a mobile transmitting post, which normally stayed with, or close to, Chêne's headquarters.

Together, the three young men had not only to adapt quickly to the different personalities and groups with which they were now to serve, but they also had to gain the local knowledge necessary for them to act and advise effectively. SOE had some knowledge of the area following the arrival of Lise de Baissac, who had dropped by parachute in September 1942, settled in Poitiers and had created 'Artist', a network of twenty-two agents in and around Poitiers and Ruffec.

But this circuit now lay fallow, with many of its members, like Monsieur and Madame Gateau, arrested or compromised. Nor had the Vienne in general seen a great deal of sabotage activity prior to D-Day, its terrain not easily lending itself to guerrilla warfare. Nevertheless, sabotage and attacks had been steadily increasing throughout the spring of 1944 to the extent that the occupying forces rarely ventured out of the major towns unless in considerable strength.

It was in Poitiers, some 50 kilometres to the north-west of Sazat, that most of the German Army's authority in the area lay, General Gallenkamp's LXXX Corps having its headquarters in the city. This Corps had remained in France since the campaigns of 1940, its tactical headquarters moving to Poitiers by the time Gallenkamp took command in April 1942. The Corps was responsible for security duties in an area stretching on the Atlantic coast from the Loire in the north to the Gironde in the south. Inland, the rear boundary was along the line Nantes–Niort–Saintes and this meant that, unusually, the command's headquarters in Poitiers were about 100 kilometres outside the Corps' area of responsibility.

In addition to LXXX Corps' headquarters, Poitiers was also the base for two reserve security divisions, the 708th and the 158th, both largely up to strength but with around 15 per cent foreign 'volunteers'. Only 40 per cent could be said to be fully trained, the balance being made up of young recruits and rear echelon non-combatant troops. In total, the Poitiers area therefore boasted some 60,000 enemy troops. From these and local Milice forces the enemy had created Unité 602 and Unité 608, two mobile, hard-hitting, quick-reaction units, also known as Sections Rapides, which were to launch numerous actions against the Maquis to the east and south of Poitiers.

Such actions were normally at the request of the Sicherheitsdienst (SD), the feared Security Police of the SS, whose headquarters were at 13 rue des Écossais in Poitiers. There, a twenty-man team was headed by SS-Sturmbannführer Herold, SS-Haupsturmführer Linn and SS-Obersturmführer Hoffmann. They ate and slept in their hotel, the Hôtel de l'Europe, in the rue Carnot, and were supported by another thirty or so agents spread throughout the Vienne and Charentes regions. If an additional hard core of troops were required for difficult operations, one of the Reich's most fanatical fighting forces, the Waffen (Fighting) SS, was also available. The 17th SS Panzergrenadier (Armoured Infantry) Division, the Götz von Berlichingen, had been based to the north-east of Poitiers at Châtellerault and Bonneuil-Matours, and although the Division's main fighting units had immediately headed north after D-Day for the Normandy beachhead, the recruits' depot remained in Bonneuil-Matours. If needed, two to three hundred SS troops could therefore be called upon.

Freed from his long and tiring period of isolation – and with the Hirsch brothers, the FFI and SAS at his side – Dédé was now at last able to play a more openly aggressive role against the Germans. At Chêne's headquarters he was still very much involved in training the maquisards, but he also played a greater part in reception committees and took every opportunity to join the FFI patrols in and around headquarters. At the Sazat farm he and Colonel Chêne arranged for the SAS to set up camp nearby and from there Captain Tonkin went out on 9 June to reconnoitre the local countryside for a new DZ to receive his SAS main party. Dédé also took the SAS to meet the local 'Amilcar' Maquis of Capitaine Robert Artaud who later recalled how, when his men stood to attention and presented arms, 'the SAS group were astonished and impressed.' It was small wonder that the SAS were surprised by a display of military order from the Maquis, for the British had been warned to expect a rather disorganised, exotic and somewhat bloodthirsty force, their main strength being an impatience to get to grips with the enemy. But Tonkin, in unfamiliar country and with no knowledge of the language, soon accepted Dédé's advice that the only sensible approach was to trust the Maquis in almost everything. With their help, he selected a suitable DZ site not far from the N147 Limoges to Poitiers road, close to a house called Montplaisir and extending over the land of Le Leché, a farm managed by a helper of the Maquis.

The next morning, 10 June, Dédé returned to the SAS camp with a visitor who had arrived at Chêne's headquarters at Sazat with important information. John Tonkin was later to recall:

> A small, very frightened and therefore highly courageous French civilian (I think he was a railway employee) arrived at our newly established base. He told us that there were eleven petrol trains on a well-camouflaged and heavily guarded series of sidings about a kilometre south-west of Châtellerault.

Both Dédé and Tonkin were well aware London had stressed that petrol was a priority target, but as many as eleven trains seemed an exaggeration; where exactly were they and how strong was the guard? If the trains were not too heavily guarded, should the SAS postpone their imminently expected main party drop and attack with what strength they already had, or could an attack wait until the SAS main group arrived? If the enemy guard were too strong, how busy were the RAF and USAAF and would they be able to bomb the trains before they dispersed?

Clearly, it was first essential to confirm the existence of the trains as quickly as possible, pinpoint their location and determine the strength of their defences. Lieutenant Stephens of the SAS, being a smallish, dark-haired Welshman with a dapper moustache, was considered most able to pass for French. He therefore borrowed some civilian clothes and together with the railwayman and one of the Maquis who spoke about as much English as Stephens spoke French, set off on bicycles to reconnoitre. Stephens certainly looked the part of a young French farmer, but he was more than a little caustic about a 120-kilometre round trip to Châtellerault. They left at midday on the 10th after Stephens, Tonkin and Crisp posed for a photograph, taken with a camera which Tonkin had brought with him.[7]

For those left behind, the remainder of the day proved eventful. At around two o'clock in the afternoon a burst of firing was heard from about 5 kilometres away and the Maquis proudly announced that four men of the 'Amilcar' group, based at Le Leché to guard the DZ area, had attacked a German convoy on the Montmorillon to Moulismes road. Five Germans were reported killed, but it was feared that the engagement would draw further attention to the area. When the time came to go out to the DZ, however, no other enemy reaction had developed and the reception committee duly took up their positions on the 'Montplaisir' DZ. It was to be a frustrating night. Not a single aircraft was heard, let alone seen, and the party eventually returned to camp in the early hours of the 11th. They were resting when Lieutenant Stephens and his companions returned, very tired and saddle-sore; they had thumbed lifts for only a small part of their journey and as a result were worn out from their pedalling. But the strenuous exercise had been well worthwhile. The young Welshman confirmed the presence of the petrol wagons and reported that they were too heavily guarded for the SAS or the FFI to attack them. He could not be sure there were eleven trains, but there was certainly a huge reserve of petrol, and the railwayman was adamant that there were eleven sidings all containing petrol wagons. Stephens had made a precise note of their location and at 5.17 p.m. that same afternoon, Tonkin had the map reference radioed in code back to England. An immediate air attack was requested.

From SAS Brigade Headquarters at Moor Park, details of the target were quickly telephoned through to the RAF's No. 2 Group and an outline operation plan was put together in time to alert the relevant squadrons at 7.30 p.m. for a low-level precision raid at dusk. Clearly the petroleum wagons could be moved at short notice, so time was of the essence and the plan involved Mosquito fighter-bombers at least preventing the trains from being taken elsewhere. If necessary, heavy bombers could then be called in to finish the job.

The attack was planned in two stages, 140 Wing at RAF Gravesend in Kent being asked to provide six crews for an immediate take-off, and 138 Wing at RAF Lasham in Hampshire required to detail a further six crews for a second attack shortly afterwards. The units chosen for the job could not be bettered, both wings already being expert at precision attacks on pinpoint targets – 140 Wing in particular had gained fame from its remarkably successful raid on Amiens prison in February 1944, when hundreds of Resistance fighters had been freed after the Wing's bombs had shattered the prison wall. The Amiens raid had involved careful preparation and planning beforehand, but the attack on Châtellerault had no such advantages and the operation remained clear in the memories of many of the aircrew who participated, largely because of the haste in mounting it.

Within 140 Wing the commanding officer of the New Zealanders' 487 Squadron was Wing Commander I.S. 'Black' Smith from Auckland, a former fighter and night-fighter pilot who had only arrived in Britain in August 1939, but had subsequently managed to rise from Pilot Officer to Wing Commander in the astonishingly short space of 11 months. Soon after 2 Group's orders reached Gravesend on 11 June, Smith was on his way to the control tower to discuss a training programme when he walked into Group Captain Peter Wykeham-Barnes, the commanding officer of 140 Wing.[8] Although 487 had no operations scheduled for that night, Wykeham-Barnes asked Smith to provide a section of three aircraft for an immediate attack. Smith immediately telephoned Flight Lieutenant John Ellacombe, one of his most experienced pilots, and gave orders to bomb up three of the squadron's aircraft.

As Smith drove quickly out onto the airfield, the sleek shapes of his squadron's aircraft came into view, dotted about the distant dispersals. There could be little doubt that for the task ahead the Squadron was superbly equipped. The fighter-bomber they flew was the RAF's 'wooden wonder', the potent Mosquito FB VI with a powerful nose armament of four .303-in Browning machine guns mounted above four 20-mm Hispano cannon. Its bomb bay could carry four 250-lb bombs and two wing stations allowed for an additional two 500-lb bombs or auxiliary fuel tanks to augment the Mosquito's already not inconsiderable range of 1,120 miles. The aircraft's maximum speed at altitude was 378 m.p.h. but more importantly, at low level it was usually capable of pulling away from the Germans' most effective fighter, the Focke Wulf Fw 190.

At the dispersals Smith met up with his navigator and the crews of Flight

Lieutenants Ellacombe and Runciman who were to fly as numbers two and three respectively to Smith. The briefing was minimal as speed off the ground had been stressed as imperative and there had been no time to prepare a navigational or attack plan. Consequently, Smith simply stood by the aircraft, told the others what the target was, where it was and how they would fly to it – and they then took off.

Over southern England, the Channel and the first leg over France, the three Mosquitos remained in cloud on instruments before letting down to ground level near Le Mans. Smith successfully located the Tours–Châtellerault railway line and knew that the target would be the first major marshalling yards that they would come across to the south down this line, sited on the edge of the town of Châtellerault. Sure enough, the yards came into sight with the petrol trains still present. Attacking immediately, Smith bombed the northern end, Runciman the centre and Ellacombe the southern end of the yards before pulling up and around onto a reciprocal course to the north for the return journey. As they did so, running in from the south came the Australians of Wing Commander Iredale's flight who had watched and enjoyed the spectacle of 487 Squadron's bombing attacks.

Bob Iredale had thrown together a three-aircraft flight of himself, Squadron Leader McPhee and Flying Officer Rowell; Iredale and McPhee had also taken part in the Amiens prison raid. With no better briefing than that which 487 Squadron had enjoyed, the 464 Squadron Mosquitos took off immediately after the New Zealand unit's contingent, but flew a separate course to the target area at low level and in wide formation, thus using the opportunity to reconnoitre as large an area as possible.

The Australians had no difficulty in identifying the target as they made their run from the south, thanks to 487 Squadron's bombing attacks already being delivered. All three aircraft reported bombing trains, wagons, troops and motor transport in and around the yards, as well as strafing the area with cannon before turning north to follow Smith's formation home. Between the target and Châteaudun the Australians remained at low level and attacked several troop trains, which were stationary in sidings. A moving railway engine was destroyed 2 miles east of Tours on the east-west railway line, and Flying Officer Rowell attacked and destroyed a transport train which was heading south. The only flak experienced came from this train and from a single 20-mm gun on the deserted airfield at Conches. All aircraft of 487 and 464 Squadrons returned safely to England.

The crews of 138 Wing's 107 Squadron at RAF Lasham had also been given a 'stand-down' from night operations on 11 June. Most of the aircrew had thus left the aerodrome to spend the evening in the nearby town of Alton. Soon after arrival, however, crews were called out of the cinema and various hostelries by the RAF Police who ushered them aboard a crew bus to be returned to Lasham.

Briefings started immediately the crews returned, with pilots and navigators being briefed separately to save time. The pilots were briefed by their commanding officer and formation leader, Wing Commander Mike Pollard, who quickly outlined the target and attack plans. At the same time, the navigators received route and weather details before joining their pilots and hurrying out to the six waiting Mosquitos, where the armourers were still fitting wing bombs.

107 Squadron lifted off from RAF Lasham at 9.10 p.m. as 464 and 487 Squadrons were already heading for home. Keeping at low level and in loose formation, the Mosquitos thundered over the English south coast at Littlehampton and crossed into France at St Valéry, west of Dieppe. Over France visibility worsened as drizzle began to fall and in an effort to maintain formation the Mosquitos switched on their navigation lights in the gathering gloom as they climbed to 6,000 feet above what became 10/10ths cloud. After some 120 kilometres the cloud began to break up and the Mosquitos dropped back down to ground level. The navigators easily picked up the River Loire, a beautiful sight in the late evening light and serving as confirmation that the Mosquitos were on track. By the time they approached Châtellerault it was dark, but they had no difficulty in identifying the target from as far away as 30 kilometres, thanks to the fires left by the two squadrons of 140 Wing. An area estimated to be 300 yards by 170 yards was in flames and smoke was already rising to 4,000 feet.

Climbing to 3,000 feet, Wing Commander Pollard called in his aircraft in turn to attack singly, allocating each Mosquito two shallow dive passes across the line of wagons, working down from those already alight. All attacks were successfully completed and, as a final gesture, Pollard personally delivered a cannon attack along the entire length of the marshalling yards. Leaving the immense fuel fires well and truly stoked, 107 Squadron's aircraft headed for home individually, in the certain knowledge of a job well done, and all landed safely back at Lasham.

In Châtellerault the town's civilian population had not escaped involvement in the dramatic attack. 'Le Glaneur', the periodical diary of Châtellerault, was unable to openly proclaim the attack's success due to the censorship of the German authorities, but later carried confirmation of the raid's effect on the town:

> Last night it was the turn of Châtellerault. Suddenly, at ten o'clock in the evening, bombs fell from the sky, hitting the station and a petrol train standing there . . . an enormous mushroom cloud of black smoke formed and hung over the area and from time to time red bonfires flared up, lighting up the entire town. An hour passed and then, again, aircraft roared overhead, aiming earthwards with bombs, tracer and incendiary bullets. This time it lasted twenty minutes. Eleven dead and twenty wounded, the latter including the Mayor, Colonel Aymard, who was hit by a bomb splinter.

A combination of local intelligence and courage from the Maquis, Dédé's organizational skills and vision, and the SAS's ability had scored an early and eye-catching success in support of the general insurrection across France.

On the same night, some 55 kilometres to the south of Châtellerault, Tonkin and his advance party, helped by the 'Amilcar' Maquis, had made their way for a second time to the 'Montplaisir' DZ to receive the SAS main party. This had originally been expected to drop into the Châteauroux area on the night of 9/10 June, but had been postponed due to Tonkin's decision to move south-west, closer to Poitiers. On the following night a Stirling of 620 Squadron took off from RAF Fairford to drop the SAS main party of twenty men and containers, but on reaching the 'Bulbasket' DZ had reported being unable to spot any signal lights in the area. The big bomber had therefore swung round for home – for the SAS aboard it was not only a disappointing anti-climax, but also the first indication of the problems that would be faced by the loss of their Eureka beacon.

A second attempt was, however, immediately made on the following night of 11/12 June, only hours after the RAF had finished their devastating attack on Châtellerault. Yet as the scheduled drop time of 1.00 a.m. approached, and the reception party at 'Montplaisir' took up position by their unlit bonfires, the growl and squeal of armoured vehicles was heard and a steady stream of shrouded headlights appeared across the fields. It took only a few moments to realize that the advance elements of the 2nd SS Das Reich Panzer Division were advancing up the nearby N147 road.

# Chapter Eleven

# Das Reich

The Maquis had reported only that afternoon that Das Reich was moving north from Limoges, heading towards the Normandy battlefront, but it had been hoped that the DZ would be cleared well before the Germans reached the area. They certainly had no desire to attack this powerful formation, which had already left a trail of death and destruction in its wake. Constantly harassed by FFI forces since it had started north, the Division's patience had already been exhausted and its troops had inflicted terrible retribution on local communities. Two days earlier the Division had hanged ninety-nine Frenchmen in the town of Tulle and now, making all haste to Normandy, Das Reich was intending to refuel from the very petrol trains at Châtellerault which had just been reduced to a distant glow on the horizon.

Conferring urgently, the SAS and their Maquis helpers decided that if the signal fires were lit in a depression, they just might not be seen from the road. The DZ would also have to be cleared very quickly, with the help of bullock carts. Everyone took up their positions, one eye on the sky and the other on the approaching enemy column, and the signal fires were lit just before the deadline.

Almost dead on schedule, the SAS main party came roaring in towards the DZ in two Stirlings of 190 Squadron from RAF Fairford. In similar fashion to the late addition of Tonkin and Crisp to the 'Hugh' Jedburgh team's drop, a five-man Phantom special forces signals team had been added to the SAS party at the eleventh hour, necessitating two aircraft, rather than just the one. The Stirlings both made one low pass over the waiting reception committee and then disappeared into the distance. After a few anxious moments, aircraft engines were heard again, but it was only one aircraft that now swung back over the DZ to make a second pass and drop twelve men and a number of containers from just 400 feet.

As their parachutes jerked open, the SAS troopers were stunned by the spectacle that unfolded below them. Instead of the dark and deserted countryside they had been briefed to expect, to one side of the drop zone a long stream of enemy vehicles in convoy could clearly be seen, their headlights stretching away into the distance. On the horizon to the north a huge fireball marked the Mosquitos' raid on Châtellerault. Worse still, the sky all around them was studded with coloured lights that had sprung out from the supply containers. From the ground the spectacle was equally alarming to John Tonkin:

Suddenly the sky was full of multi-coloured lights – green, blue, white and red – three to a container! There must have been at least thirty-six and probably forty-five. I had never heard of this idea before, and didn't know what they were. What was for sure was that they presented a grave danger to us for, almost immediately, all the German convoy lights went out, they stopped, and we could no longer hear their engines.

We moved <u>very</u> fast. I did not need to give any orders! Men were smashing the bulbs everywhere and we were frantically collecting Sergeant Jessiman and his 11 men who had dropped at the same time. The aircraft had disappeared and, most ominously, there was neither light nor sound from the Germans.

We collected everything and got to blazes out of it. When we were at a reasonably safe distance, an abusive Jessiman told me it was the latest idea. The lights were each on the end of three spring-loaded arms (like an umbrella), which were held in a sleeve on each container. The intent was that, as the container parachute opened, the 'umbrella' was jerked out of the sleeve and hung by its electrical cord below the container, but unlit. On the container hitting the ground, some sort of switch was operated which lit the lights, thus enabling one to find the containers easily! Jessiman told me that base wanted me to report on their usefulness. I did so next morning . . . !'

Only later was it realized that the malfunctioning lights may well have been a blessing in disguise. Almost certainly the Germans must have believed themselves under air attack. The combination of low-flying aircraft and coloured lights in the sky would have seemed very similar to the target-marking tactics carried out by Allied aircraft prior to bombing. The prudent reaction for the Germans would therefore have been to black out the convoy and lie low. Apparently this is exactly what happened and the enemy would seem to have taken to the road-side ditches, wondering what fearful new weapon was being launched against them.

Sergeant Jessiman, who led the new arrivals, brought the unwelcome news that the main party had only consisted of a much-depleted strength of twenty SAS and the five-man Phantom team. This was due to SAS Brigade Headquarters having received a priority request from SHAEF for attacks on the 'Lot' railways west and north of Poitiers, too distant for 'Bulbasket' to reach. Two officers and twelve men, in four groups, had therefore been dropped 'blind' the previous night on or near the vital lines, with orders to march cross-country to join Tonkin after they had carried out their sabotage.

So instead of an expected strength of fifty, the SAS now had only twenty-three men, missing not only the fourteen troopers of the 'Lot' parties dropped the night before, but also the five Phantom and eight SAS men who had been in the second Stirling over 'Montplaisir'. The pilot of this aircraft had spotted the lights of the enemy convoy and quickly consulted Captain Roger Sadoine, the Phantom commanding officer. The latter felt that the ground activity presented too much risk, but the Stirling pilot was under orders to drop his paratroopers come what may, rather than return to England with them. The big aircraft therefore flew on until, some 25 kilometres to the south-east, a suitable area of open high ground was spotted and the troops and containers were dropped without further incident.

Back at 'Montplaisir' the SAS and their Maquis helpers were quickly marching north-east, distancing themselves as rapidly as possible from the Das Reich convoy which was showing signs of emerging from cover. They soon reached La Jarrouie, a farm just south of the town of Montmorillon. The 'Amilcar' group normally operated in and around this farm and the SAS were shown to a wooded area close by where they pitched camp. As the SAS troopers bedded down in their sleeping bags their Maquis escort group posted sentries, alert for any patrols from Das Reich and watching the vivid glow in the sky to the north where OB-West's trains carrying the petrol that was vital for the swift refuelling of Das Reich on its way to Normandy had been completely destroyed by the RAF.

For the local German forces there was little sleep that night. In addition to the attack on Châtellerault and the appearance of the strange lights dropped from the air close to Das Reich, two acts of railway sabotage had been reported. The first was the responsibility of the energetic SAS officer, Lieutenant Stephens, who after only a few hours' sleep had gone out to blow up a road/rail bridge on the branch line south-east of Montmorillon, making sure the charge went off no earlier than 2.00 a.m. on the morning of the 12th. This would therefore only be after the drop of the SAS main party just 15 kilometres away at 'Montplaisir'. The second, timed to coincide with Stephens's attack, was by Dédé and Chêne's FFI maquisards cutting the 'Lot 2' line at the same time, south of Poitiers.

The SAS troopers at La Jarrouie were in high spirits and keen to start operations. The warm June weather and the deceptively peaceful countryside combined to give the promise of pleasant days ahead, mixed with high adventure. For many it was their first experience of a foreign land and the dangers of war seemed far distant. In reality, however, the nearest enemy troops were only 12 kilometres away at Sillars Camp, a large ammunition dump, and all the activity south of Montmorillon was unlikely to go unchallenged. On 12 June, Tonkin signalled Brigade HQ that the area was 'lousy with enemy' and he asked for jeeps to be sent as mobility was now a serious problem for his party of twenty-three. The following day he reported that 200–400 Germans were looking for them and had clashed with local Maquis forces, inflicting several losses. Dédé received reports of the Germans patrolling within 9 kilometres of the SAS base and he therefore arranged with Chêne for the 'Amilcar' group to provide a dozen volunteer maquisards who would be permanently attached to the SAS party to procure food, maintain contact with the local population and act as guides for operations at night. The Frenchmen were led by Jean Dieudonné ('Maurice'), one of Robert Artaud's trusted lieutenants. Dédé also organized three cars and a small lorry, requisitioned to help Dieudonné transport the SAS group that night to a new camp on the western side of the N147 road near the village of Nérignac, well away from the enemy's patrols to the south and west of Montmorillon.

Meanwhile, more horrifying news of the passage of Das Reich through the area had reached Chêne's headquarters. On 10 June, in one of the most infamous crimes of the Second World War, one of the Division's units had killed 642 civilians and razed the village of Oradour-sur-Glane in the Haute-Vienne, only some 70 kilometres south-east of the 'Montplaisir' DZ. Many of the maquisards wanted to launch immediate revenge attacks on Das Reich, but Dédé was to the forefront of those who realized that the German Division was simply too powerful to be challenged. Chêne agreed with him that it was better to let the Division now pass through the area and so avoid any further acts of reprisal. Consequently, the Haute-Vienne FTP immediately shelved plans for a large-scale attack on Limoges, but it did not deter Lieutenant Crisp of the SAS laying mines on the night of 12/13 June in the path of Das Reich along the Limoges to Poitiers road in the Fôret du Défant.

While the British developed their own operations in the area, Chêne's maquisards were far from idle and by 13 June Dédé was able to report back to England that the Paris–Toulouse and Paris–Bordeaux railway lines had been put out of action, at the same time confirming 'all Vienne at your orders.' For the next few days, however, Dédé continued to help the SAS establish their presence and arrange for supply drops from England, both for the British troopers and for the local Maquis groups. A new DZ was found at the farm Primo la Coupe, near la Font d'Usson, but a supply drop on the night of the 16/17 failed when a Stirling of 196 Squadron from RAF Keevil could not find the DZ and returned to England with seventeen containers still on board. More successful was a Stirling of 299 Squadron, also from Keevil, which found the DZ arranged by Captain Sadoine to the south-east near Azat-le-Ris. Despite very bad weather conditions, containers were dropped and the occasion, later colourfully recorded by Sadoine, provides a vivid description of the enthusiasm of the Maquis for such operations:

There was nothing clandestine about my first what the French call *un para-chutage*. Once the containers were released from the aircraft there was considerable drama. Albert (the local *Maquis* chief) began the proceedings by shouting 'Attention! Everyone! The *bidons* descend'. Everyone present repeated this advice to Bobo or Alphonse or Pierre, or whoever was nearest, to 'have a care that the sacred *bidons* do not crush thee!'

Once the containers had landed, the parachute stakes were on. The winner was whoever could roll and hide away the most parachutes before being spotted by someone else. The bullock carts then came up with much encouragement from the drivers such as: 'But come, my old one, to the *bidons* advance.' Then began the preliminary discussions as to how the first container would be hoisted on to the cart and who should have the honour of commencing. I found that I had to go through the motions of beginning to hoist one end myself before, with loud cries of 'But no, my Captain! Permit!' or for example 'My Captain, what an affair!' my helpers would then get on with the job. Once, however, the drill for clearing the DZ was understood, the helpers were of the greatest value, and we succeeded one night in clearing the DZ in seventy minutes. This was very good as it included four containers that had fallen in trees.

On 17 June two of the four separately dropped SAS railway sabotage parties reached the main group with encouraging reports of their exploits since their drop on the night of 10/11 June. Lieutenant Morris and his three men had been dropped some 5 kilometres out from the Poitiers–Tours railway, which was their target. One of the party was missing and presumed to have suffered a parachute malfunction, but despite this setback Morris and the two others had continued, found their target and had blown both railway tracks over a culvert a few kilometres to the south of Châtellerault.

Like Morris, Sergeant Holmes and his two men had the Poitiers–Tours line as their target and had been dropped accurately some 30 kilometres to the north of Châtellerault. They removed 15–20 feet of rail under a bridge carrying the D760 road, near to Noyant de Touraine and then set off on their 90-kilometre trek to reach the main party camp. Heartened by their reports, Dédé had Pierre Hirsch signal to London on the 17th, confirming that the railway lines Paris–Limoges, Paris–Bordeaux and Paris–Toulouse were 'constantly being destroyed and made useless as far as German traffic is concerned'.

The arrival of the additional SAS troopers underlined the lack of mobility still suffered by the British force, though plans were already in hand to remedy the situation. That night at 'Primo la Coupe', a suitable DZ site that had been identified between the villages of Usson-du-Poitou and Queaux, an extensive air operation lasting three quarters of an hour saw four Halifax aircraft of the RAF drop 4 jeeps, 4 more SAS soldiers and 22 containers, while a single Stirling dropped an additional 17 containers of arms. In preparation, four large holes had been dug in a wood close by in order to bury the cradles which held the jeeps, together with the huge 90-ft parachutes which had carried them, and these were quickly covered over after filling. One jeep was found to have suffered a twisted chassis, but all were fit for action, engines roared into life and the convoy of four jeeps, along with the local vehicles already in use, turned left out of the DZ field onto a narrow farm road.

As they did so a storm of gunfire erupted. The lead jeep swerved into a ditch and overturned, but the SAS and maquisards recovered quickly and returned a withering fire at their unseen assailants, believed to be a German patrol. They feverishly struggled to pull the crashed vehicle out with another jeep and had it righted again in a matter of moments. By a miracle no one was hit and the only injury was to one of the SAS troopers whose fingers had been crushed when the jeep rolled over. But as the joint SAS and Maquis force again sped off, the night's drama was not yet over. Crossing the River Vienne, they arrived at the D11 road, south of Persac, only to find another large German convoy crawling along it. The road had to be crossed for the maquisards and SAS to reach their camps, so they quietly stood off several yards from the road for a few minutes and when a short space showed they hurtled straight across, presumably much to the surprise of the Germans, who were later learned to be yet more units of the Das Reich 2nd SS Panzer Division, heading northwards to Poitiers. It may well have been a patrol of the Division that had been sent to investigate the DZ, for the convoy would almost certainly have detected the protracted aerial activity.

With additional fuel tanks, the SAS's American-built Willys jeeps had a range of some 700 miles and each was fitted with a rapid-firing Vickers 'K' .303-in. machine gun. Proven in combat during the Regiment's operations in North Africa and Italy, the rugged and speedy jeeps enabled the SAS to range farther afield in their offensive operations, but the four of them could still only hold sixteen men at any one time. Consequently, when increased German activity in the area suggested a precautionary move of camp from Nérignac, Dédé and the Maquis still had to provide requisitioned vehicles to move the entire SAS force.

The new SAS camp was some 5 kilometres further south, but there was still no appearance here of Captain Sadoine's Phantom radio team and the remaining eight SAS who had been dropped blind near Azat-le-Ris. Having already made one unsuccessful foray to try to locate them, Captain Tonkin suspected that he had been deliberately misdirected by the local Maquis group in Sadoine's reported camp area, an understandable move if Sadoine had arranged supply drops of arms for the group.

From the new SAS camp Tonkin therefore immediately took one of the jeeps out and this time succeeded in reaching the Phantom operating base near Azat-le-Ris where at last he met Sadoine. The latter proved to be a 23-year-old Belgian who had escaped to England at the time of the Dunkirk evacuation, 'Sadoine' being a nom de guerre and, indeed, the name of another officer (Captain John Sadoine) in the Phantom organization. A radio fanatic, he had subsequently volunteered for Phantom where he felt his specialist knowledge would be of greater use than in his original unit. Despite a lack of operational experience, his radio skills and fluency in both French and English should have stood 'Bulbasket' in good stead, yet Tonkin found that Sadoine had settled down into what was a seemingly peaceful existence. The SAS troopers who had dropped with Sadoine had soon become impatient as the Phantom officer appeared disinclined to make contact with, and support, the SAS main party. Two experienced NCOs, Sergeant Eccles and Corporal Bateman, had therefore already taken matters into their own hands by going out on the night of 13/14 June to the branch line south of Sadoine's base. Eccles had laid charges on the front wheels of a locomotive in the station at Le Dorat, while Bateman destroyed the points just to the south. Not content with this excellent start, the two NCOs attacked the points again two nights later after repairs had been made. While the SAS troops were therefore happy to see Tonkin, and keen to join his main party, Sadoine still displayed a strange reluctance to follow the SAS commander back, claiming simply that he was not yet ready to do so, despite having procured two cars locally to provide mobility.

Though Sadoine's hesitancy was irritating to Tonkin, the latter was nevertheless not over-concerned. Like Tonkin, Sadoine held the rank of Captain and the SAS officer therefore put the signaller's reluctance down to an unwillingness to come under the orders of someone not only from another unit, but also of no more than equal rank. Moreover, for radio support Tonkin could still rely on his own SAS radio operator, Corporal Chick, supported if the need arose by Troopers Adamson and Hill who were trained signallers as well. Messages could also be sent by Pierre Hirsh on Dédé's SOE radio. Sadoine and his radio operators were therefore of no great value in the field so Tonkin, for the time being, shrugged off Sadoine's attitude and returned to the SAS main camp with Sergeant Eccles and four others, the absolute maximum he could carry in the jeep. For the moment Bateman and two other SAS troopers remained with the Phantom team, but on 22 June Sadoine was sent a radio message from England, clearly instructing him to join Tonkin. When he had still not appeared the next day, Tonkin sent Lieutenant Morris over to the signallers' camp. On arrival, Morris found Sadoine effectively 'pulling rank' on him and maintaining that he was still not ready to move. Exasperated, Morris returned with Bateman and his two troopers to report the situation, but the pressing demands of operations allowed little time to worry over the situation.

On the night of 20/21 June, two SAS parties attacked the railway lines both north and south of Poitiers, while the same night brought the delivery of a further twenty-four containers of arms and supplies, courtesy of the RAF, to a reception organized by Captain Tonkin. SOE were expecting a similar, routine, supply drop the same night and Jacques Hirsch was therefore sent by Dédé to a DZ near Pouillac, 3 kilometres south-west of Adriers. The site was relatively small and, surrounded as it was by barbed-wire fencing, it had been designated a 'non-personnel' ground.

It was therefore a surprise when Hirsch and his helpers found themselves welcoming the members of yet another Jedburgh team, this being 'Ian', delivered by a USAAF special duties B-24 Liberator. Its members were Major Gildee ('Oklahoma') of the American OSS as Team Leader, Captain Desfarges (real name Delorme, 'Maine') of the French BCRA, and as radio operator, Sergeant Bourgoin ('Mayo'), also of the OSS. Major Gildee and Captain Delorme landed easily, but Sergeant Bougoin's parachute had not opened as quickly as it should and though he managed a good landing, the two radio sets which accompanied him were both damaged.

The next morning Jacques Hirsch took the three new arrivals by car to Le Petit Bois, a large house on the outskirts of the village of Luchapt. It was to here that Dédé had moved with Chêne's headquarters and he now questioned the newcomers as to their mission. He heard that Gildee's briefing in England had specifically included the instruction 'to impress upon all concerned that a general uprising must not take place in the Département of Vienne, and to mount continuous attacks against rail lines Bordeaux–Poitiers–Tours and Bordeaux–Niort–Saumur'. Other than that, Gildee's main purpose was to assist Dédé with the arming and training of the Maquis, and with railway sabotage. Dédé was not impressed. He knew there was little that this new team could achieve in his own immediate area as everything was already in hand by himself and the Hirsch brothers, supporting Chêne's existing and efficient co-ordination of all the local Maquis groups. Instead, Dédé, with Chêne's approval, felt that 'Ian' could be of much more use in the south-west of the Vienne and the north of the Charente region where there was still an urgent need to arm and train the Maquis. Gildee was not overly pleased with this proposal, but had little choice other than to accept the judgement of Dédé, the experienced man in the field. But first, the 'Ian' team had to wait five days with Dédé, awaiting the delivery of two replacement radio sets. In the event, just one more was dropped and this, too, was smashed as it landed. Fortunately, Sergeant Bourgoin managed to repair one of the two original sets and team 'Ian' departed on their revised mission for the Bir-Hackeim Maquis, based near Chasseneuil-sur-Bonnieure, 35 kilometres north-east of Angoulême in the Charente.

Before 'Ian' left, Dédé and Gildee had another disagreement when Dédé was critical about the proposed use of American fake money that the Jedburgh team had brought with them, a move which Dédé recognized could only alienate the French ultimately. Whether Gildee heeded Dédé's advice is not specifically recorded, but on arrival in the Charente he made arrangements for a loan of 12 million francs of real money to support the local FFI's efforts. Thereafter, 'Ian' played a vital role in helping organize four battalions of Maquis in the area, but on 2 August the team ran into a column of 400 enemy troops in the village of Pleuville. As their car came under fire and crashed, Gildee and Delorme managed to escape, but Sergeant Burgoin was shot down and killed.[1]

After his initial negotiations with the 'Ian' team on the morning of 21 June, Dédé's next task had been to visit the SAS and obtain their commitment to joint operations with the Maquis. These were planned to harass units of the German 277th Infantry Division which was reported to be moving through the area, though no contact had actually made with the enemy during the day. Instead, only 5 kilometres away, enemy search parties were spotted heading in the direction of the SAS camp. As soon as night fell the British troopers made a rapid move to the north and a new base was set up near Persac, by the River Vienne. From there the SAS continued sabotage attacks on the local railway lines, roaming the countryside more or less at will in their jeeps and sometimes staying away from camp for several days if the target were distant. One such operation involved Sergeant Jessiman and a small SAS team staying out by the 'Lot 1' line in the adjoining Indre region for a number of days, undoubtedly advised by Dédé who knew the area well. On the night of 22/23 June, Jessiman cut the line in two places south-west of Eguzon, not far from where SOE's Lieutenant Schwatschko had come to his tragic death only two weeks before.

By 24 June, Chêne's headquarters staff had moved again, to the Château La Combe, between Adriers and Nérignac. Here, an admiring description of Dédé and the Hirsch brothers was penned by Max Survylle, the FFI's Press Officer:

'[Samuel] had the face of a child, slightly marked by acne as if an adolescent. He was very sporty and seemed to consider the war a sport, in contest against the *Boche* whom he detested. He would leap into his car, driven by his number two, as if he were off hunting. And whenever they had to use a road frequented by the enemy he would perch on the car's back seat, his rifle at the ready, with a gleaming eye glancing into the distance, almost wishing the enemy to appear. He frequently joined the patrols around Bernard's [Chêne's] HQ, loving the opportunity to prepare his rifle. He knew all the weapons used extremely well.

He introduced a programme of physical training, followed by weapons tuition, for the young and inexperienced *Maquisards*. At seven in the morning they would parade on the lawns of the Château and start with

British Army exercises, followed by a demonstration of boxing or the martial arts. A run of two or three hundred metres would finish off the session before practice on stripping and reassembling weapons – over and over again. And when they returned to HQ, Samuel was always still the freshest.

Samuel's adjutant [Jacques Hirsch] went under the nom de guerre of François and was a different type altogether. No-one knew much about him other than that he was a Parisien who lived in London [sic] and spoke halting English. He was a big man, with a thick-set face and intelligent eyes. He was normally almost silent, distant and quite the opposite of his brother, Pierrot [Pierre Hirsch], with whom it was always a pleasure to chat. But they were both clever, with great intelligence.

Pierrot was the radio operator of the team, a modest enough role but one that was both difficult and dangerous. And I would say he had the heaviest workload of anyone at the *Etat Major*. Night and day he had to send and receive messages, and encode and decode, and still somehow find time to eat.

On 28 June, Chêne's headquarters were the setting for a dramatic scene. Only eight days earlier Chêne had written to all his Maquis leaders, setting out clearly and unequivocally his expectation that his groups would follow, to the letter, a directive already issued by General Koenig in London. The directive addressed the conduct of the FFI while under arms and stipulated that there were to be no personal acts of vengeance. In his covering order, Chêne went on to spell out in some detail how he expected the Maquis to set up military tribunals to deal with traitors and collaborators. He stipulated that a defence must be arranged in all cases, but also that if the death penalty were imposed, then the execution must be carried out quickly. On 28 June exactly such a tribunal, chaired by Chêne, heard the case of Van Hellepute, a Belgian accused of spying for the Germans and brought in by the 'Gilles' Maquis. Albert Dupont, the FFI's interpreter who had been attached to the SAS, but who had now returned to Chêne's headquarters, acted as Van Hellepute's defence, but a guilty verdict was found and the death sentence was pronounced. Two of the SAS men, Corporal Sam Smith and Trooper Brown, witnessed the outcome, as recalled by Smith:

At this base, 'Topper' Brown and I had rather good relations with the senior *Maquisard*s. At one drinking session, an invitation to witness the execution of the Belgian spy was accepted. At 8 a.m. the following morning, we gathered at the execution site and the grave was dug. The Belgian (half-carried and half-dragged) was brought into the opening. After his cry for mercy was rejected, he pulled himself together, stood to attention and when asked if he wanted to say anything, pleaded with the firing squad (I was asked to join this but declined) not to shoot him in the throat.

Dédé, too, was developing a good rapport with the Maquis groups in his new area. Towards the end of June he sent Jacques Hirsch to establish contact with the heads of the Resistance in the Haute-Vienne while he himself concentrated on the rapidly expanding Group D of Maquis, which covered almost all the lower half of the Vienne-Sud. This was commanded by Lieutenant Colonel Blondel ('Michel'), a former regular officer of the French Army, supported by Commandant Bourdet ('Marcel'). Blondel's original Maquis groups were centred on Asnières-sur-Blour and Luchapt, yet as volunteers increased he split his command into no less than fourteen distinct groups, recognizing the danger of grouping all his forces into only a few, easily located, places. But as numbers grew, there were too few weapons and not enough co-ordination, the latter exacerbated by the fact that both Blondel and Bourdet were often engaged elsewhere. But so close was the understanding and bond between Chêne and Dédé that Dédé was permitted unlimited freedom of action to help with the training and command of the Maquis. Chêne was perfectly aware that his command was still largely dependent upon the SOE and the British for almost all its arms and other military supplies, a situation not altogether to the liking of General de Gaulle's Delegué Régionale Militaire (DRM) for the Vienne, Georges Héritier. But the Vienne-Sud arrangement worked. Neither Chêne nor Dédé were overly concerned with political sensitivities, though they were both astute enough to recognize and allow for them. So while the BCRA almost certainly did not formally authorize Chêne to continue the liaison, Dédé nevertheless continued to spend much of his time either with Chêne's headquarters or touring, advising, supplying and supporting the Vienne-Sud Maquis groups. He soon found that air supply operations, in particular, were one of the most effective means by which special forces advisors could demonstrate their bona fides to local Resistance forces.[2] And when the arms and explosives arrived, Dédé then showed himself to be expert in their use, his instruction to the maquisards covering the Sten gun, Lee Enfield rifle, grenades, sticky bombs and in most cases the Bren gun and bazooka, which were issued one per group. The groups of the Vienne-Sud with which Dédé had most contact were: 'Gilles' (together with its sub-groups 'Baptiste', 'Gilbert' and 'Cram'); 'Le Chouan'; 'Lagardère'; 'Jacky'; 'Michel'; 'Jalladeau'; 'Gaucher-Bonnet'; 'Vauquois'; 'Fernand'; 'Amilcar'; 'Fracasse'; 'Anatole'; 'Les Etudiants'; and the L'Isle-Jourdain Gendarmerie. But ironically, while training of the largely amateur Maquis was still progressing, Dédé found himself troubled by problems arising from the presence of the highly trained soldiers of the SAS.

By late June the SAS main party had gathered in all its men and Dédé had established a good relationship, particularly with Captain John Tonkin and his fellow officers, a mix of veterans and the inexperienced. Tonkin, though young, had seen action with the SAS in North Africa and Italy and his behind-the-lines operations in Italy were recognized by his being entitled to wear the coveted SAS parachute wings above his left breast, rather than on his right sleeve.

Lieutenant Tomos Stephens was a high-spirited regular soldier who had served with the South Wales Borderers before joining the SAS. He came to France bursting to start operations against the Germans, whom he hated, and when Dédé noticed the small covered pipe that the young Welshman frequently smoked, Stephens confided that it was his good luck talisman, having kept his father safe through the First World War.

Lieutenant Peter Weaver, at thirty-two years of age, possessed rather more experience of military life than his fellow officers. He had first sampled army life as a private soldier in the Royal Tank Regiment, but had then bought himself out in 1934. A talented sportsman, he captained England at hockey and played cricket for Hampshire, but was never able to settle in a job for long. In 1937 he had re-enlisted as a part-time soldier in the Territorial Army's Royal Engineers and when war came he was immediately called up in 1939 and commissioned as an officer in the Dorset Regiment. Subsequently posted to one of the secret Auxiliary Units, he commanded a group of these specially trained forces whose task it would have been to harass the Germans in the event of an invasion of Britain. After the threat of invasion had passed, in late 1943 Weaver and many of his men took up the offer to volunteer for the expanding SAS. Typically stubborn, he refused to adopt the new red beret of the British airborne forces and, once in France, continued to wear the unique beige-coloured SAS beret. It was to stay there throughout 'Operation Bulbasket' and in photographs taken during the operation clearly distinguishes Weaver.

Lieutenant Hugh Morris, a South African, was somewhat more taciturn, but had seen useful active service in the North African campaign where he had served in the South African Army. He had transferred to the SAS there in its early days, but had not taken part in the Sicily or Italy campaigns. 'Operation Bulbasket' was therefore his first experience of irregular warfare, but he proved to be the SAS group's best administrator and organizer for managing the radio work.

Lieutenant Richard Crisp was perhaps the most unusual in that he certainly did not fit the typical mould of a special forces SAS officer. Still only twenty years of age, the stage had been his first love and he had seriously contemplated registering as a Conscientious Objector before deciding that the evil of Hitler and the Nazis was greater than the evil of war itself. He therefore registered for his call-up and was commissioned into a tank unit of the Royal Armoured Corps. In February 1944, however, his parents had been surprised to receive a letter from their youngest son with the news that he had volunteered for the Special Air Service. Despite his quiet and gentle nature, however, once in France he established his reputation as the group's road-mining expert, developing a technique of spreading dirt across the road at intervals and compelling the enemy to stop and sweep constantly after the first explosion. If the location were suitable, a long burst of Vickers 'K' machine-gun fire from a jeep added to the enemy convoy's discomfort before Crisp and his men withdrew.

Yet while the officers and men of the SAS appeared a capable force, Dédé's attention was claimed by two concerns, namely the security of their base camp, and the actions of Captain Sadoine, leader of the Phantom signals party supposedly attached to the SAS.

Tonkin had again moved the main SAS camp on 25 June as a precaution against location by the enemy and had established a camp in the Forêt de Verrières, to the west of the N147 Poitiers to Limoges road. While still within

124

easy reach of their DZ at la Font d'Usson, the Verrières site was some 15 kilometres further north-west of the SAS's previous camp at Persac, and further away from Chêne's headquarters. Verrières was also no more than 25 kilometres from the German forces in Poitiers and enemy jamming of Tonkin's radio was immediately encountered, showing that their transmissions were being monitored. On 28 June the camp's numbers had been swollen by the arrival of more SAS troopers from the separately dropped railway line sabotage parties. Trooper Brown, the missing man from Lieutenant Morris's party, had in fact merely landed some distance away from his comrades and had set off on his own to reach the main party. Picked up by a local Maquis group, he was passed on to Colonel Chêne's headquarters where Dédé arranged for him to reach Tonkin at Verrières.

With Brown had also come the parties of Corporal Kinnivane and Lieutenant Weaver. Both groups had been dropped blind in the early hours of 11 June and should have landed on adjoining DZs in order to attack the 'Lot 4' railway line which ran from Niort to Saumur. From the very start things had gone badly wrong for Kinnivane and his two men. Disastrously, all three had landed in the middle of the square at Airvault, a small town close to the 'Lot 4' line. Unfortunately the town held a German garrison and the three SAS men came under heavy fire the moment they landed. Compelled to abandon all their explosives and equipment in order to escape, Kinnivane and one other soldier were eventually able to meet up again in the countryside thanks to assistance from the local Maquis. Of Trooper Biffin there was no sign and it was later learned that he had been taken prisoner.[3]

Weaver and his three men had landed to the west of Parthenay, some 25 kilometres west of where they were supposed to attack 'Lot 4' and almost 90 kilometres from Tonkin and the main party. Realizing they were still far from their target, they remained in hiding throughout the next day then marched all night towards the railway. They succeeded in blowing the line and derailing a train on the night of 13/14 June before setting off south-eastwards to find Tonkin. They marched for ten nights, making cautious contact with isolated farms for food. Once, moving through a wood, the SAS were startled to hear American voices and came across an officer and a sergeant in American uniforms. These were Lieutenant Anstett and Sergeant Watters, two of the three-man Jedburgh Team 'Hamish' which had dropped on the night of 12/13 June. Sitting alone in a clearing they were surrounded by an enormous stock of weapons and equipment, radio gear, food and money. The Americans generously offered the British some of their money, but Weaver declined, accepted some food instead and the SAS continued on their way.

When they eventually reached their pre-arranged rendezvous near Montmorillon on 24 June, only to find no sign of Tonkin and the main party, a friendly farmer undertook to help them and alerted the local 'Gilles' Maquis group. In no time at all a car bursting with heavily armed maquisards arrived and the SAS were whisked off to a nearby village where they were greeted joyously as conquering heroes. Wine flowed freely, pretty girls queued to kiss them and food appeared from every house. Weaver was worried at the lack of caution shown, but was reassured when told that all the Germans were in Poitiers. From the village the SAS were then taken to the Maquis camp where they found the French had weapons, but little idea what to do with them. For three days Weaver and his men trained the maquisards until they realized that their hosts were keeping their British visitors to themselves. Weaver therefore had to insist upon being taken to Tonkin's camp and the maquisards reluctantly took his party on to Verrières.

The next night, 29 June, two of the SAS NCOs, Sergeant Eccles and Corporal Bateman, failed to return from a sabotage attack on the railway yards at St Benoît, just outside Poitiers. No shots had been heard by the trooper waiting with their jeep, so capture seemed likely and Tonkin ordered a move of camp as a precaution. But only the next day, the two SAS men returned to the same camp site in the woods at Verrières. Although Captain Tonkin was well aware of the dangers of remaining too long in one place, where informers or German radio direction-finding might pinpoint the camp, there was also a need to remain within easy reach of suitable DZs for supply drops and to find camp sites with an adequate water supply. The summer of 1944 proved to be one of the driest for many years, with drought conditions throughout the region. For a camp holding anything up to seventy men of the SAS and Maquis, a constant supply of fresh water was therefore a major concern. The new site to where the precautionary move had been made proved to have inadequate fresh water, whereas Verrières benefited from a good clear stream that ran through the woods.

Dédé was also concerned that so many of the soldiers remained immobile. Although the SAS had requested five more jeeps to be dropped, these had not been forthcoming, consequently most of the troopers had little to do other than relax around their base camp for much of the time. The group had now been in France for up to three weeks, but the war and the invasion sometimes seemed far distant. As a result, some were lulled into a false sense of security by the thought that it would probably only be a few weeks before the advancing Allied armies overran them. As boredom set in, the SAS men began to get impatient and the 'Amilcar' Maquis reported that two or three of them had sauntered in to the village for a drink at the bar and to chat up the local girls. Some of the latter had already been up to the camp in the woods, hoping perhaps to attract the eye of the brave young men who had come from England to fight for their country. This lapse in security was compounded by sightings of a strange car slowly touring the area. This was suspected to be a radio direction-finding vehicle, and added to fears that the Germans already had information that caused them to pay particular attention to the area

But it was the issue of Captain Sadoine's Phantom signals party that gave Dédé most cause for concern as he now became personally and directly involved. Word had reached him at Chêne's headquarters that not only was Sadoine still refusing to join up with the main SAS group, but also that he had been telling his Maquis helpers that the SAS were a danger to everyone as they would inevitably attract a German attack.

This was highly disturbing news to Dédé. He had not yet met Sadoine, but he liked and trusted Tonkin and his group. The SAS had proved enthusiastic for action, while Sadoine had achieved nothing more than arranging a few arms and supplies drops and had shown more interest in securing the services of a decent camp cook from the Maquis. But if the report were true, Sadoine was putting the SAS at risk and was guilty of cowardice.

Consequently, Dédé sent a car and message asking Tonkin to join him at the FFI headquarters, which the SAS officer described as being near Lathus-Saint-Rémy, some 35 kilometres to the south-east of the SAS camp. After a fast drive through the French countryside, Tonkin arrived to find Dédé in a grave mood, accompanied by Colonel Chêne, Blondel, leader of Groupement D of the Vienne-Sud and Marcel Robichon, leader of the 'Vauquois' Maquis.

Dédé outlined the startling news to the SAS Captain, stressing that it came from absolutely reliable and trusted Maquis group leaders. They had reported that Sadoine was not only reluctant to join Tonkin, but had been actively encouraging the local Maquis forces to keep away from the SAS group. Sadoine seemingly considered that the SAS's mode of operations represented not only a danger to themselves, but also to any Frenchman helping them, and also to his own team of Phantom signallers. The French described him as having become obsessed by the idea that the SAS operations would lead to his own capture and execution. In view of the Allied invasion, Sadoine no longer saw any purpose to 'Bulbasket' and had even suggested that the only solution was the elimination of Tonkin and his officers.

Tonkin was stunned by the information, yet both Dédé and Colonel Chêne were agreed in what they thought should be done. As a British officer, now of senior rank having just been promoted Major with effect from 30 June, Dédé felt there was only one option – to court-martial Sadoine in the field. If the accusations were proven, Sadoine would be found guilty of treachery and executed. This he urged Tonkin to do, without delay, but Tonkin could not bring himself to act. Sadoine was from another unit and, as such, was not Tonkin's direct responsibility. To judge and possibly execute a brother officer was a decision not easily made and, instead, Tonkin pledged to place Sadoine under close arrest as soon as possible. It was not Dédé's preferred course of action, but he acknowledged the extent of Tonkin's dilemma and therefore accepted the SAS commander's proposal, on condition that the SAS would be responsible for the custody of Sadoine. This having been agreed, Tonkin was driven back to Verrières,[4] but before he was able to do anything about Sadoine, disaster struck.

Around midday on 3 July an exhausted Maquisard from the 'Amilcar' section attached to the SAS reached the FFI headquarters. Jean Dieudonné told how at dawn a strong German force had encircled and then attacked the SAS camp at Verrières. Dieudonné had managed to escape from the woods and had spent the rest of the morning taking refuge in a cabbage field. Realizing that the SAS might still need help, he found a bicycle and set off to reach the 'Vauquois' Maquis, only to find that the group, having heard the noise of the battle, had already dispersed into the countryside and hidden their arms. Dieudonné therefore continued on to Chêne's headquarters. It would seem that Dédé was temporarily away when Dieudonné arrived, possibly in preparation for a supply drop he was supervising that night, but Chêne immediately allocated fifty men under one of his officers to set off back to Verrières. They arrived at the village around two o'clock in the afternoon, but saw that the Germans already had many of the SAS troops in captivity and were assembling the men of Verrières in the village square. In the face of a clearly much stronger enemy, and wanting to avoid civilian casualties, the Maquis stood off and awaited the departure of the Germans. Reprisals against the men of the village looked certain, but the Germans suddenly seemed to change their minds and began to pull out.

One reason for the hurried departure of the Germans was subsequently suggested by Robert Artaud, commander of the 'Amilcar' Maquis. A messenger had been sent by motorcycle from Chêne's headquarters to inform him that the SAS party and his own detachment had been attacked in the Forêt de Verrières. Lacking sufficient vehicles, but having to react quickly, Artaud assembled just two lorries, packed in forty-five men and set off. One kilometre from Verrières Artaud and his men split up into small groups to slip into the village. They arrived just after the Germans had left and found all the men of the village still assembled in the square. It was Artaud's belief that the change of plan by the Germans was due to the fact that the two lorries he had with him had both lost their exhausts. They could be heard from 6 kilometres away and sounded like a convoy of dozens of vehicles. Artaud was therefore convinced that the Germans had heard what they took to be the approach of a large force of Maquis and had chosen to avoid another fight.

This may well have been wishful thinking, for the German force had little to fear, having consisted of no less than 400 troops assembled by SS-Obersturmführer Hoffman, acting second in command of the Poitiers SD. It was Hoffman who, having already had information that the SAS camp was some-where in the Forêt de Verrières, had sent agents to the area on 1 July to pinpoint the camp's exact location. They were soon able to report back to Poitiers and Hoffmann immediately began to gather a force to mount an attack. The main component was the 17th SS Panzergrenadier Division's holding battalion, based at Bonneuil-Matours. Other troops came from the Poitiers Feldkommandantur, a number of radio units and a Reconnaissance Bicycle Squadron of the 158th Security Division, the latter specializing in anti-Maquis operations such as the SD now planned at Verrières. By dawn on 3 July the enemy had managed to encircle the forest holding the SAS camp quietly and achieved complete surprise when the attack was launched. Only eight of the SAS and four maquisards escaped the net, the remainder all being captured alive. For the seven maquisards who were caught there was instant retribution, for they were im-mediately shot on the edge of the forest at La Couarde. At the same spot Lieutenant Stephens of the SAS, wounded but still blazing verbal defiance, provoked his captors too far and was beaten to death with a rifle butt. His body, together with those of the executed maquisards, was later thrown into the village square in Verrières.

When Dédé returned to Chêne's headquarters on the 4th, it was after an eventful night when he had received an unexpected but welcome gift. Manning

128

a drop zone to receive a routine delivery of arms and supplies, he had heard a low-flying aircraft some time before the time arranged for his own operation. Passing directly overhead, the aircraft dropped a package that Dédé retrieved, opened and found to contain 1,200,000 Francs. With the money he also found documents, inscribed with the name 'AIL', that appeared to be from some form of intelligence organization, though not from SOE. When he later radioed London, Dédé obtained Colonel Buckmaster's confirmation that SOE had not sent the money, but was ordered to use it anyway. This did not prevent a local rumour that Dédé had kept the money for his own use.[5]

On arrival at FFI headquarters, however, Dédé's good humour at his new-found riches instantly evaporated. Aghast to hear of the German attack at Verrières, he hurried to the area and went to the La Roche farm, home of Monsieur Bonnet and the pre-determined rendezvous point that Dédé had agreed with the SAS in case of problems. There he found Dieudonné still in shock that so far he seemed to be the only survivor. Throughout the remainder of the day they waited, but no one else showed up and it was decided they would stay the night in the hope that others might still come in.

The next day they were joined by three SAS troopers who had been away on a rail sabotage mission and who, having heard from local people of the battle, had come straight to La Roche. They were shaken to find themselves the only SAS personnel there and, in the expectation that there might not be any other SAS who had got away, Dédé began to discuss with them what their future role might be. Depressed at the thought of what might have happened to their comrades, they settled down in the farm's barn, but were cheered some-what when eight SAS survivors, including Captain Tonkin and Lieutenant Weaver, trickled in over the next twenty-four hours, gathered from local farms and other hiding places by the 'Vauquois' Maquis. In addition, another maquisard from the SAS camp, Denis Chansigaud, arrived at La Roche. He told of several wounded and many captured and had personally witnessed the killing of Lieutenant Stephens. The losses were considerable. Lieutenant Stephens had been killed and thirty SAS men, three of whom were badly wounded, had been captured, along with their medical orderly, Corporal Allan and a downed American fighter pilot, Lieutenant Bundy, who had only just been brought to the camp on 1 July. Shot down by flak in his Mustang over the Normandy beachhead on 10 June, Bundy had dutifully followed his escape and evasion briefing which, making no allowance for the invasion, dictated heading south for neutral Spain. Living off the land and walking only at night, the resourceful young pilot had managed to cover some 300 kilometres before being discovered on their farm near Jardres by the friendly Guillon family. Welcoming and hiding Bundy, they had subsequently passed him on to the local Maquis. But with the worst possible timing he had then been sent, at Dédé's suggestion, to join the SAS who would be best placed to arrange his evacuation and return to England. He had arrived in the SAS camp just in time to be captured.

129

Despite his own escape, Tonkin was now so despondent that he told Dédé he might withdraw south towards Spain in order to return to England. But Dédé encouraged him to come to terms with the situation and to think instead how he might continue with a smaller force, helped by the return, the next day, by another SAS party that had had the good fortune to be away from Verrières at the time of the attack.

Before the move to Verrières, SAS Brigade Headquarters had requested Tonkin to investigate attacking La Martinerie airfield near Châteauroux, the Priority A target that had long engaged the attention of Southgate and Dédé. Recent intelligence reports suggested that, despite recent bombing attacks, there were still some thirty Junkers dive-bombers and night fighters parked under the trees and that flying activity had resumed. When transport and fuel had finally allowed, Lieutenant Morris had therefore left the SAS camp by jeep on the night of 30 June with one trooper and a maquisard as guide in order to attack the airfield. First they needed more explosives, so they travelled some 40 kilometres to the south-east where they joined a Maquis headquarters in a wood near Azat-le-Ris. From there they were led to the elusive Captain Sadoine's camp in another wood a few kilometres away. In the afternoon of 2 July the group, accompanied by Sadoine, set off for the explosives dump created by the Phantom team, but an encounter with a herd of cows led to the jeep swerving off the road and overturning. Only Sadoine was unscathed, while the other three were fortunate to escape with minor injuries. The jeep was pushed upright but, with its steering damaged, had to be taken to a nearby farm. The sabotage party spent the night sleeping there with Sadoine's party, but at dawn were woken by gunfire in the far distance. Later they received the news of the disaster at Verrières. Unable to return to their base camp, their overriding concern was to avoid causing any trouble for the farmer. The jeep was therefore pushed down a small track and covered with foliage. They were driven to the village of Oradour-sur-Vayres where they were hidden in a house while they recuperated for another two days before retrieving the repaired jeep and joining Tonkin's survivors near the Forêt de Plessac (also known as the Forêt des Vieilles Forges). Their jeep was now the only one left to the SAS.

The disaster at Verrières was a timely warning that the enemy were still a danger, despite their reluctance to venture into the countryside except in force. Early in the month, in an incident unrecorded by Dédé, but clearly remembered by Colonel Chêne, a German patrol caught the two men by surprise. Neither was armed at the time, and they had no option but to run for their lives, pursued by bursts of machine-gun fire that were fortunately wide of their mark. July also saw the strong German SS unit from Bonneuil-Matours attack the camp of the 'Baptiste' sub-group of the 'Gilles' Maquis near Bélâbre, killing many, with only a few losses of its own. But the FFI were not to be deterred and a radio message from Dédé on 7 July reported attacks on the Germans in their barracks at Magnac-Laval, in the open at Joussé, and in ambushes at Lussac-les-Châteaux. To cap it all, the following day saw another audacious Maquis operation in the very heart of Poitiers, under the noses of the Germans.

The Hôtel-Dieu hospital in the city was used by the Germans for treatment of any of their prisoners who were wounded. Two such captives were members of the 'Lagardère' Maquis who had been wounded and taken by the Germans in an action at Bonneuil-Matours on 11 June. Despite their wounds, the captured maquisards had been brutally interrogated at length by the Poitiers SD before they had been allowed treatment at the Hôtel-Dieu under close guard. But one of the two prisoners, Henri Baudinière, was the brother of André Baudinière, leader of the 'Lagardère' Maquis. On learning of his brother's transfer to the hospital, André seized his chance, realizing that his brother could be executed at any moment. Lieutenant 'Thomas' and two other maquisards simply drove into the hospital's courtyard at 8.00 a.m. and, while one man kept guard over the getaway vehicle, the two others entered the building armed with sub-machine guns. The German guards were surprised and held at gunpoint while the two wounded men were found and helped from their beds. Moments later, and without a single shot having been fired to raise the alarm, the maquisards were speeding from the city in triumph.

There was a sad irony. Without the 'Lagardère' Maquis knowing it, the three wounded SAS soldiers captured at Verrières had been in the very same ward as the maquisards, watched over by the same guards. It would have been a simple matter to have rescued them at the same time, had the situation been realized and adequate transport provided. Seemingly, however, neither the wounded maquisards nor the wounded SAS were aware of each other and the opportunity was lost. Realizing they had come perilously close to losing their precious captives, the SD acted swiftly, hastening to the hospital the same evening and returning the SAS men to the security of the Feldkommandantur cells. It was the last that anyone saw or heard of the three wounded men.

The survivors of the SAS group had regrouped in the Forêt de Plessac (Fôret des Vieilles Forges) on 5 July, a move of some 35 kilometres south-south-east from Verrières. The SAS had not yet operated in the locality, but Dédé recommended it since it was an area where the Maquis were strong and consequently afforded some sense of security. Having lost the services of his own signallers, captured at Verrières, Captain Tonkin was now in urgent need of replacements and he therefore immediately sent Lieutenant Weaver and Corporal Rideout, with six maquisards and adequate transport, to bring in Sadoine's Phantom group. On their arrival, Sadoine was placed under close arrest as Tonkin had agreed with Dédé, and the Phantom signallers transmitted to England the next day to confirm that all the surviving SAS and the Phantom group were now concentrated together and were again ready for operations. There were just eighteen left out of the original strength of fifty-four and, following instructions received from England, Tonkin was to begin to look for a suitable landing strip in the area west of Limoges in order to arrange an air evacuation of his party. In the interim, in a move again organized by Dédé, the SAS decamped some 30 kilometres to the west on 9 July and joined the strong Charroux Maquis group where they were able to help with weapons and explosives training, and planning small-scale sabotage attacks. There, a measure of relaxation came Captain Tonkin's way when Dédé invited him to attend the 14th of July Bastille Day celebrations which Chêne's headquarters had sanctioned to take place in the small town of Luchapt. In what was still, theoretically, enemy-held territory, Blondel's maquisards staged a military parade and Tonkin took the salute from a smartly turned-out guard of honour. The local population crowded the streets and joyfully welcomed this blatant disregard for the enemy, knowing almost beyond all doubt that they were witnessing their last Bastille Day under German occupation.

# Chapter Twelve

# Revenge

While the FFI were savouring their Bastille Day parade in Luchapt, an even greater humiliation for the enemy was being prepared in England on the same day, aimed at the German units responsible for the Verrières attack, and the murder of Lieutenant Stephens and the seven maquisards.

Surviving British records suggest that requests for an air attack came from both the SAS, via Dédé and Pierre Hirsch's radio set, and from the 'Hugh' Jedburgh team. Both had obtained map references for the exact location of a German camp alongside the River Vienne at Bonneuil-Matours, 22 kilometres north-east of Poitiers. Identified as being the barracks of the holding battalion of the 17th SS Panzergrenadier Division, the camp therefore housed the unit that had provided most of the force used in the operation at Verrières on 3 July. 'Hugh' actually pinpointed the Château de Marieville, an imposing residence sited on a hill on the east bank of the River Vienne, but although the house had been requisitioned by the Colonel commanding the battalion, the SS troops were in less-solidly constructed barracks along the lightly wooded west bank of the river. The Vienne, and a nearby bridge, provided excellent reference points for an air attack.

From Special Forces Headquarters Dédé's message was passed to the headquarters of the SAS Brigade where no time was wasted in using their established contacts with the RAF's No. 2 Group to seek revenge for the brutal murder of Lieutenant Stephens. When the call reached the RAF it came at the busiest time of the war when No. 2 Group's squadrons were faced with constant demands for round-the-clock air operations, above and immediately beyond the invasion area in Normandy. They might therefore have been excused for turning down the SAS's plea for help. Typically, they did not, and it was immediately appreciated that Bastille Day would provide the most fitting date for a powerful act of retribution.

Air Vice-Marshal Basil Embry, the Air Officer Commanding No. 2 Group, considered the task important enough to travel down himself from Group Headquarters in Berkshire to 140 Wing, which had by now moved to RAF Thorney Island near Portsmouth on the English south coast. There, on 14 July, he personally briefed the fourteen crews detailed to carry out the operation and although the day had been cloudy, the evening promised to be fair and suitable for a precision attack. The operation was therefore timed to reach the target at dusk, hopefully catching the maximum number of Germans in the barracks for their evening meal.

Embry made it clear that the attack was to be a reprisal operation against the German unit responsible for clubbing to death a British officer taken prisoner of war. He wanted to fire up his crews with a passion for revenge and described how the Germans had 'bashed somebody's head in'. He also stressed to the flyers that a Bastille Day attack would serve to raise the spirits of the French people on such a symbolic day. This time the attack was only to be undertaken by 140 Wing and so 464 and 487 Squadrons were joined by their sister 21 Squadron.

The decision was taken not to attack the solidly built chateau, but to aim instead for the barracks where there would be a greater and more vulnerable concentration of the enemy. Six Mosquitos were to be equipped with special new incendiary bombs, which were delivered to the airfield by American trucks shortly before take-off. Four aircraft with high-explosive bombs would first open up the target, the incendiaries would then be dropped and finally more high explosive would be delivered to spread the effect around. Other aircraft were detailed to patrol the road alongside the River Vienne and shoot up any approaching reinforcements. Describing the plan, Embry cold-bloodedly urged his crews to 'let the bastards burn', but nevertheless realized that any hint of a reprisal operation could provoke the Germans into 'tit-for-tat' tactics. His final memorable words were therefore: 'If you get shot down and taken prisoner, don't shoot your mouth off about retaliation. You can't out-piss a skunk!'

There was no mention of any SOE or SAS involvement and none of the aircrews were aware that British special forces were operating so far behind enemy lines.

Of the fourteen Mosquito crews briefed, four came from each of 140 Wing's three squadrons and were led by the respective commanding officers. They were joined by two crews from the Wing's headquarters staff, those of Group Captain Peter Wykeham-Barnes and his Wing Commander (Flying), Reggie Reynolds.

All aircraft took off in the evening shortly before 9.00 p.m. and formed up in formation for the trip across the Channel. At 2,000 feet the Mosquitos safely skirted the Cherbourg peninsula, but a few moments later were rocked by explosions as a heavy flak battery on the Channel Island of Alderney opened up. The fighter-bombers swiftly scattered in what was described as 'a relatively disciplined way' before reforming once the guns were outdistanced.

Over the Bay of St Michel the Mosquito formation was met by an escort of twelve Mustang III fighters from 65 Squadron RAF. Based on the continent at B7 Airfield, Martragny, the Mustangs were able to afford the Mosquitos extra protection during the daylight stage of their flight over enemy-held territory, making the combination of Mosquitos and Mustangs a formidable force should the Luftwaffe attempt to interfere. Together, and still in strict radio silence, the fighter-bombers and their escorts crossed the French coast near St Malo and then dropped to just 50 feet near Rennes. Shortly afterwards the Mustangs turned back for Martragny which, as day fighters, they wanted to reach before night fell.

Just before reaching the target, the Mosquito flights climbed to the planned bombing height of 1,000 feet and then swept in to the attack. With no cloud and excellent visibility, the target was easily identified alongside the river and although small-arms fire spat out from a number of doorways on the approach, the only opposition of any real concern was a 20mm gun wildly firing tracer from the roof of a nearby large house. After the first aircraft had released their bombs, smoke enveloped the gun position and the tracer stopped.

No warning had been given of the fighter-bombers' approach and the townspeople only heard the roar of Merlin engines as the Mosquitos pulled up from the river valley, causing the onlookers to believe that the aircraft had glided in with engines cut in order to surprise the Germans. In reality, the sheer speed and low altitude of their attack had ensured that the Mosquitos were on the target before the Germans had time to hear their approach and organize themselves.

The bombs used were a mixture of eleven seconds' delay and instantaneously fused high explosive, along with the new American M76 phosphorous incendiaries which were effectively the first napalm bombs. The attack on Bonneuil-Matours therefore constituted the first operational use of the weapon in Western Europe. As the last crews called 'bombs gone' over the target they reported the area and buildings carpeted in flames, the majority of bombs having fallen in the target area with only a few overshooting towards the neighbouring village and a couple on the east bank of the river.

But for the SS troops their ordeal was far from over. As they stumbled from the blasted remains of their barracks a growling crescendo of noise rose above the roaring of the flames as the Mosquitos banked sharply and dived back into the attack. Through the rising smoke the graceful aircraft streaked in with their nose cannon and machine-guns spitting venomously, hosing down any of the black-uniformed figures unlucky enough to be caught in the open. Knowing something of the reason for the raid, the Mosquito crews were in no mood for pity and night was falling before they left the blazing target, all returning safely to England.

Behind them the RAF had left a scene of savage destruction. All seven barrack blocks had been blasted and, as planned, the SS had been caught during their evening meal of lamb stew. They had only just returned from a successful anti-Maquis operation and there were estimated to be some 400 enemy troops in camp at the time of the attack. One wayward bomb, on the opposite river bank, had only just missed the Château de Marieville and had consequently given the SS headquarters staff a severe, if unintentional, fright.

Throughout the night the village's inhabitants feared reprisals, but happily none came as the Germans occupied themselves with transferring their wounded to Poitiers. A number of local men were compelled to help lift bodies into lorries, but otherwise the local people were left unmolested. Quietly, they celebrated the raid which had caused their unwelcome lodgers to choke on their evening meal, the more so as the Germans' stew was made from sheep stolen from local farms. A couple of days later the German camp was completely abandoned when the SS survivors left Bonneuil-Matours for good. Local Gendarmerie records suggest that the enemy suffered some 80–100 killed and wounded. The raid had been a complete success.

But while the RAF had been more than happy to divert their resources to avenge the SAS's Lieutenant Stephens, Brigade Headquarters had only limited plans for the future use of the 'Bulbasket' survivors. Instead, it was decided to pull out what was left of Tonkin's troop and replace it with a large contingent of the French 3rd SAS in 'Operation Moses'. As an advance party, two French SAS officers therefore parachuted in on the night of 15/16 July, west of Parthenay and accompanying another three-man Jedburgh team, 'Harold'.

Designed to support the Deux-Sèvres region that Dédé had recently visited in early July, 'Harold' consisted of Major Whitty ('Ross'), as the British commander, Lieutenant Jolliet (serving as Rimbaut, 'Tyrone') of the French BCRA, and Sergeant Verlander ('Sligo'), a British radio operator. As they arrived, arms and equipment were already being parachuted into the area to an organization that Dédé had started. In all these operations he had been working in close co-operation with the Délégué Militaire Régional of Région 5, Eugène Déchelette ('Ellipse'). But the Deux-Sèvres suffered from local tension between the AS commanded by Colonel Proust and the FTP Maquis led by Lieutenant Colonel Robin, the latter allegedly having been favoured by Dédé in the matter of arms supplies. How this claim first arose is not clear, but Lieutenant Claude Gros ('César') had also been sent to the Deux-Sèvres by the BCRA, the Free French Secret Service in London. Gros appears to have mistrusted Dédé's intentions in arming FTP units and although it was Dédé who had arranged for 'Harold' to be sent to improve matters, it seems it was probably Gros who persuaded Whitty to radio a complaint to London, suggesting to Special Forces HQ that Dédé had too much sympathy with the communists. Certainly, it was more often the case that F Section agents stayed clear of their local FTP groups, discouraged as they were by the instinctive suspicions of the communists and their disinclination to depend upon the services of a foreign, capitalist power. The FTP also had a reputation of ignoring potential German reprisals for their sabotage and ambushes, but Dédé was one of the more far-sighted SOE agents to appreciate that, properly armed, supplied and advised, the FTP Maquis could be as effective as anyone in harassing the Germans. And, despite his own well-heeled background, Dédé had the sensitivity, tact and diplomacy, coupled with a passionate hatred of the Germans, which soon won over even the most untrusting and left-wing FTP maquisard.

Whitty eventually realized the truth of the matter and concluded that the problem lay with Robin who had not been distributing weapons and supplies as expected by Dédé. He had instead been keeping them all for his own FTP groups and Whitty soon put this right by taking over distribution and ensuring that AS groups in the area received their fair share. Given Dédé's excellent relations with Colonel Chêne, and with the AS groups in the neighbouring Vienne, there can be no truth to the suspicion that he favoured the FTP in Deux-Sèvres. Indeed, an incident later recounted by Colonel Chêne showed that Dédé could be decidedly unimpressed by communist doctrine, or any political cant. This occurred when Dédé and Chêne visited an FTP Maquis in the Limousin region and questioned the group's three young leaders as to their arms requirements. Once the practicalities were over, one of the three maquisards began a little speech, which left little doubt as to his political leanings. But before he got far, Dédé interrupted him with the words 'I came here to find out what you wanted in the way of weapons. I didn't come to listen to a sermon. If you're going to continue preaching, then all I have to say to you is *merde*!' After which all went well.

The accusation of communist sympathies was certainly a claim that carried no weight with SOE in England. Surviving records show that from late June to mid-July Dédé (through Pierre Hirsch) was 'continually radioing invaluable intelligence, such as German camps, holding reprisal units, and information regarding movements of divisions'. Dédé's file also noted that he and his men had developed a simple tactic for blocking the important RN148 road, whereby trenches were dug every 2 metres, effectively blocking the road. On 11 July two German divisions were reported to be held up for lack of petrol, which had been stolen by the Maquis; and the 110,000 volt cable feeding the German submarine base at Rochefort, over 150 kilometres away on the Atlantic coast, was cut, rendering telephone communications useless. The Germans were again attacked in their barracks at Magnac-Laval on 16 July and the enemy lost many men in an action at Joussé on the 20th. A puzzling note, left on Dédé's personal SOE file by Colonel Buckmaster in April 1945, also records Dédé or his men killing a German general at Angles on 20 July. Given that the nearest Angles was some 200 kilometres away, it is a mystery as to why this was credited to Dédé and he made no claim himself to this coup de main.

Meanwhile, and in contrast to the drama of the Germans' successes at Verrières and Bélâbre, the air attack on Bonneuil-Matours and the continuing escalation of FFI attacks, ambushes and sabotage, events in the field for the remaining British SAS party were relatively low key. Numbers in camp had increased on 15 July by the arrival, at last, of Captain Sadoine and his Phantom party, together with a cache of arms, supplies and four vehicles. They were followed by several USAAF pilots brought in by the Maquis at Dédé's suggestion, the first being Lieutenant Flamm D. Harper, known as 'Dee', on 16 July who had been brought down in his Lockheed P-38 fighter while attacking the enemy's ammunition depot at Sillars Camp. The American's impression of Dédé as a British officer came over fifty years later when Dee Harper could still vividly recall their meeting in the SAS camp:

> I met Samuel twice at Captain Tonkin's camp. A very impressive man. He was very reserved, a distinguished individual. Both times he was dressed in his uniform with a swagger stick, he looked like he had just stepped out of a band box and was strolling down Oxford Street in London. He even wore his rank. He was only introduced to me as 'Samuel' . . . but Tonkin, Morris and Topper Brown all told me stories about the man.

Two days later, four more USAAF airmen arrived, Lieutenants Bradley and Scott, and Sergeants Gross and Norton, who had been shot down some six months before, but had then managed to escape from a POW camp. Another two downed

American flyers, Sergeants Ward and Hitchcock, had suffered sprain injuries and for the time being remained at a farm in the area in order to recover. While most of the Americans were happy to help the SAS with cooking, labouring and general camp chores, there were three exceptions. One of the young sergeant air gunners was terrified at the thought of what might happen to him if discovered in the company of the SAS and the Maquis and consequently wanted to play no part whatsoever in their activities. By contrast, Lieutenant Bill Bradley and Lieutenant Dee Harper could not wait to get to grips with the Germans again, the latter in particular taking every opportunity to help with operations and telling Tonkin, 'I see no reason why the lack of an aeroplane should stop me fighting.'

But then, as the SAS prepared to receive further supply drops, their plans were again interrupted by reports of German troops moving into nearby Charroux. Concerned at the limited strength of the SAS's depleted party, Dédé arranged for Captain Tonkin to return eastwards, joining another strong Maquis group in their camp on a farm at Asnières-sur-Blour, west of the Limoges–Poitiers road. This was to prove a good, secure base and an easily identifiable DZ was established immediately next to the camp. The nearest Germans were now some way to the north, so it was considered safe enough for the SAS men to enjoy a little bit of local life. Frequent visits were paid to the café in the village of Asnières, using the kitchen not only for drinking and eating, but also for passing and receiving messages since a radio set was kept there. Friendly rivalry with their Maquis hosts also led to the SAS challenging the French to a game of football on a field north of the farm. And further cementing of the Anglo-French relationship came when, on 25 July, papers and an identity disc arrived from the crash site of an Allied aircraft some 10 kilometres to the south of Asnières. The aircraft had been a Stirling of 620 Squadron RAF, one of the squadrons responsible for the regular resupply of the Maquis, but it was not known what had brought the four-engined former bomber down on the night of 22/23 July with the loss of all Flying Officer Oke's crew on board. When it crashed, fire had engulfed the aircraft, making identification of the bodies a grim and difficult task, but the local 'Foch' Maquis and the people of nearby Brillac arranged a burial with full honours in their village cemetery. As a mark of respect Dédé, Lieutenant Weaver and one other SAS soldier attended the funeral of the six dead airmen.

In mid-July, when Dédé had first met the chiefs of the Haute-Vienne Maquis (after initial contact had been made by Jacques Hirsch), there had been consideration of the SAS survivors helping train the swelling Maquis groups in that area, but the lack of linguistic ability among the SAS proved to be an insurmountable barrier. In a message received by London on 21 July, Dédé had already reported that there was now one single, unified, FFI movement in the Vienne, armed and financed by him, of about 1,300 men and this must have further convinced London that there was no useful role left for Tonkin's men. In reply, London had therefore requested that Dédé should temporarily return to England for a short debriefing session and fresh instructions, and that he should take advantage of the aircraft that would shortly be sent to pick up the survivors of 'Operation Bulbasket'. The SAS subsequently received a radioed message to cease operations and to stand by to receive a specialist who would help them find and prepare a landing ground so that their party and Dédé could be flown out to England. In the early hours of 29 July a Stirling therefore thundered low over the Asnières DZ and dropped Lieutenant Surrey Dane of 1st SAS Regiment, together with twenty-four containers and four panniers of supplies.

David Surrey Dane, another of the SAS's enthusiastic and capable young officers, had been frustrated at not yet having seen action in the war. He had left his medical studies at Cambridge University to join the Army, but had missed inclusion in the main SAS parties dropped into France after D-Day as he had been selected to attend an RAF-run course on the selection, preparation and operation of clandestine airstrips. Before departure he had been thoroughly briefed by SOE's F Section staff in London, who had advised him of three sites to be reconnoitred, and he was provided with the instructions for an evacuation airlift of Dédé and all 'Bulbasket' SAS personnel back to England.

When he parachuted into the Vienne, Surrey Dane immediately hit it off with Dédé whom he quickly summed up as a natural leader and a crucial go-between in the often complex relationships among the different Maquis groups, and between the British and the French. It was a situation that fulfilled Surrey Dane's quest for adventure, but he was also soon to find that war had its ugly side:

The morning after I had parachuted in to join John Tonkin, he took me to visit a group of *Maquisard*s hidden a few hundred yards away from the SAS camp. They were using an old pigsty as a shelter and I can remember having to bend down to look inside and greet their leader. Sitting next to him on the floor was a young woman whose head had been shaved. This made a lasting impression on me, as she was the first shaven-headed woman collaborator I had seen. It was explained to me that they were holding her until some enquiries about her collaboration had been completed. I never saw her again.

When I returned to camp one evening after being away during the day, one of the SAS soldiers told me what had happened to her. Word must have come through that she had committed a serious crime. Perhaps she had been the mistress of a German officer. The trooper saw her being taken past the SAS camp to a nearby wood by two members of the local *Maquis*. One carried a spade and the other a Sten gun.

After a while there was a burst of automatic fire and later the two men reappeared, one carrying the fur coat she had been wearing. They said that before they shot her she removed the coat and gave it to them saying that it would be of more use to them than to her.

I thought at the time and have thought many times since how lucky we were in Britain not to have been occupied by the Germans. It meant we were spared this sort of killing.

Corporal Sam Smith and Trooper John Fielding of the SAS also never forgot the incidents they witnessed at Asnières involving alleged spies and collaborators, Fielding remembering:

139

I believe there were two executions by the *Maquis*, one being the French/Canadian spy and the other one a woman. These two were executed in the wood adjacent to the DZ.

Both the man and the woman were brought through our base and I also recall seeing the woman being informed of her pending execution the following morning – she was taken into the field between our base and the farmhouse and the group could be seen standing on the horizon.

The young woman was alleged to have fraternized with the Germans and had been held prisoner in the camp for some time. She was in her thirties, a graduate of Poitiers University and spoke perfect English when she chatted amiably with the British soldiers. She had no great fear for her own fate, for she did not think her crime serious. Smith found it particularly difficult to accept the 'crime' of the woman and before his death in 1989 he wrote of his bad memories:

The other prisoner was a woman from Poitiers. I got to know her very well – not intimately. She was a university graduate and a very intelligent person. Her 'offence' was socialising with the Germans. She asked Brown and I to visit her in Poitiers after the war. One afternoon, drinking with the French, she was singled out and taken to the far side of the field. I asked if she was being told to leave as she had told us that this is what she was expecting. The reply that she was to be executed next morning horrified me – could I have done anything?

This is something I have lived with all these years.

The post-war memoirs of FTP Maquis leader Camille Olivet ('La Chouette') poured scorn on such accounts. Responding to another author's claim that collaborators and spies were executed by the FFI,[1] Olivet wrote: 'All these assertions are false and would be worthy of a serialised novel.' Dédé's reports to SOE make no mention of such incidents, yet the SAS survivors of 'Bulbasket' definitely recalled at least three such executions after Verrières, and Captain Tonkin believed there to have been five. One was the case of the French-Canadian spy mentioned by Fielding and in which Dédé took a personal part.

At Chêne's headquarters a supposed Canadian soldier, a private, had arrived, having been passed down an escape line from the fighting in Normandy. Dédé and the FFI commanders had suspicions about the man and it was crucial that the suspect be tested, as by then he would have known many of the escape line's safe houses and helpers. Dédé therefore sent a car to collect Tonkin and when the SAS Captain, in uniform, entered the room, Dédé barked at the suspect, 'Don't you stand to attention when an officer enters the room?' The man sprang belatedly to attention, whereupon Dédé stared at him and, after a few moments silence, observed, 'He has his hands flat against the sides of his legs. No Canadian soldier stands to attention like that.' The stranger was led outside and immediately shot. Recalled and recorded in detail by John Tonkin, this incident was never reported nor mentioned by Dédé, but there is evidence elsewhere in remaining operational files that this type of action was no more than expected

# PLAN OF STATIONER ORGANISATION
## December 1943 - May 1944
(prior to and following Southgate's arrest in May 1944)

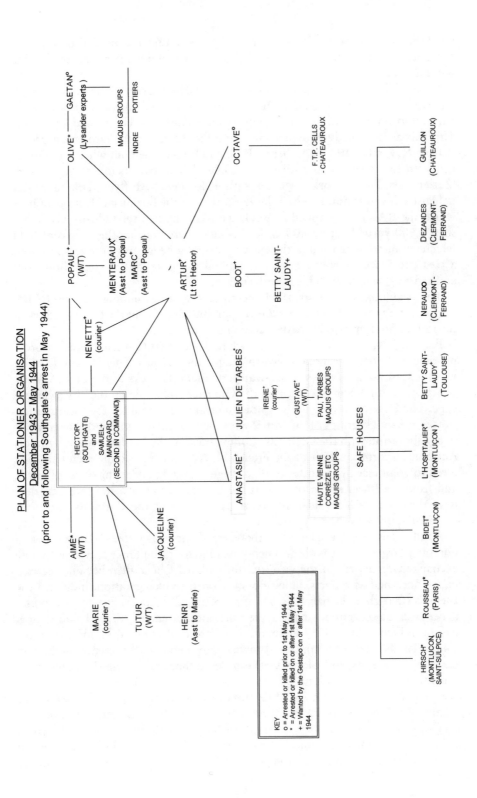

KEY
o = Arrested or killed prior to 1st May 1944
* = Arrested or killed on or after 1st May 1944
+ = Wanted by the Gestapo on or after 1st May 1944

by SOE. Documentation from the 'Hugh' Jedburgh team conceded that 'it was extremely inconvenient to take prisoners . . . we avoided it as far as possible without inhumanity.'

Meanwhile, the SAS's Lieutenant Surrey Dane had surveyed the three possible airstrip locations identified by SOE and had selected the one on part of Foussac Farm, north of Montmorillon and close to the hamlets of Haims and Villemort. This was a site already known to SOE and the RAF, and the farmer confirmed that, in November 1943, another pick-up had been carried out when a Lysander delivered two agents and returned to England with two members of the SOE 'Zetland-Dahlia' network, together with a downed RAF flyer. The particular field used then was not, however, large enough for the Lockheed Hudson aircraft which the RAF now planned to send, the twin-engined type ideally needing a strip 1,600 yards long by 800 wide. Luckily, there was another adjacent field which permitted extension of the existing strip if a hedgerow were removed and a tree cut down. Surrey Dane code-named the potential airstrip 'Bon Bon' and returned to report to Dédé and Tonkin.

The beginning of August 1944 therefore saw time running out for Dédé's responsibility towards the SAS's 'Operation Bulbasket', but the first two days of the month brought two more devastating air attacks.

Back in July, an FFI report on the 24th had been first to warn of enemy forces massing in Poitiers for a major sweep against the Maquis. Their assembly point was the Caserne des Dunes, a pre-war permanent barracks of the French Army which stood on a prominent hill in the Quartier Abboville on the city's eastern edge. The Caserne des Dunes was now the training school for the local *Francs-gardes*, the shock troops of the Milice who specialized in 'anti-bandit' operations in collaboration with the Germans. Commanded in the Poitiers region by Louis Aussenac, a former officer of the French Navy, some 300 young men had been lured to volunteer by the offer of high wages. Largely under thirty years of age and from the lower strata of French life in terms of ability and intellect, they nevertheless added considerably to the resources of the Germans and were despised above all others by loyal Frenchmen.

A radio message to England had therefore already suggested the barracks as a bombing target, along with an enemy headquarters building and a telephone exchange which were in the vicinity. But Colonel Chêne then became increasingly concerned as reports, albeit possibly open to exaggeration, indicated the enemy's strength in the barracks was approaching 2–3,000, suggesting the imminence of a major action. At the same time another enemy force, 1,800 strong, had been identified at Saint-Germain-de-Confolens, some 70 kilometres to the south. The FFI feared a concerted pincer movement by the enemy might trap many of their units, so Colonel Chêne ordered that another message should be urgently radioed to London.

In England it was again No. 2 Group of the RAF who were informed of the details of the target on the morning of 1 August 1944 and an operation was quickly planned for the same evening in the belief that, like the raid against Bonneuil-Matours, this would catch most troops in the barracks, which were an easily-identifiable feature on the outskirts of Poitiers. Twenty-five Mosquito crews of 140 Wing were briefed at 6.00 p.m. and Group Captain Wykeham-Barnes again chose to lead the attack. Joining him were ten aircraft from 21 Squadron and fourteen, including two reserves, from 487 Squadron RNZAF. Twelve crews of 464 Squadron RAAF were briefed for a second attack after dark.

First into the air from RAF Thorney Island at 7.40 p.m. were Group Captain Wykeham-Barnes and the 21 Squadron formation led by Wing Commander Dennis. Immediately behind 21 Squadron, Wing Commander Smith led the twelve main force and two reserve aircraft of 487 Squadron. At the French coast the Mosquitos were met by a fighter escort of 20 Mustangs, 12 from 19 Squadron RAF and 8 from 65 Squadron RAF based in newly liberated Normandy. The Mustangs were briefed to accompany the Mosquitos all the way to the target in Poitiers and although the fighters missed the rendezvous on the coast due to poor visibility, they picked up their charges a little later. By this time it had been decided that the two reserve Mosquitos were not needed and they had turned for England. It was therefore a combined force of twenty-three Mosquitos and twenty Mustangs that thundered on over the French countryside.

The plan called for an approach from the south, those aircraft armed with instantaneously-fused bombs attacking in a shallow dive from 1–2,000 feet and those using eleven seconds' delay fuses coming in as low as 100 feet. The weather was clear with visibility of at least 15 kilometres and as the Mosquitos swung round to the south of Poitiers to begin their bombing runs, the Mustangs pulled wide and upwards, ready to spot and engage the flak defences or, more unlikely, any Luftwaffe response. There could have been no better spectacle for patriotic Frenchman watching from the ground.

Despite the Caserne des Dunes being a permanent and well-established barracks and therefore undoubtedly defended by flak guns, the speed of the Mosquitos' approach ensured the crucial element of surprise. The enemy had no time to react before the roar of aero engines and the crump of exploding bombs told them of the RAF's arrival, the fighter-bombers wheeling around the hilltop like hornets disturbed from their nest. The majority of bombs were seen to fall in the target area and the last aircraft to clear the area reported it covered in smoke from the incendiary bombs which had taken a good hold. In just minutes the deadly attack was over and the Mosquitos streaked for home. The pilots of the Mustang fighter escort, circling protectively overhead, were later to record their praise for the accuracy and weight of the Mosquitos' attack, saying they had 'never seen a target so thoroughly pranged'. No enemy aircraft were encountered and neither was any flak reported, so the Mustangs were released to make their own way home at low level.

All the Mosquitos returned safely to England with the exception of 'T-Tommy' of 21 Squadron which, though badly damaged by flak, managed a safe forced landing in a large field close to Mazières-en-Gâtine, some 55 kilometres west of Poitiers. After a walk due south of 100 kilometres the two crew members reached the village of Jarnac, on the River Charente near Cognac. There they were taken in by the Chambon family, long dedicated to the Resistance, and hidden until the Allies overran the area in September 1944.

In the days following the attack, good aerial reconnaissance photographs were obtained and showed considerable damage inflicted on the target. In his '2 Group Operations and News Bulletin' of 5 August, Air Vice-Marshal Embry congratulated his crews warmly:

Reconnaissance photographs have since shown that this was a very clean attack; only three bombs have fallen outside the barrack area and these have not damaged civilian property. Nearly all the bombs have found their mark in barrack buildings. Of three large barrack blocks, one is 3/4 destroyed and the other [sic] is completely destroyed by high explosive at its western end and the western part has suffered severe fire damage, causing partial collapse of the roof.

Seven other buildings and buildings lining the walls of the barracks have been destroyed or gutted by fire, containing possibly 40 or 50 motor transport vehicles. The activity of the barracks is confirmed by the presence of horse exercise rings and ambulances are seen at the main entrance, some twelve hours after the attack.

It has been reported that 150 enemy troops were killed and more than that number again injured.

The casualty report came from an FFI claim radioed back to England on 3 August, but a Milice document discovered after the war lists a total of forty-three French personnel killed. Numbers of Milice wounded, and any German losses, were not recorded.

One final aspect of this attack clearly shows the extent of the political rivalries that, despite the efforts of Dédé and Colonel Chêne, continued among the supposedly fraternal FFI commanders. In a quite remarkable distortion of the facts the FTP leader, Camille Olivet, described an entirely different version of events in his post-war memoirs. Claiming it was he who had first identified the enemy force in the Dunes barracks, he related how he then pressed Dédé to radio for a bombing attack. While this aspect may be true, Olivet went on to say that he supposedly listened as Dédé's radio operator (presumably Pierre Hirsch) succeeded in diverting four Mosquitos already taking part in an attack on the railway station at Tours. He describes the Mosquitos' leader speaking over the radio in an American accent until it was discovered that he was, in fact, another Frenchman. In reality there was no such diverted air operation from Tours; there were no means by which anyone on the ground in France could have spoken by radio to the Mosquitos; twenty-three Mosquitos participated, not four; and the RAF leader was Englishman Peter Wykeham-Barnes, not a Frenchman.

The RAF had not yet finished with the enemy's forces in the Vienne. After the bombing of the barracks at Bonneuil-Matours on 14 July, Maquis forces had tracked the surviving German SS troops to a new headquarters at the Château du Fou, 11 kilometres south of Châtellerault. This news reached Dédé who passed it on to the remaining SAS party to again radio England for another retaliatory air attack.

The RAF's response came the very next day after the raid on Poitiers. This time it was the Mosquito fighter-bombers of 107 Squadron, from RAF Lasham's 138 Wing, which were to deliver the blow, seventeen squadron aircraft being joined by a Mosquito Mk IV aircraft of the RAF's Film Production Unit (FPU). The Mosquitos crossed into France over the Cap de la Hague and dropped to low level for a zig-zag course in order to confuse the enemy's radar. This time there had been enough time for No. 2 Group's planners to build an accurate scale model of the chateau, working from aerial reconnaissance photographs. All crews were told that the target housed SS troops, but there was no mention of a link with earlier operations, nor of the reprisal nature of the attack.

Each wave was given a portion of the target upon which to concentrate, the first two groups attacking in quick succession at ground level with delayed-action bombs and the third in a shallow dive with instantaneously fused bombs. Weather conditions were excellent, with no cloud and visibility of at least 20 kilometres; the moderate but inaccurate flak experienced en route did nothing to distract the aircrews from their task.

The attack was to be on the front of the chateau, the final approach being over beautiful formal gardens and a fine courtyard before bombs were released in the front entrance area. Dozens of SS troops poured from the shattered building, fleeing for the supposed safety of nearby woods, but the Mosquitos broke formation and dived back into the attack at ground level. Streams of cannon and machine-gun fire snaked after the running Germans, mowing many of them down before they could reach the cover of the trees. Even those who did were not left in peace. The aircrews had been warned that some of the SS were camped in the woods, so the Mosquitos comprehensively strafed the trees before the flyers turned for home. At least twenty-eight bombs hit the target, the centre and south wings were left burning and the north wing was also hit several times. All crews returned safely to England, although one aircraft was written off on landing.

Interpretation of most of the photographs taken proved impossible due to under-exposure and the filming from the FPU Mosquito was hindered by dense smoke shrouding the target.[2] There was no subsequent report from either Dédé or the SAS in the field, so it was left to 107 Squadron's operations log to record a simple conclusion on the operation: 'All those taking part thoroughly enjoyed themselves.'

With the end of 'Operation Bulbasket' now imminent, SAS Brigade Headquarters continued with plans to replace Tonkin's survivors with 'Operation Moses' of the French SAS. On the night of 2/3 August another eight men were therefore parachuted onto the Asnières DZ, including Lieutenant Cameron, their British SAS liaison officer. Cameron, together with the commanding officer of Operation Moses, had been given advice similar to that received by Captain Tonkin before leaving England, to liaise closely with Dédé and to trust him for the best interpretation of the local situation.

With the arrival of more of the French SAS, Captain Tonkin was then free to leave the area and move his party closer to the site chosen for the return to England. 'Bon Bon' was some 40 kilometres north-east of the Asnières camp and still in need of a considerable amount of hard labour in order to accompany the RAF's Hudson aircraft. A north–south run of a minimum of 1,000 metres was required and would entail the removal of considerable hedgerow. Work therefore began, organized by Lieutenant Surrey Dane, with Lieutenant Morris driving the SAS's remaining jeep which was used to pull an agricultural harrow. For four days the SAS and the American USAAF evaders sweated in the fields, and during the daytime of the 5th, a move of camp was made to a site north of Lathus-Saint-Rémy, to be closer not only to 'Bon Bon', but also to Chêne's FFI headquarters and the protection of its strong Maquis forces – for the Germans were still proving dangerous. On 4 August a so-called 'Repression Column' had brought terror to the village of Vigeant, where twenty-two civilians and eighteen maquisards were executed as part of a *ratissage* through the region, looking to flush out and destroy Maquis groups by provoking them with the taking and execution of civilian hostages. In their looting, pillaging and raping, the Germans were also shamefully helped by numerous Milice, and the next day they continued their assault on Lussac where a force from at least three Maquis groups lost some twenty men in a vain attempt to hold the town's bridge.

With increased German activity in the countryside, Dédé arranged for the two injured American airmen, Ward and Hitchcock, to be brought in from the outlying farm where they had been recuperating and on the 6th, with all preparation finished, he joined the SAS in tuning in to the BBC for confirmation of the evacuation operation. First came the BBC News in French and then, as usual: 'Voici les messages personnels.' A long string of coded messages followed until eventually the one hoped for – two aircraft would be landing that same night. The men cheered with delight.

The RAF's 161 Special Duties Squadron was the ony one experienced in pick-up operations and therefore it was the Squadron's 'C' Flight that provided two twin-engined Lockheed Hudsons for the job. On the outbound journey the Hudsons carried not only a cargo of arms to resupply the Maquis but also a total of eleven more French SAS of 'Operation Moses' to replace the 'Bulbasket' team. For Lieutenant Surrey Dane, waiting with Dédé, it was the culmination of his airstrip training when, at 0130 hours, they detected the drone of approaching aircraft:

Dead on time we heard an aircraft in the distance and set fire to the small bonfire which was to act as a beacon. The first of the Hudsons appeared against the moonlit sky and as it circled our airstrip, we exchanged a pre-arranged Morse code signal and then turned on the five torches that formed an inverted 'L' marking the 'runway'. Without further delay the Hudson came in to land, switching on its landing lights at the last moment. The plane bounced high into the air after touching down and then disappeared in a cloud of dust. A couple of anxious minutes later it reappeared taxiing to the take-off point . . . very soon half our SAS party were aboard and the Hudson was starting down the 'runway' for take-off. Again it disappeared in a cloud of dust and there were more anxious moments before we saw it climbing away safely. The second Hudson had been circling the airstrip and now came in to land. It made a smoother landing and took on board as many of the remaining members of Bulbasket as it could, leaving a few of us to be picked up on another occasion. I cannot remember how long it took from the time we heard the first Hudson until the second one was airborne and away. It was probably less than twenty minutes. All lights had been on for the shortest possible time and I was fairly confident that the operation had passed unnoticed by our enemies.

The combined capacity of the two Hudsons enabled Dédé, Tonkin and twelve other SAS, Sadoine (still under open arrest), two of his signallers and three of the USAAF flyers to be picked up. Dédé found he was in the Hudson piloted by 161 Squadron's commanding officer, Wing Commander Alan Boxer,[3] and although the trees at the end of 'Bon Bon' had appeared uncomfortably close on take-off, the remainder of the flight was relatively uneventful. Light flak searched for them at one point on the return journey, but did little to trouble the pilots. Before long the English coast was in sight, but low on fuel and warned of foggy conditions back at Tempsford, the Hudsons let down to the south-coast fighter airfield at Tangmere, the forward base of 161 Squadron. All passengers were offloaded and, while the SAS underwent a day's medical tests, Dédé was driven up to SOE headquarters in London for briefing.

# Chapter Thirteen

# Victory

When Dédé arrived in London on 7 August 1944 it was with a formidable record of achievement. He reported that he was now supplying and arming 5,000 men in the Vienne, 3,000 in the Haute-Vienne, 2,000 in Deux-Sèvres and 2,000 in the Vendée. But he was so very tired. The responsibilities of a more active role, and the additional demands coming from the reception of the SAS and Jedburghs, had demanded a great deal from a man who had spent well over a year living in constant danger. A supply drop reception could entail sitting out on a DZ for four to five hours, and coupled with the need for operations during daylight hours, tiredness became a major challenge, making it all too easy to let one's guard slip as a result. Yet even without the dozens of drops made to the Jedburghs and to Major Staunton's now separate 'Salesman' circuit around Limoges, Dédé's debriefing showed a remarkable record of achievement in air operations alone since Southgate's capture at the beginning of May.

**Table 2:** Supply drops, 1944

| 1944 | Operations | Containers | Packages |
|---|---|---|---|
| May | 19 | 296 | 85 |
| June | 50 | 1,137 | 376 |
| July | 36 | 1,077 | 342 |
| August | 20 | 726 | 206 |
| Totals | 125 | 3,236 | 1,009 |

In London, this stood Dédé in great stead in his first personal experience of the combined Free French headquarters (EMFFI) in Bryanston Square, to which F Section of SOE had moved. Dominated by the FFI and the BCRA, the headquarters were not the most welcoming building for a British agent, especially one who had experienced some disagreement in the field with the BCRA's agent, Lieutenant Gros. The ill-founded suspicion that Dédé had been more sympathetic to the communists rather than the Gaullistes could also have been expected to lead to some difficulty, but such was not the case. On the contrary, Dédé seems to have arrived with glowing recommendations from Colonel Chêne and the DMR's in France, and to have won over the Free French to such an extent that they decided he should be decorated immediately. On 12 August, he therefore proudly received, from the hands of General Koenig, the Croix de Guerre avec Palme.

But there was no time to savour the moment, for the very next night Dédé returned to France, eager not to miss the final acts of liberation from an enemy now in full flight. His new mission had been confirmed as a continuation of where he had left off: working with and advising Chêne's headquarters and arming and training the Maquis. To help him, Dédé unofficially turned to a newly made friend.

When the two Hudsons had brought Dédé and the SAS survivors back to England, eight men had temporarily been left behind. These included the recently arrived SAS airstrip specialist, Lieutenant Surrey Dane, supported by two of Sadoine's Phantom signallers. Their job was to wait for a third flight into 'Bon Bon', which came on the night of 9/10 August when Colonel Heflin, commanding officer of the USAAF's 'Carpetbaggers' special forces unit, the 492nd Bombardment (H) Group, brought in a twin-engined C-47 (Dakota) transport aircraft. This delivered another batch of eight men of a total of forty-six from the 3rd French SAS for 'Operation Moses', and then brought back Surrey Dane, his signallers and the remaining five downed American flyers. Dédé, having seen how pleased the young SAS Lieutenant had been to see action at last, guessed that Surrey Dane was frustrated at having been brought out of France so soon. A quick telephone call proved him right, finding Surrey Dane on extended leave (automatically granted to those returning from behind-the-lines operations) at his parents' home, and bored. Might he be interested, instead, in returning to France to help with Dakota air operations and weapons training for the Maquis? In all likelihood, Dédé suggested, the task could even be accomplished within Surrey Dane's leave, avoiding the red tape of seeking temporary release from the SAS. Surrey Dane jumped at the offer and reported for briefing by F Section.

When Dédé and Surrey Dane parachuted back into France on 13 August 1944 they returned just in time to confront what was arguably the greatest danger faced by the region throughout the war – on 15 August Allied landings took place on the south coast of France. Faced with the likelihood of being trapped between the Allied forces advancing from the south and those already to the north, the enemy ordered a general retreat towards Germany for their units in the south and centre of France. Their route, however, was now threatened by thousands of armed maquisards, determined to avenge the long years of occupation of their country. Any sort of movement in less than considerable strength would therefore be suicidal for the enemy. The Maquis were still only lightly armed, but were now more than capable of ambushing and destroying the smaller German units fleeing through their territory.

Altogether, the Germans had gathered together around 80-90,000 men for a fighting retreat across France, including sailors, airmen and a host of support units. Most were on foot with only a few more fortunate riding on bicycles, horse-drawn vehicles or the few motorized vehicles that still had sufficient fuel.

Organized into three groups, it was clear they would only be passing through Dédé's area of operations, but the retreating columns, often several kilometres long, were normally preceded by strong and aggressive advance forces. These were designed to clear the route ahead by neutralizing any Maquis found, and appropriating billets and provisions. This brought unprecedented levels of looting, pillaging and raping, for these enemy forces were not staying in the area, were desperate for supplies and had nothing to lose. Nor did the despised Milice. Scenting defeat in the air, they sank to desperate acts of torture and murder on their prisoners before eventually ridding themselves of their uniforms and attempting to blend into the civilian population. In similar fashion, the Poitiers SD and Gestapo managed to slip out of the city on 22 August.

Among the more unusual enemy troops were Indian soldiers and former members of the Soviet forces. The latter so-called Russians were from the German Army's Ostbattalionen and in reality were largely from the non-Russian southern Soviet Union, of Armenia, Azerbaijan, North Caucasus, Turkestan and the Volga Tartar. Many of these volunteers had regarded the Germans as liberators of their homeland and after volunteering they were trained in Poland and Germany. When based in the West, however, these troops tended to suffer from low morale, since they had enlisted to fight the communists. Consequently, there were instances of mutiny and many desertions to the Maquis.

But of the enemy's forces, none were now to gain more notoriety in the region than the Indian troops, some 2,500 men in total, of the Indische Freiwilligen Legion der Waffen SS, more commonly known as the Legion Freies Indien (the Free Indian Legion). This mechanized infantry unit had recently come under SS control after transferring from the regular Wehrmacht where it had been titled the Panzergrenadier Regiment 950 (Indische). Largely officered by German SS, a majority of these troops were Moslem, with lesser elements of Hindus and Sikhs, the latter appearing particularly incongruous in their German uniforms topped by turbans. They came from prisoner-of-war camps, having been captured in Libya when fighting for the British, but then freed in return for volunteering to serve in the German Army and swearing allegiance to the movement of Germany's (and Japan's) ally, the self-proclaimed Indian National Government of Subhash Chandra Bose.

What was originally the Indisches Infanterie Regiment 950 had first seen defence duties in Holland before deployment to France on coastal-defence duties in the area of Lacanau, covering from the mouth of the Gironde river, opposite Royan, to the Bay of Arcachon near Bordeaux. Ironically, in April 1944, they were inspected there by Generalfeldmarschall Rommel, who had been responsible for their original capture in Libya. Despite Rommel's praise for their efforts on the long expanse of coast that they defended, the Indian troops suffered generally from a lack of respect in the Wehrmacht. Their German officers held a low opinion of the fighting potential of the Indian Legion, exacerbated by a lack of language skills, which made communication difficult between officers and men. This did nothing to help the morale of the Indian troops, especially after D-Day when they realized that they would soon be pursued by the Allies who would inevitably regard them as deserters and traitors.

The Legion remained at Lacanau until over two months after the Allied invasion of Normandy. However, following the Allied breakout from the Normandy bridgehead, and with the growing threat of Allied landings on the Mediterranean coast of France, the Indian unit was at risk of being cut off. On 8 August 1944 the Free Indian Legion, like all the national legions of the German Army, was transferred to the control of the Waffen-SS and became the Indische Freiwilligen Legion der Waffen SS under the command of SS-Oberführer Heinz Bertling. On the 15th, the same day that the Allied landings took place on the French Riviera, the Legion left Lacanau to begin its retreat to Germany. The first part of their journey was by rail, the 1st Battalion of the Legion relocating to Mansle, 80 kilometres south of Poitiers, while the 2nd and 3rd Battalions stopped in Angoulême and Poitiers respectively. After a few days' rest the Legion took to the road once again and news soon reached Dédé and Colonel Chêne's headquarters of the terror that some of the Indian troops were bringing to the towns and villages they passed through, in Bonneuil-Matours, Chauvigny, Antigny and especially Bonnes where heavy drinking led to the reported rape of ten local young women and girls.

On the morning of 23 August a lorry-borne column of the Indian troops was attacked and stopped by the 'Le Chouan' Maquis outside Chauvigny. While the enemy took cover and awaited reinforcements, 'Le Chouan' was joined by elements of the 'Baptiste', 'Cram' and 'Lagardère' groups. Contrary to Colonel Chêne's standing orders which aimed to avoid reprisals against the civilian population, this enlarged Maquis force, encouraged by the latest BBC broadcasts announcing that Paris had been liberated on the 24th, decided to blow up the town's road bridge across the River Vienne and to hold the enemy there. The plan had an inauspicious start when the leader of the 'Baptiste' Maquis, still standing on the bridge, was killed when the explosives went off. The operation then failed completely when, reinforced, the enemy troops crossed by a railway bridge and boats. These enemy troops then occupied Chauvigny for three tense days from 25 to 28 August, taking a hundred hostages and killing five local men. It must have been Dédé who arranged for Allied air attacks on the Indians' positions on the 27th, an action that undoubtedly encouraged them to move on. But it was only the courageous intervention and pleading of their Mayor that saved the inhabitants from disaster, since the German officers had vowed to raze the town. The region breathed a sigh of relief when the Indian regiment finally moved on out of the area at the end of the month.

Elsewhere, the 'Cram' Maquis was in action near Ingrandes in the latter half of August, the 'Adolphe' group was active against the enemy north of Gençay, and the 'Joel' Maquis at Usson-du-Poitou. Many of these actions were against smaller German forces, retreating to the east on their own and without the protection of the three large organized columns. They presented potentially easier pickings for ambushes, but they reacted ferociously and inflicted many losses on both the Maquis and the civilian population.

The 'Renard', 'Bayard' and 'Richard' groups nevertheless fought a pitched battle against a strong enemy force on 28 August south of Civray, drawing in reinforcements from other local Maquis groups. The Germans proved too strong, however, and entered Civray itself as the Maquis fell back in disarray. There had been too few men and weapons, and not enough co-ordination, the latter exacerbated by the fact that both senior commanders, Blondel and Bourdet, were engaged elsewhere. Again, the civilian population and town looked certain to suffer, but were spared when the occupying Germans discovered some of their troops already receiving medical care from a French doctor in the town. By the end of August, the RN151 road, from Poitiers to Châteauroux, was firmly under the control of Maquis groups 'Gilles', 'Lagardère', 'Gaël', 'Le Chouan' and 'Cram'. The 'Thiers' and 'Claudiers' groups covered the D725 road between La Roche-Posay and Preuilly-sur-Claise, and were successful in calling in, via Jedburgh 'Hugh', an Allied air attack on an enemy column retreating along the highway. Allied strafing of retreating German units also took place on 31 August/1 September at Villedieu du-Clain, Smarves, Croutelle, Saint-Julien-l'Ars, Archigny and Pleumartin.

When Dédé returned from England with Lieutenant Surrey Dane he had also been briefed that he would form part of an inter-Allied team that would serve with Colonel Chêne's FFI headquarters. This team was created by the addition of another British officer, Lieutenant Wallace (real name Ivan Justin Woolf) who had landed by Dakota at Le Blanc airfield on 26 August and joined up with Dédé at the FFI's headquarters, then at Jouhet, on the 29th. He was joined by two American lieutenants, Blackwell and Macarthy, of the Office of Strategic Services (OSS) who parachuted in. All the new arrivals were answerable to Dédé, Wallace helped Surrey Dane with Dakota and Hudson landing operations (all of which passed off well) and the Americans specialized in weapons training with the Maquis groups.

The last Germans left Poitiers on the evening of 4 September 1944 and the next morning the Maquis entered the city in triumph, led by Colonel Chêne with Dédé at his side. There was an unseasonable downpour as they arrived at the Hôtel de Ville (city hall) where they met Monsieur Schuhler, the newly-appointed Commissaire de la République. They sang the Marseillaise national anthem and gave orders for the French flag to be raised again at last over the city. While hundreds waited patiently outside beneath a sea of umbrellas, it took an embarrassing twenty minutes for a Tricolore to be found.

Next stop was the Préfecture, to bring to an end the administration of the Préfet of the Vichy regime. He was waiting in full uniform and wearing all his medals (he was a former naval officer) and offered champagne. But the crowd had been shouting their angry disapproval of this official, so the champagne was refused and the Préfet, stripped of his authority, was confined to his apartment. In a moment of tragic farce during the visit, the cook of the Préfecture was killed when he accidentally shot himself while inspecting a Sten sub-machine gun.

Dédé and his group of Surrey Dane, Wallace, Blackwell, Macarthy and the Hirsch brothers now worked from the Hôtel de Ville as their headquarters and on Sunday, 10 September 1944 they attended the extensive liberation celebrations in front of the building. Standing behind a microphone, and having insisted on Dédé being at his shoulder, Colonel Chêne addressed the huge crowd. He described how the Maquis and FFI had played their part in the struggle for liberation, but he also made sure that Dédé's own part, and the contribution of Britain, were not overlooked. As Chêne finished, Colonel Blondel gave the command for a march past of contingents from the Maquis groups that had come under Chêne's command. It was a memorable sight. The proud maquisards, bearing their unit flags, swung past with heads held high, group after group. Many years later Colonel Chêne described it thus: 'There was a particular expression on every face. I never, in the course of my career, saw an expression like it. It was one of confidence and pride. Never have I felt such brotherhood. I was proud to have commanded these men.'

According to official governmental figures, the Vienne *département* had only some 3,300 maquisards in June 1944, but there were 11,500 registered at the time of liberation only three months later; 3,000 of these marched through Poitiers that day and Dédé calculated that he had directly helped arm at least that many. The celebrations were perhaps Dédé's finest moment. Certainly, it remained Pierre Hirsch's most treasured memory of Dédé, taking his rightful place alongside Colonel Chêne and suffering little of the animosity or suspicion that many SOE agents were to face elsewhere from the new French authorities. On the one hand, General Koenig had just agreed to grant an equivalent rank in the French Army to those French who had received British Army commissions through SOE. But on the other, General de Gaulle had given orders that those declining the offer, and all non-French F Section agents, should leave France as soon as possible. Many received just forty-eight hours' notice, but for Dédé the order came only via a recall message from London, rather than from the local civil or military authorities. Colonel Chêne would surely never have approved such a move in Poitiers, paying tribute instead to Dédé's 'great impartiality and great efficiency'. There was, however, an embarrassing moment during a speech at a celebratory dinner after the parades when the Commissaire de la République, Monsieur Schuhler, praised General de Gaulle, President Roosevelt and Comrade Stalin, but overlooked King George VI of England and Prime Minister Churchill. Stony-faced, but in a dignified manner and without a word, Dédé rose and left the room.

But despite the unswerving support and loyalty of the local FFI, Dédé nevertheless had to follow the order he had received from England. Consequently, on 14 September he quietly packed his few belongings and bade farewell to Chêne, Olivet, Blondel and his other close brothers-in-arms. Accompanied by Lieutenant Surrey Dane, he climbed aboard an aircraft at Le Blanc airfield and a few hours later he was back in England.[1]

Shortly after his return, Dédé was required to write a final report for Colonel Buckmaster, though he was once again reticent about his own activities and clearly did not wish to go into any great detail:

I am writing the following to wind up my activities in France. Since the 13th August, when I was parachuted for the second and last time, nothing much happened except for the liberation of the region assigned to me, by men who were armed by our section only, and required no help from any other organisation.

He acknowledged that the two British lieutenants, Surrey Dane and Wallace, had been of great help, being sure that steps would already have been taken to reward them. In respect of the three French 'officers', Jacques and Pierre Hirsch and Jacques Dufour, who had helped him, he stressed that they:

> have done splendidly, and deserve an award of some kind. I cannot speak too highly of them; they have been very sincere patriots from the beginning, and understood that France would only be saved if Frenchmen were willing to help their allies in helping them.

He also went on to praise the two Americans sent to him in August, Lieutenants Blackwell and Macarthy of the OSS, saying:

> These officers are of a very high standard, and deserve promotion and decoration. If they had been sent to me earlier on I would have entrusted them with any task whatsoever, so much confidence had I in them. May I suggest that a strong recommendation be made about them to their C.O.

In respect of the ordinary, but courageous, people of France he singled out several who had helped him before D-day, and who he considered to be worthy of some form of compensation, as well as an award:

> Mlle. GUILLON, rue de la République, CHÂTEAUROUX.

> MARC's parents (of ROBERT L'HOSPITALIER), rue de Rimard, MONTLUÇON, who have suffered through us since they sheltered our W/Ts; and it was at their house that HECTOR and AIMÉ were arrested.

> M. & Mme. NERAUD and their daughter Colette, 37 rue Blatin, CLERMONT-FERRAND, who were arrested by the Gestapo because of us. The daughter we used as courier quite often.

> Mlle. Pillar ALVAREZ, 14 rue Brauhauban, TARBES, known as IRENE to our service.

> The farmer at AUCH, whose address you have and who operated BOOT (Eureka Beacon).

> ARTHUR's and POPAUL's parents.

> M. CHANTRAINE, rue Diderot, CHÂTEAUROUX, who was our main helper in this region.

> Mme. de ST. LAUDY, 12 rue Ingres, TOULOUSE.

Dédé also recorded those who did not deserve any financial recompense, starting with Madame Lebas, his landlady at 24 rue de la Gare in Châteauroux. Though

154

noting she had been arrested by the Germans when the enemy had been looking for him after Southgate's arrest, Dédé felt she deserved no praise, being convinced that she would have thrown him out had she known the truth. Among other undeserving causes he also mentioned Schwatschko's helpers, many of whom claimed to be owed money. He had not agreed to pay these people since he was aware that Schwatschko used to promise money to almost everyone with whom he was on good terms. Dédé had not forgotten that it was one of Schwatschko's helpers who had accused him of having stolen the million francs that had been meant for an agent of the British SIS. As Dédé now took care to report, he had obtained agreement from Buckmaster by radio and had simply used the money for Resistance work.

# Chapter Fourteen

# Britain's Gratitude

In addition to Dédé's report, Colonel Buckmaster received even more tangible evidence of the 'Shipwright' circuit's achievements when, on 20 September, Jacques Hirsch arrived in London, followed by Pierre on the 23rd, and shortly after by Jeanne and her parents who were flown out of France by Hudson. But even as Dédé welcomed his friends during their brief stay in England, SOE headquarters were considering what further use he might serve. On 20 September 1944, Colonel Buckmaster had written to Gubbins, head of SOE, to report that he had put Dédé forward 'for work in the Far East for which his qualifications render him particularly suitable. Alternatively, if this does not materialise he would like to be considered for work in Germany, but he does not speak German.' Buckmaster concluded: 'I have a great admiration for this young man who has every time come up to scratch when a particularly tricky job had to be done.'

With France liberated,[1] SOE's F Section and Jedburgh Section had returned from EMFFI in Bryanston Square to SOE headquarters at Baker Street, and it was there that the returning SOE agents and British Jedburgh team members were given the choice of returning to their units or joining SOE's Force 136. This was the 'work in the Far East' to which Buckmaster referred, involving behind-the-lines operations by what were still termed Jedburgh teams, against the Japanese in South-East Asia. To Dédé, already finding it difficult to settle to the relevant peace and quiet in England, this sounded appealing. A note on his SOE file, signed by Buckmaster, suggests that Dédé had struggled more than most to make the transition back to peace, and, worryingly, seemed in need of living fast and dangerously. This addiction to danger must therefore have been the motivating force when, after again volunteering, Dédé had a short interview with Force 136's recruiters and a final F Section debriefing on 14 November 1944 by Major Angelo.[2] Formally transferred from F Section the next day, Dédé sailed for India on the 19th, carrying orders for further service in the Far East as a Jedburgh.

His route was via Cairo and it was agreed that once in Egypt he could take a few weeks leave with authorization to fly on to Mauritius. The latter arrangement was helped by the fact that Dédé's brother Colo had been posted back to Mauritius from Britain, and was based at the new RAF airfield at Plaisance. It therefore proved a simple matter for Dédé to hitch a ride in one of the regular

RAF Dakota flights that had just commenced to his home island. Exactly a month after leaving a Britain still suffering from German air raids and V weapon attacks, Dédé found himself sitting down at a dinner thrown in his honour by the Club de Curepipe and Automobile Club of Mauritius. Though feted by others, however, Dédé was soon brought back to reality when he went for lunch in the family home, dressed in his British officer's uniform. Aghast at the sight, Old René immediately banished his son, vowing that he would not entertain that uniform at his table. The Maingard ancestors would undoubtedly have approved of the censure.

Once home, Dédé took some time to overcome his stretched nerves. He discussed a few aspects of his wartime activities with his parents, but his mother and father did not mention them to anyone else. His parents had received regular telegrams from the War Office in London, simply stating 'Maingard well' and while they had guessed that he might be in France, they had never known it for certain until his return. Even when Colo was in England, he had no idea what Dédé was doing.

Regarding his longer-term future, Dédé had doubts whether he could continue his accountancy studies in England, but was inclined to return permanently to Mauritius as soon as possible and to work with Rogers and Co. Véronique, the 'baby' of the family, was the only sibling still at home during Dédé's leave. Only twelve years old, she was nevertheless conscious of the nervous tension in her brother and noticed how uneasy he was unless seated with his back to a wall, even in the family home. Frequently preferring his own company, he was initially reluctant to take up his rifle again, but his father eventually persuaded him to do so and Dédé disappeared by himself into the island's interior for several days on a hunting trip, clearly in need of time and space to clear his mind. It therefore came as no surprise when he decided he could not continue to the Far East as a Jedburgh.

Instead, Dédé cabled London on 27 December 1944, asking SOE to withdraw his commitment to a posting to India, but requesting any further work with Colonel Buckmaster. Back in Baker Street a flurry of signals and correspondence exercised SOE's senior officers and administrators. Eventually, on 13 January 1945, an unnamed SOE officer wrote on Dédé's personal file: 'I see no point in sending this officer to India to become a problem for Force 136', also noting that SOE did not have the authority to demobilize army officers. If there was no more SOE work for Dédé, then the British Army would have to decide on his future, SOE's file note concluding: 'if the Army send him to India, that will not be our affair.'

As a result, on 22 January 1945, a coded telegram marked 'Secret' was sent in reply to Dédé. Expressing regret that there was no further work available with Colonel Buckmaster, the message nevertheless ordered Dédé to return to England, promising that alternative work would be sought within SOE, but that if nothing were found he would be posted back to the British Army. This did not sound encouraging, but in the face of a formal order of recall, Dédé had no alternative but to bid farewell to family and friends and begin the long, tedious journey back to England. He only reached London in mid-March 1945 where,

157

still officially attached to ME 80 (India), he soon appreciated that he posed a problem for SOE's planners.

Their first offer was for Dédé to work in Germany in civilian clothes for, despite a lack of German language skills that would have made him unsuitable for any clandestine role, in March 1945 SOE had been involved in the decision to form the Special Allied Airborne Reconnaissance Force (SAARF). This would have consisted of 120 teams, organized similarly to the Jedburghs, which would have been dropped into Germany to protect Allied prisoners of war and other foreigners felt to be at risk from extermination by the Nazis as the Third Reich finally collapsed. But the job didn't appeal to Dédé. Seeing Pearl briefly at a party, he made no mention of his abortive trip to serve in the Far East, but confided that he wished to return to Mauritius as soon as possible with the intention of joining Rogers and Co., and playing a part in bringing about diversification of the island's economy, particularly through tourism. He was already formulating a vision that was to shape the rest of his life, a vision of a series of first-class hotels for the island, served by the air transport that was now possible due to the opening of an aerodrome at Plaisance.

To this end, on 27 March 1945, he visited Baker Street for a heart-to-heart talk with Vera Atkins who proved sympathetic to his misgivings about the future. Miss Atkins wrote to Colonel Buckmaster that same day,[3] but her appeal came too late to spare Dédé a 'refresher course' and from 1 April 1945, Dédé was posted to STS 41 at Gumley Hall near Market Harborough in Leicestershire, yet another of SOE's imposing country houses. The six-week course of special forces training was in preparation for the SAARF missions, and on completion, his appraisal by the commandant on 19 May 1945 read: 'A very intelligent type who has had a fair amount of operational experience which he has put to good use here. He is very quick to grasp new ideas, and has shown great keenness throughout. His work has been very satisfactory.'

But all this was now academic for, while Dédé was at Gumley Hall, the war in Europe had ended with the Germans' unconditional surrender on 6 May, making the SAARF teams redundant. In late May he therefore made a special declaration and formal application for permission to relinquish his commission. In view of the fact that Dédé had volunteered for such dangerous work, and had achieved so much, there was little that the British authorities could do. He was therefore officially sworn out from SOE, 'relegated to unemployment' with effect from 2 June 1945 and ceased to be 'specially employed'.

As events would have it, Dédé's departure from SOE proved to be only just ahead of the organization's demise. In delivering the news of SOE's imminent disbandment, Colonel Buckmaster wrote to Dédé in June 1945 to give his home address and to encourage participation in maintaining contact with former colleagues, an aim which was ultimately to lead to the founding of the Special Forces Club in London, and the Amicale Buckmaster network of former SOE agents, Resistance and FFI fighters across France. Buckmaster wrote:

> though we shall be wearing civilian clothes, and shall perhaps be dotted about all over the globe, the spirit of F Section, forged in four years of hard

common endeavour, will never be extinguished. We want to see you often, we want to have your news, and we want to feel again, from time to time, that lively excitement with which we awaited the return of a Lysander, or the thrill of pride and joy when we deciphered a perhaps mutilated telegram, announcing yet another masterstroke!

and he concluded: 'how very proud I am to have been associated with you in the wonderful work you have done, and in the astonishing friendship which exists among us all'.

There now remained only the issue of how Dédé's service to Britain was to be adequately recognized – on 21 June 1945 it was formally announced that he was to receive the Distinguished Service Order (DSO) military decoration from King George VI.[4] On 26 June 1945 Colonel Buckmaster wrote with his 'heartiest congratulations' for the 'excellent work which you carried out in France'.

Dédé was thrilled, writing home to his father with the news of his own award and of a decoration for his friend and fellow Mauritian SOE agent, Marcel Rousset. Under the code name 'Leopold', Rousset had parachuted into the Sarthe region of France in March 1943, but was arrested the same autumn in Paris. A daring escape from the Germans, and an eventual safe return to England after fighting alongside the Resistance during the liberation of Paris, had brought him a well-deserved Military Cross (MC). The same letter home signalled Dédé's taking up work again with Falk, Keeping in the City for three months only from the end of June.

On 16 October 1945, resplendent for one last time in his British Army uniform, Dédé was personally invested with his DSO by King George VI in a ceremony at Buckingham Palace, and finally, on 20 December 1945, Major Maingard was officially demobilized from the British Army. In addition to the DSO, he also received the 1939–1945 Star and the France and Germany Star, and as he handed in his uniform, Dédé at last put to rest the spirits of those of his ancestors who had fought the British over hundreds of years.

# Chapter Fifteen

# New Horizons

Post-war Mauritius, as Dédé was quick to realize upon his return in early 1946, was ripe for development. The technological advances that the recent conflict had brought were now the tools with which far-sighted businessmen could further their ambitions. Hitherto, Mauritius had been one of the most isolated places in the world, being some 855 kilometres off the east coast of Madagascar and 1,800 kilometres from mainland Africa. But the war had involved hundreds of thousands of men and women traversing the globe. Dédé was certain that people would have the desire to see more of the world in peacetime as well and that the advent of long-range passenger aircraft would enable them to do so. He was determined that many of them would go to Mauritius.

Thankfully, the island had remained largely undisturbed by the war. On several occasions Japanese or German submarines and surface ships had prowled the waters around the island and had managed to sink a few merchant ships. And at the height of Japanese power in 1942, the British authorities in Mauritius seriously feared a Japanese invasion of either Madagascar or Mauritius, but this threat had receded after the Japanese defeat at Midway in June 1942. The British used Port-Louis and Grand Port as naval bases, as well as building an airfield at Plaisance, a seaplane facility at Baie du Tombeau and a large telecommunications station at Vacoas. Moreover, despite its small size and population, Mauritius had contributed loyally to the Allied war effort and many volunteers had served overseas, not least the disproportionate number of Mauritians who, like Dédé, had joined SOE. There were thus many young people who were returning home with wider horizons and confidence in their own abilities. Dédé, and his brother Colo, were two such men.

The Rogers company, where both Dédé's father and Colo (since 1942) were now partners, had faced hard financial times during the war, but had managed to survive the labour unrest that had plagued the island's sugar cane industry. After the death of Eric Rogers in 1946, new partners joined and were receptive to the ideas of the young Maingard brothers, whose overseas experiences had opened their eyes regarding the possibility of developing the Rogers business in the fields of shipping, tourism and aviation. The latter was particularly attractive – the RAF aerodrome at Plaisance had been established in November 1944 and its long, hard runways made it suitable for development as a civil airport. The brothers had also forged good contacts in Britain and France and the first of these paid off when Rogers secured the contract to represent RLAF (Réseau des Lignes Aériennes Françaises), which later became Air France. RLAF had begun operations to Mauritius from Madagascar and Réunion in February 1945 and their first flight from Paris, via Algiers, arrived at Plaisance in October of the same year, after a total journey time of six days.

Despite having served as a pilot in the war, Colo's main interest was shipping rather than aviation, while Dédé, who did not particularly like flying, was nevertheless enthused by the business opportunities fostered by air travel. Consequently, when Rogers and Co. became a limited company in March 1948, and Dédé became a major shareholder in the firm, he was made responsible for setting up an aviation department. He threw himself energetically into the task, opening an agency office in Port-Louis and setting up a ground-handling service at Plaisance airport where, in addition to the Air France contract,[1] he then secured the contract to act as agents for the British national airline, BOAC. This was soon followed by similar arrangements for South African Airways and the Australian Airline, QANTAS. With the company's business stability secured, Dédé was ready to develop the next stage of his vision.

The first election win of the island's Labour Party also took place in 1948, a success seen as ominous to some of the old ruling classes of French and British backgrounds. Dédé was nevertheless far-sighted enough to see that the Labour Party could be a positive force for the future of Mauritius, and he therefore shrewdly stayed clear of expressing any political allegiances. In similar fashion to how both the Gaullistes and communists in the Resistance had recognized him as a true friend of France, so too did the politicians of Mauritius realize that his heart was firmly committed to the island and its development for the common good, as well as for his own profit as a businessman.

Yet as Dédé developed his new career, he remained tight-lipped about his SOE service, not even discussing their respective operations with Jean Larcher. His parents learned a little, but there was only one other person who heard some of the details. Jacqueline Raffray had become engaged to Dédé in 1947, but had then joined her parents in England when her father, Sir Philippe Raffray, became the London representative of the Mauritian Sugar Syndicate in the same year. Her sister, Françoise, had already married Colo, Dédé's brother, in London a couple of years earlier and the expectation was that Dédé should now cement the family alliance. Consequently, in the late summer of 1949, he left Mauritius and travelled to Europe to tour his wartime haunts in France. The local population and his former comrades in arms were overjoyed to welcome him back and the local press made much of his brief visit to the Vienne in September. From France he continued on to London and on 8 October 1949, Dédé married Jacqueline Raffray at Westminster Cathedral.

Impatient to continue with the rapidly expanding business of Rogers and

Co., Dédé lost little time in returning to Mauritius with his bride. As the company continued to diversify, Dédé's sights were now firmly set on developing a tourism industry for Mauritius. With expansion of the airport, and the airlines using it, the means were now available to bring holidaymakers to the island, and Dédé was determined that they would have luxury accommodation when they arrived. In 1952 a large colonial house in Curepipe was transformed into Le Park Hotel to cater for transit passengers and airline crews, QANTAS being the first users as they had to base a crew permanently in Mauritius for their Australia to South Africa route. An existing travel agency, the Mauritius Travel and Tourist Bureau (MTTB), was taken over to promote and market Mauritian holidays, and another subsidiary, the Mautourco company, was developed to meet, greet and transport the crews and passengers, and to provide a car hire service. Le Park was the first investment of Dédé and Rogers in the hotel industry, and was followed in 1954 by Dédé's construction of a restaurant and a small complex of family holiday bungalows on the south-west coast. This he called Le Morne Plage, in recognition of the good fortune he'd had by being at Montluçon Plage on 1 May 1944, thereby avoiding arrest by the Gestapo.

In addition to these new accommodation developments, Rogers diversified widely. In 1955 the M/V *Mauritius* was launched, the start of a range of shipping activities through a number of companies, most importantly the Mauritius Steam Navigation Company. The same year, Rogers became the local partner of Cementia, a Swiss company, in the building of a cement bulk terminal in Port-Louis and then forged a partnership with United Molasses of the UK in Mauritius Molasses Ltd (now a subsidiary of the Tate & Lyle international conglomerate), building the bulk installations for the export of molasses.

All this brought more financial rewards, but in December 1956 a link with the past was severed when Dédé's father, Old René, died. Three years later more change came when the first open elections were won in 1959 by Dr Seewoosagur Ramgoolam's Labour Party and in 1968 Mauritius became an independent country within the Commonwealth of Nations.[2] With Queen Elizabeth II as Head of State (represented in Mauritius by a Governor General) and Sir Seewoosagur Ramgoolam (knighted in 1965) as the first Prime Minister, a new era awaited both Mauritius and Dédé.

Dédé's own part in the island's political changes was peripheral, though he was an admirer of Ramgoolam's philosophy of racial and religious tolerance, and social harmony. Yet when the notion of independence had begun to gain ground at the start of the decade, Dédé was troubled, feeling that the island did not yet have the strength to go it alone and that it still needed the guiding hand of Britain. Nevertheless, and despite his upbringing in a wealthy European family, Dédé became a trusted friend of the new Prime Minister, cementing a friendship that was to help enormously as he concentrated on expanding his business interests. He was now a leading member of the Board of Rogers and Co., the Chairmanship of which was held by Colo, while Dédé was Chairman of New Mauritius Hotels (NMH) founded in 1964, the Mauritius Travel and Tourism Bureau and Mautourco.[3]

Hotels and tourism were Dédé's abiding business passion above all else, but he was astute enough to recognize that this industry would be dependent upon the airlines, and he wanted more control over this critical supply line. At the same time, the Prime Minister of Mauritius recognized that there could be no better symbol of the island's new nationhood than an independent national airline, formed to ensure adequate passenger flight availability to meet the country's growing capacity for tourism. Ramgoolam therefore discussed the matter with Dédé and the latter was entrusted with the task of establishing the new airline. There was no public finance available to finance the venture, but Ramgoolam was confident that Dédé would have the right business contacts to broker a deal. Prior to independence, he had found no difficulty in remaining close to the ruling British authorities, undoubtedly helped by what little was known of his wartime SOE record. By the 1960s Dédé had been leaning somewhat more towards Air France, rather than BOAC and British interests in Mauritius, but in looking for partners and investment for his new airline, Dédé typically took a diplomatic line and began negotiations with both his old trading partners. Air France, BOAC and the government of Mauritius each took a 27.5 per cent stake in the new company, while Rogers and Co. held the remaining 17.5 per cent. Together they founded Air Mauritius Ltd in June 1967 and at the first Board meeting held in the company's Port-Louis headquarters, Dédé was appointed Chairman. As the symbol of Air Mauritius, the Phaeton, the straw-tailed tropical bird native to Mauritius and much admired for its graceful flight, was chosen. On 5 December 1967, the designation 'MK' was allocated to the airline by the International Air Transport Association (IATA) and operations, as a ground handling company only, started in May 1968, the company being initially managed by Rogers before it set up its own management structure.

Thanks to his commitment to this high-profile example of independent nationhood, and his developing close personal friendship with Sir Seewoosagur Ramgoolam, Dédé enjoyed a good relationship with the Mauritian government. Although a socialist, the Prime Minister was quick to appreciate that skilful and well-connected leaders of industry such as Dédé were essential to the future of the island. It was known and appreciated that Dédé kept all his wealth, and therefore his commitment to the future, on the island. It was perhaps an echo of his wartime skill of winning the confidence of the right and the left in the Resistance. In the same way that the wartime French had been left in no doubt as to Dédé's love for their country, so now did Ramgoolam and his government realize that their new airline's chief was first and foremost a Mauritian, his loyalties then extending to France and to Britain, in that order. But while Britain came third in his affections, the British government were no less appreciative of Dédé the businessman than they had been of his performance as a wartime secret agent. For on 30 December 1969 (though with as much regard for Dédé's correct full name as SOE had once displayed), the *London Gazette* reported the award of a CBE:

> The Queen has been graciously pleased, on the advice of Her Majesty's Mauritius Ministers, to give orders for the following appointments.
>
> Ordinary Commander of the Civil Division of the Most Excellent Order of the British Empire:
>
> Amedee Hugnin MAINGARD DE VILLE ES OFFRANS DSO
>
> For services to tourism and the hotel industry.

Former friends and colleagues of Dédé agree over his character traits in these years. As an individual, Dédé retained the intelligence, strong will and charismatic qualities of a born leader that had served him well throughout the war. His personal charm and aristocratic manners were always supported by a smart dress code that further emphasized his natural authority. But at the same time he was a modest man, at ease with all levels of society. It was noted that he would queue with everyone else for his flight at Plaisance airport, and he had a welcome habit of calling in to see his staff at the airport when a delayed flight kept them on duty to an ungodly hour. Yet he was not always easy to fathom. There was a contradiction in his character that made him value other opinions, yet give every indication and reaction to suggest he did not welcome an opposing point of view. One example was when a group of counter staff created a fuss over what they considered to be low pay. Dédé was less than sympathetic and left them in no doubt that he was the boss, and that he did not tolerate dissension. Some thought him too autocratic, perhaps a little crazy, being still affected by the war. There were stories that he still held a deep-seated revulsion for Germans and that he could not stand to hear New Year fireworks. Yet there were also descriptions of Dédé's acute sense of humour and his reputation as a leg puller.

Many remember him for his affection and generosity, both in spirit and material help, normally given privately and discreetly. On one occasion, a local Catholic priest, of modest means, was seen to have a new Mini, but it was only when teased about the supposed riches of his church that he revealed the car to be a gift from Dédé.

As a businessman he was sharp, inventive and, above all, far-sighted. His word was known to be his bond, earning him trust and respect, especially in financial circles. But the generous side to his character could cloud recognition of the fact that several of his inner business circle of colleagues and friends did not possess Dédé's ability to plan strategically and long term. The results were occasionally disappointing, for example when supposedly loyal suppliers were found to be taking advantage of Dédé's support and generosity. If the best deal were not always obtained, Dédé displayed the ruthless streak that had been necessary during the

164

war. Any business partner identified as having been disloyal was immediately cut out of the loop – there was no forgiveness, no way back. This approach was the same for any friend who betrayed his trust. Always self-controlled and loath to display any strong emotions outwardly, Dédé would also adopt the tactic of completely ignoring the person from then on.

Dédé lived for his work, leaving only limited time for his family which now included Jan, born in 1950, Didier in 1951, and Véronique in 1953. Yet he still somehow managed to maintain a wide range of social activity. He had been a founding member of the Rotary Club of Port-Louis in 1964 and later became a director of the organization. He was an avid bridge player and was passionate about golf. At weekends he was happiest in the company of his close male friends, preferably at his hunting lodge when the season permitted. Yet despite such friendships, Dédé remained reticent about his war, as if a door on his former life had been firmly closed when he returned to Mauritius in 1945. Rarely did he talk of his experiences although, as modest as ever, Dédé once commented that he would not have achieved anything during the crucial months of the war had he not been helped so much by Jacques Hirsch. He also once confided that his insistence on being early for appointments and meetings was a legacy of his wartime exploits, explaining that lives had then depended on his never being late.

On another occasion, Dédé attended a dinner at the home of the first French Ambassador to Mauritius, Raphaël Touze. During the conversation, Touze mentioned that he came from Poitiers where he had heard many admiring stories of a Mauritian, code-named 'Sam', who had served as a British agent in the area during the war. Expressing the wish that he might one day find this 'Sam' in Mauritius, Touze was delighted at the end of the evening to be quietly told by Dédé that he was the former agent. Otherwise, 'Sam' was no more, and it was normally only an occasional letter that resurrected echoes of the past. A number of wartime comrades, chief among them Pearl and Henri Cornioley, kept in touch and met on Dédé's occasional business trips to Paris and London. Pearl, Henri and their daughter spent almost a month in Mauritius in 1974 as Dédé's guests, and Colonel Buckmaster also visited.

But mostly, Dédé had little time to look back. He had added to Le Park in 1962 with the opening of purpose-built tourist hotels at Le Morne Plage and at Le Chaland in the south-east of the island. One of Dédé's happiest moments was when he opened the hotel at Le Morne where it became his regular habit to stop each Thursday, during his hotel visits, to walk through the grounds, relaxing and thinking, or to play a round of golf there. This was also the spot where the Maingards kept one of the original modest beach bungalows for another forty years. With its corrugated-iron roof and modest construction it was an incongruous sight among the modern luxury development until it was eventually demolished.

The late 1960s and early 1970s saw rapid development for Rogers and Co., consolidating its shipping activities but also becoming a diversified conglomerate. It invested in the import, storage and distribution of cement on the local market as well as in the export of molasses. Three local companies, Scott and Co., Roger Fayd'herbe and J.M. Goupille were taken over and New Mauritius Hotels, in particular, was at the forefront of expansion. But in 1971, social and industrial unrest resulted in a state of emergency and the following year saw the start of an economic recession. New Mauritius Hotels was forced to downsize its workforce and for it and the MTTB the situation became financially precarious. Added to this came a crisis over control of Rogers and Co.

In 1969 the company had reached its limit of investment that would enable further expansion – there had been a considerable call on start-up capital and revenue income took time to build. On at least four occasions when the situation looked desperate Dédé had tendered his written resignation from the Board to Colo, but it was always refused. Without an injection of capital, however, Rogers and Co. was doomed to stagnate when there were so many business opportunities still beckoning. Against Dédé's better judgement and his clearly stated fears for the future, a majority of the Board voted to accept an offer from the Lonrho international company to buy a 51 per cent controlling share in Rogers, in return for investment funding being made available. The deal included an agreement that the Rogers Board could continue largely unchanged, and despite Dédé's concerns, all initially appeared well. Rogers weathered the economic doldrums, and expansion and development of the company continued, thanks to the additional investment from Lonrho. But as Rogers's fortunes soared, the company's value rose dramatically and Lonrho chose to cash in on their investment. In 1972 they informed Rogers that they had decided to sell their controlling 51 per cent share and though they had a willing buyer, Rogers were offered first option of buying it back. But the cost was now considerably in excess of what Lonrho had paid for it, the value of the company having trebled. His worst fears realized, Dédé nevertheless argued passionately that the Board should find the money to buy the company back, even at the inflated price. The alternative was unthinkable, that Lonrho would sell out to just anyone and control would be lost forever. It was the lowest point in Dédé's business career, but the rescue was achieved, involving restructuring and merger with and investment by several Mauritius-based companies who purchased the Rogers shares that had belonged to Lonrho. These developments brought autonomy, money and new ideas into Rogers, and helped it to continue its expansion, though the same year also brought a frustrating end to what was potentially the biggest business venture conceived by Dédé.

This was a huge project, christened 'Projet Suroît', *suroît* meaning south-west in old French. Its location was to be a sizeable expanse of the coast leading from Black River to Le Morne, where Dédé planned a development that was to include hotels, residential houses and a golf course. He bought a sugar estate called Bel Ombre which included Chamarel in the interior and Case Noyale along the coast, and a beautiful property a few kilometres north, called Les Salines Koenig. It would have been Dédé's masterpiece, but the scale of the project, together with the need for road diversion, and even the relocation of an entire village, called for considerable foreign investment, which the government would not allow on a point of political principle. Though Dédé went so far as to bang his fist on the Prime Minister's desk, Ramgoolam would not be swayed and the scheme was shelved.

In compensation, Rogers's freshly secured stability was also the platform for

166

Dédé to fulfil another of his greatest ambitions, for Air Mauritius passenger flights had at last commenced on 13 September 1972. A humble six-seater, twin-engined Piper Navajo was leased from Air Madagascar (it wore a Madagascar registration, but was painted in Air Mauritius livery) to offer scheduled flights to the island of Rodrigues, just over 350 nautical miles away.

While almost all Dédé's energies were taken up with business challenges in the early 1970s, a dramatic incident in 1971 nevertheless meant that he had to relive some of his wartime exploits. That year a reunion was held in Paris of former *résistants* from France, Holland and Belgium. Among those who attended was Albert Dupont, who had served alongside Dédé at Colonel Chêne's headquarters and had been temporarily attached to the SAS 'Bulbasket' team as an interpreter. At the reception Dupont found himself seated next to a veteran of the Belgian Resistance. On hearing that Dupont had operated in the Vienne region, the Belgian told him of a man in a mental home in Belgium who also claimed to have fought in the Vienne. At some point this individual had been badly wounded during the war and had ended up in the psychiatric institute at Leuze, suffering from total amnesia for over twenty years or so. Over the last four years he had slowly started to recover some memory and about two years before he had started calling himself 'Captain Tonkin' and claimed that he had operated with the Resistance in the Vienne.

Dupont was astounded. He had heard little of the fate of the 'Bulbasket' team since the war, yet he clearly recalled Tonkin. Pressing the Belgian for more details, Dupont was shocked to hear that 'Tonkin' claimed the SAS had been betrayed, repeating again and again that 'it was the radio operator who betrayed the group to the Germans.' This was dramatic news for Dupont and the other former *résistants* of the Vienne, as it was thought that the accusation was directed at Pierre Hirsch, hitherto accepted to have served Dédé loyally and having been decorated for doing so. Hirsch, now a respected figure in France, suddenly found himself under the gravest suspicion of having been a double agent of the Germans. The matter required urgent resolution.

As a first step Albert Dupont had written to the patient in Leuze and discovered that he was registered under the name of Octave Dupont. In an exchange of correspondence, there could be no doubt that 'Tonkin', or Octave Dupont, had definitely been involved with 'Bulbasket', possessing as he did detailed knowledge of many aspects of the operation.

Determined to pursue the matter, Albert Dupont travelled to Belgium. He found a wreck of a man whom he could not identify for certain after the passage of so many years, but they talked of incidents that only a participant could have known. 'Tonkin' revealed that his true nationality was Belgian and that he had never uttered a word in French during the war for security reasons because of his relatives in Belgium. Having only met the SAS officer for a few days in 1944, Albert Dupont was prepared to believe that the patient was indeed John Tonkin. Returning to France, Dupont reported the matter to the Resistance veterans' headquarters in Paris who in turn contacted Colonel Maurice Buckmaster in England. Buckmaster quickly wrote to Mauritius, where Dédé was immediately suspicious and concerned. The physical description and a photograph of 'Tonkin' supplied via Albert Dupont did not match Dédé's recollection of the young SAS officer at all; the height and hair colour were both wrong. Above all, Dédé would never, even for a moment, doubt the loyalty of Pierre Hirsch.

While controversy continued to rage in France, Colonel Buckmaster was using his extensive network of contacts to try to get to the bottom of the affair. Using Foreign Office and MI6 sources, he soon confirmed Dédé's belief that the real John Tonkin did not match the description of the mental patient discovered by Albert Dupont. Indeed, Tonkin was known to have been a mining engineer in northern Australia from 1953 to 1961 and his last known address was in Melbourne. This information was relayed back to Albert Dupont who, by co-incidence, had a brother in Melbourne whom he therefore telephoned without delay. Yves Dupont rang the first J.E. Tonkin he could find in the telephone directory and reached John Tonkin's wife, Heather. Initially cautious, Heather rang her husband at work.

John Tonkin lost no time in calling Albert Dupont in France, his initial hope being that the hospital patient might be one of three missing SAS troopers from 'Bulbasket', Ogg, Pascoe or Williams, whose bodies had never been found. He also corresponded with Dédé, but it seemed there was only one way to find out for certain the identity of the mystery patient. Accompanied by his wife, Tonkin set out for England.

On arrival he made contact with the SAS Regiment who had been conducting their own enquiries and, before continuing on to Belgium, Tonkin had discovered the identity of the man in Leuze. David Dane,[4] the former SAS Lieutenant who had worked so well alongside Dédé, had been sent the photograph taken by Albert Dupont of the patient. Despite a drastic change in facial features, the patient was recognized by Dane as Captain Sadoine, commander of the Phantom signals team attached to 'Bulbasket' and the man whom Dédé had thought should have been court-martialled in the field.

Colonel Buckmaster had passed this identification to the Belgian authorities for further research, but it became apparent that the Belgians had known nothing of Sadoine's British Army service with Phantom. All they were certain of was that, on the liberation of Belgium, Sadoine had been called up for his own country's army as an infantry private under the name of Octave Dupont. His service record was erratic and plagued by absences, but after just two months he was wounded in the lower back, in action on the Rhine in early 1945. Though his physical injuries eventually healed, he was also found to have amnesia, with no memory of his past. No relatives could be traced and there was not even proof that Octave Dupont was his real name. In such condition he was transferred to the Saint-Jean-de-Dieu Institut Psychiatrique in Leuze and had remained there ever since, working in the Institute's gardens and calling himself either 'Octave Dupont', 'Don Varrenes' or, most recently, 'John Tonkin'. Before leaving for the Continent, Tonkin consulted with a medical expert on Sadoine's reported condition. There was no known case of injury inflicted amnesia recovering after so long a time and therefore Tonkin was advised that the cause of Sadoine's amnesia had to be hysterical, the condition of a man who had a strong reason not to want to identify with his old self.

At the Institute, Tonkin first met the relevant staff and Sadoine was then brought into the room. He immediately greeted Tonkin by name, but appeared terrified by his presence. The Belgian had clearly paid a terrible price for what amounted to a combination of severe stress and battle fatigue, and had obviously been completely unsuited to duties behind enemy lines. And as to the claim it had been a radio operator who had betrayed the SAS, Tonkin believed that he was witnessing an inverted confession to the betrayal by Sadoine himself, confirming the wartime reports of Dédé and the Maquis. Pierre Hirsch had to be cleared of all suspicion as soon as possible.

By chance, Dédé had recently been in correspondence with the village of Rom in the Deux-Sèvres region of France, where the local community was planning a memorial to the fallen SAS of 'Operation Bulbasket' in the forest of Saint-Sauvant.[5] Business commitments in Mauritius meant he would be unable to attend the unveiling ceremony in June 1973 (he instead sent a wreath with the request that it be placed on the memorial by the youngest serving soldier present), but on hearing Tonkin's news, he was extremely angry that suspicion was falling on Pierre Hirsch. Resolved to make absolutely certain that Hirsch was cleared beyond doubt, Dédé therefore flew to France in May 1973 ahead of the planned ceremony and in a two-day visit marked by an official reception in Poitiers, he made public the discovery of Sadoine in Belgium and pledged his support of Hirsch to the local Resistance veterans and historians.[6] At the reception his old comrades congratulated him on his latest French decoration, for in 1972 the French government had made Dédé a Chevalier of the Légion d'honneur in further recognition of his wartime service in the French cause. Dédé wrote later that he was saddened to see that several of his old friends had aged greatly over the intervening thirty years, but acknowledged that he himself, at fifty-four, was 'greyish and fattish'.

Returning to Mauritius, Dédé still had a long way to go with development of his fledgling airline. In April 1973 he initiated joint operations with Air India on the Mauritius–Bombay route and in November Air Mauritius entered the jet age when weekly flights were inaugurated on the Mauritius–Nairobi–London route using a leased BAC Super VC10 aircraft still in British Airways colours. In January 1975 the Piper Navajo was replaced when Air Mauritius made its first outright purchase of an aircraft, this being an 18-seater de Havilland Twin Otter that began services to Réunion and Rodrigues the following month. Later that year joint operations also began with Air Madagascar using a leased Boeing 737 on the Mauritius–Tananarive–Maputo–Johannesburg route.

In the latter half of the 1970s, business prospects looked good. In the hotel sector New Mauritius Hotels went from strength to strength, and in aviation Rogers retained their 17.5 per cent stake in Air Mauritius, while the government took a larger shareholding of 42.5 per cent; British Airways and Air France reduced to 15 per cent each as Air India took 10 per cent. The Super VC10 was replaced in November 1977 by a Boeing 707 leased from British Airways. Painted in Air Mauritius livery and named 'City of Port-Louis', it continued to ply the flagship Mauritius–London route, while in the autumn of 1979 a second Twin Otter was bought for inter-island services. The same year Queen Elizabeth

II visited Mauritius and Dédé was prominent among those presented to the Queen, to the extent that Her Majesty briefly used the family's beachside bungalow at Le Morne between functions. It seemed nothing could go wrong – until Dédé fell ill.

The normally energetic man was visibly tiring and after a series of tests came the bleak diagnosis of leukaemia. Typically, Dédé faced his illness with courage, supported by his strong faith, and never complained. But the best possible medical attention was needed and Dédé therefore left Mauritius with Jacqueline for treatment in Paris, fully committed to battle with the cancer.

Sadly, strength of spirit was not enough. The treatment completed, Dédé returned to Mauritius, but was powerless as his leukaemia took a firm hold. As the seriousness of his illness became general knowledge, the French government moved swiftly in January 1981 to upgrade his Légion d'honneur from Chevalier to Officier, this following another French award, the Médaille de l'Aéronautique in December 1980, in recognition of his long association with Air France.

From Britain came word that a knighthood was to be considered for at least one of the Maingards, but Dédé again felt that his older brother, Colo, had a stronger claim to the award.[7] Before the issue could be decided Dédé's condition worsened and at 7.30 a.m. on 12 January 1981 he died at home, aged just sixty-two, at Lamivoie, Black River.

# Chapter Sixteen

# The Trail Today

For those wishing to follow the trail of Dédé's career and achievements, wartime and post-war, numerous reminders remain.

In England, most of SOE's establishments can be found today in much the same condition as when Dédé visited them. The Baker Street headquarters buildings in London are externally little changed, F Section's Norgeby House having reverted to offices for Marks & Spencer. A little further down the road, Orchard Court retains its original elegance as an imposing apartment block and in Northumberland Avenue, the old hotel where Dédé had his first SOE interview with Major Jepson, is now office premises. Stepping into the little-changed lobby and reception area, one is in little doubt that this was a hotel, and there are plans for it to be so again. SOE's women agents who belonged to the FANY are included on the FANY memorial at St Paul's Church in Knightsbridge, and close by, the Special Forces Club's staircases display galleries of wartime SOE and other special forces personnel. A photograph of Dédé, in uniform, heads one series.

In Surrey, both of the Preliminary Special Training Schools attended by Dédé, at Wanborough Manor and Bellasis,[1] have returned to use as private residences. In the Church of Saint Bartholomew adjoining Wanborough Manor there is a memorial plaque to the SOE agents.

In the Highlands of Scotland, the properties that housed the paramilitary group of training schools remain, other than Meoble Lodge where Dédé was quartered. This property burned down post-war and was replaced by a more modern house of the same name. Two of the former training establishments, Arisaig House and Garramor, have become hotels catering for the tourism industry in this beautiful yet remote area, while at Camusdarach a campsite offers superb panoramic views of the offshore islands. Inverie House, on Loch Nevis, can still only be reached by boat and consequently the village boasts the most isolated pub in the British Isles.

Of the parachute training establishments near Manchester, both Tatton Park and Dunham Massey are open to the public under the management of the National Trust, while Fulshaw Hall currently provides offices for several private companies. Ringway aerodrome has been developed into Manchester airport, now the third largest in Britain and one of the busiest international airports in

Europe. Of the other aerodromes used by SOE and Dédé, RAF Tempsford lies disused, though wartime buildings and a hangar are in evidence, as are remains of the runways and perimeter track. Seemingly marooned in the middle of the old airfield, the barn of Gibraltar Farm is accessible by public right of way and has a plaque and a grove of trees in memory of the aircrews and agents who flew from Tempsford. Inside the barn, the concrete equipment bays and shelving remain where Dédé was issued with his parachute. At Tangmere on the south coast near Chichester, the old aerodrome likewise lies disused. Housing development encroaches on much of the site, but the old control tower and parts of runways and perimeter track remain and a museum on the site records SOE's operations from there. The cottage used by F Section and 161 Squadron is a private residence just outside the airfield.

Thame Park, former home to SOE's radio school, has probably had the most chequered recent existence. Post-war the house and grounds remained in settled ownership until 1982, belonging to the heir to the Raleigh bicycle fortune, Sir Frank Bowden. Thereafter, work started on refurbishing the property as a hotel, but in 1992 all work came to a stop and the house then stood empty for many years. Fittingly, however, the park and the house featured in numerous films and television dramas. Many scenes from the classic war film 'Saving Private Ryan' were filmed in Thame Park, the grounds taking on the guise of the hinterland of the Normandy beaches, while the interior of the chapel was used to depict a French church. In 2000, the 1,200-acre estate was put up for sale and the house, park, chapel and lake were bought for restoration (continuing in 2007) as a private residence.

Beaulieu remains the ancestral home of the Lords Montagu and is now one of Britain's foremost visitor attractions as a motor museum. A commemorative plaque in the cloisters of the Abbey, unveiled by General Gubbins in 1969, marks the passage of SOE's agents under training, and in March 2005 a new permanent exhibition was opened as an adjunct to the museum, describing SOE's use of the estate. SOE's headquarters building, The Rings, was demolished soon after the war due to its dilapidated state, but The Vineyards remains little changed in external appearance from its wartime days.

Gumley Hall, the school for Dédé's refresher training in 1945, fell into decline in the 1950s and the hall was eventually demolished in 1964. The gardens are now overgrown with trees and scrub, and the only reminders are occasional parts of pathways and steps.

Across the Channel, a network of clubs throughout France, 'L'Amicale Buckmaster', became the old comrades' association for those who had served F Section. These veterans were much involved in the F Section memorial at Valençay, inaugurated on 6 May 1991, the fiftieth anniversary of the despatch of Georges Bégué, F Section's first agent, to France. The memorial came about following the compilation of a roll of honour of F Section's agents who lost their lives, the list having then been passed to the Amicale Buckmaster. Two members of the Amicale des Anciens Résistants Nord Indre-Vallée du Cher, Pearl Cornioley and Monsieur Paul Guerbois (a young officer in a Maquis with which Pearl had worked), convinced the mayor and town council that it was in Valençay itself, the hub of early F Section activity, that a monument should be erected. A charitable association raised the necessary funds and oversaw the building of the monument, the town provided a splendid site and the council of the Indre *département* assisted in the project by making it the centrepiece of a roundabout. The memorial, named the Spirit of Partnership, was dedicated in honour of the 104 members of SOE's F Section who died for the liberation of France, and did much to heal the last vestiges of bitterness felt by former agents over the way they had been treated at the end of the war on the instructions of General de Gaulle. Of those commemorated, thirteen were connected with Dédé or his circuits in France:

Lieutenant E.A. Allard

Lieutenant P.A.H. Geelen (served as Lieutenant P. Garde)

Lieutenant M.L.M.A. Larcher

Lieutenant M. Leccia (served as Lieutenant G. Louis)

Section Officer C.M. Lefort

Sergeant R.M.A. Mathieu

Lieutenant J.A. Mayer

Ensign E.S. Plewman

Captain B.D. Rafferty

Captain C. Rechenmann

Lieutenant A. Schwatschko (served as Lieutenant A. Shaw)

Ensign V.R.E. Szabo

Captain G.A. Wilkinson

Of these, only Larcher and Schwatschko have graves, both in France. Allard, Geelen, Leccia, Mayer, Plewman, Rafferty, Rechenmann, Szabo and Wilkinson were all executed in concentration camps in Germany and have no known graves, although they are commemorated on the Brookwood Memorial at Brookwood Military Cemetery near Woking in England. Geelen and Leccia are incorrectly listed there by the false names under which they served, Pierre Garde and Georges Louis respectively, and have been the subject of a request to the Commonwealth War Graves Commission to rectify the error. The memorial lists 3,500 men and women of the land forces of the British Commonwealth who died during the Second World War and have no known grave. Cecily Lefort, likewise executed in a concentration camp, held a commission in the Women's Auxiliary Air Force (WAAF) and is therefore commemorated instead on the Air Forces Memorial at Runnymeade in Surrey, England where 20,000 air force personnel with no known grave are listed.

In the Indre, a plaque at Briantes, near La Châtre, records the arrest on 27 April 1944 of Leccia, Allard and Geelen of the ill-fated 'Labourer' party, all subsequently executed at Buchenwald. There is also a plinth to them near Néret in the Indre, alongside the road from the Chateau d'Acre where they parachuted on 6 April 1944.

Dédé's apartment in Châteauroux at 24 rue de la Gare remains above commercial premises. Not far outside the town, Dédé's former Priority A targets, the airfield and aircraft works at La Martinerie and Déols, have survived. La Martinerie is now the base of a transport and logistics unit, the 517e Régiment du Train of the French Army, while Déols is busy civilian airport.

Some 60 kilometres to the south, the bravery of the young SOE Lieutenant Schwatschko has been permanently acknowledged in the town of Eguzon by the naming of rue du Lieutenant Olive. Schwatschko, killed at Eguzon on the night of 7/8 June 1944, was buried in the local civilian town cemetery. At the head of his grave plot the standard Commonwealth War Graves Commission military headstone records him as 'A. Schwatschko served as Lieutenant A. Shaw, General List, 7th June 1944'. Intriguingly, the next but one grave is that of a German soldier killed in the war. It has a civilian headstone from his family, but no date of death is recorded, leaving one to wonder if it was the German corporal shot by Schwatschko.

In the Vienne, there are numerous reminders of the SOE, FFI and SAS operations. In the city centre of Poitiers the rue du Général Chêne ensures that the region's wartime FFI leader is not forgotten. At La Couarde on the outskirts of the village of Verrières, an imposing memorial lists Lieutenant Stephens of the SAS and the seven Maquis dead of 3 July 1944, and an annual service of remembrance is held there.

In the Vienne and Deux-Sèvres a memorial route, Les Chemins de la Liberté, marks several of the scenes of actions linked to Dédé and was the creation of Doctor Bouchet, Jacques Papineau and Maurice Fuzeau. The latter, a former *maquisard*, has also been instrumental in recent years in setting up illustrated information boards and a plaque in Bonneuil-Matours in the Vienne, scene of the Mosquito air raid on the SS barracks there on 14 July 1944.

In Mauritius, Dédé's outstanding war record remains little known. Instead, the name of Amédée Maingard is best known as the visionary business leader responsible for creating the island's tourism and airline industries and this is marked by a Foundation in his name, approved by the Mauritius Parliament in 1992. The Foundation's Board selects citizens of Mauritius to receive financial grants towards the costs of approved studies in air transport or tourism. Further recognition of Dédé's contribution in these fields came in January 2001 when the Amédée Maingard Lounge, for use by First and Business Class passengers, was inaugurated at Sir Seewoosagur Ramgoolam International Airport.

Consequently, the striking bronze bust of Dédé, unveiled on 2 August 2001 by the Minister for the Arts and Culture, Motee Ramdass and the Minister for Tourism, Nando Bodha, shows him as a suited businessman. Sculpted by Zsuzsanna Szemök, it stands on public view in front of Rogers House in the rue John Kennedy in Port-Louis and was the inspiration and twenty-year ambition of Dédé's brother-in-law, Louis René Dalais, and an organizing committee of René Noel, Guy Hugnin, Robert Rivalland and Alain Antelme. Sponsorship funding for the project came from Rogers, New Mauritius Hotels and Air Mauritius, with other support from the General Construction Co. Only the inscriptions of the British and French military decorations, the Distinguished Service Order (DSO) and the Croix de Guerre, hint at the hidden wartime history, now at last revealed, of this remarkable man.

# Chapter Seventeen

# The Players

The players in the grand drama that was Dédé's war enjoyed mixed fortunes. Of SOE's personnel, all ultimately lost their jobs after the service was disbanded, and while some continued careers in SIS, most returned quietly to civilian life. Major General Colin Gubbins was highly decorated by several countries and knighted by Britain for his astute leadership of SOE, but was nevertheless given no option of returning to his regular Army career. He became a successful businessman and was active in circles advocating a united Europe before he died in 1976.

Colonel Maurice Buckmaster rejoined the Ford Motor Co., but later became a consultant for the French champagne industry and was President of the Institute of Public Relations from 1955 to 1956. He wrote two books (*Specially Employed*, 1952, and *They Fought Alone*, 1958) on his wartime service, though they suffer somewhat from not always being factually correct. In 1969 he featured in an interview, as also did Denis Rake, in the controversial French film *The Sorrow and the Pity: Chronicle of a French City Under the Occupation*. Initially banned in France and not released until 1971, the film documents the experience of Clermont-Ferrand during its occupation and criticizes the French upper classes for collaboration. It has been re-released in recent years and is currently still widely available. Buckmaster kept in touch with Dédé and there were post-war links between the public-relations work of Buckmaster and his son when the latter undertook a tourism survey of Mauritius. Buckmaster died in 1992.

Both Buckmaster and his assistant, Vera Atkins, were deeply affected by having, unintentionally, sent some agents to their deaths. Vera Atkins made it her goal to find out what happened to each one, feeling that she could not abandon their memory. After an early post-war investigative trip to the Continent, her work seemed doomed when SOE was disbanded, but she managed to engineer semi-official support from SIS and returned to Germany. Thanks to her linguistic skills and headquarters background she was uniquely equipped to spend most of a year questioning concentration camp officials and combing through remaining German records to pick up the trail of each of the missing agents. Her reports appear in many of the F Section agents' files and were vital when they later formed the basis of the roll of honour to the 104 dead of F

Section on the memorial at Valençay in France.[1] Finally demobilized in 1947, Vera remained throughout the rest of her life as a rich seam of help, inspiration and information for researchers of SOE. As Secretary of the Central Bureau of Educational Visits and Exchanges, she was also much involved in fostering Anglo-French relations and devoted much effort to keeping alive the spirit of SOE and the Resistance. In 1987 she was appointed a Commandant (the order's highest rank) of the Légion d'honneur by President Mitterand and she died in 2000, aged ninety-three. Although it has never been conclusively proved, a story persists that Buckmaster and Atkins inspired the author Ian Fleming (a wartime officer in Naval Intelligence whose path would have crossed theirs) in his creation of 'M' and Miss Moneypenny in the James Bond novels.

The two other Mauritians who joined SOE with Dédé, Jean Larcher and Marcel Rousset, both qualified as agents and undertook operations into occupied France. Larcher took part in 'Scullion I' and 'Dressmaker' in April and August of 1943 before transferring to the Commandos and serving in the Near and Far East with distinction. He was decorated with the Military Cross in 1945, but returned home to Mauritius without his brother, Maurice, who was killed while serving with SOE.[2] Further recognition of Jean's wartime service came in 2005 when the French government made him a Chevalier de la Légion d'honneur.

Marcel Rousset, like Dédé, qualified as a radio operator. He dropped into France in March 1943, but was captured by the Gestapo in Paris. After a spell in a fortress prison in Germany he was brought back to Paris by the SD who wanted his help in a radio game with London. Seizing a chance opportunity, however, Rousset managed to escape and remained hidden in Paris until the city's liberation when he took an active part in the fighting. Of all the SOE wireless operators captured by the Germans, Rousset was one of only two to avoid execution and he ended the war with the Military Cross and the Croix de Guerre avec Palme.

The original members of the 'Stationer' circuit all survived. Southgate enjoyed poor health for some time as a result of his twelve months in German captivity, but he was fortunate to have been one of the very few SOE agents to emerge alive from Buchenwald in May 1945. He was decorated with the DSO and the Légion d'honneur, and post-war returned to his business in France where he lived until he died. He was highly regarded as one of SOE's very best agents, though a series of newspaper articles, 'The Casebook of Colonel Hector', that appeared in the *Today* newspaper under his name in 1964 verged on the sensationalist and raised eyebrows.

Those not so fortunate as Southgate at Buchenwald included the thirty-seven Allied officers murdered there on 14 September 1944. Several among them had crossed Dédé's path: Captain Rechenmann, Lieutenant James Mayer, Lieutenant Geelen, Lieutenant Allard and Lieutenant Leccia. Captain Rafferty and Captain G. Wilkinson were also to die later at Buchenwald. Rechenmann was awarded a posthumous MBE (Military), Mayer a posthumous Mention in Dispatches, and Rafferty a Military Cross and Croix de Guerre. Lieutenant Schwatschko, killed and buried in Eguzon, received a posthumous Mention in Dispatches.

Of the female agents connected with Dédé or his circuits, Ensign Eliane Plewman was one of four SOE women taken from their cells at Dachau in the early hours of 13 September 1944. In a small courtyard next to the crematorium they were forced to kneel on the ground and all four were executed by a single shot through the back of the neck. Their bodies were cremated.[3] Ensign Violette Szabo and Section Officer Cecily Lefort died at Ravensbrück on 25 January and 1 March 1945 respectively. Lefort was awarded a posthumous Croix de Guerre while Violette Szabo became one of the best-known tragic heroines of SOE thanks to the book *Carve Her Name With Pride* and subsequent film of the same name. She too was awarded a Croix de Guerre by the French, and a posthumous George Cross, Britain's highest civilian award.[4]

By the time Jacqueline Nearne had recovered from the stress and fatigue of her first mission, it was too late for her to return to the field. She was, however, flown back out to France to join Buckmaster, Pearl and Henri Cornioley for the 'Stationer' part of the 'Judex' mission, a post-liberation tour of F Section's main operating areas to thank the local people who had helped their agents and networks. Jacqueline also starred in a British propaganda film, made in 1945, but not screened until 1946. Entitled *Now It Can Be Told*, the film also featured Harry Rée and followed the two agents through their training and insertion into France. SOE's Special Training Schools and RAF Tempsford feature in the film, which can still be bought today in VHS video format. Buckmaster clearly had great affection for Jacqueline and when recommending her for an MBE he wrote: 'A grand girl, full of common-sense and charm. Her sense of security was unequalled by anyone else in the field. She did a tremendous amount of un-spectacular, hard and uninteresting work, which she always discharged faultlessly. I think the world of her.' Jacqueline was also awarded the Croix de Guerre by the French; she later ran protocol for the United Nations and died in London in 1982.

When Pearl Witherington returned to England in September 1944, her mother was astonished to learn that her daughter had been in France, let alone that she had led some 1,500 *résistants* and had been the only woman to head an SOE circuit. After the war Buckmaster wanted to recommend her for a Military Cross, but as a woman she was deemed ineligible and was instead awarded an MBE (Civil). She returned the medal with a note saying that she did not deserve it as she had done nothing civil and it was eventually replaced with an MBE (Military), which she accepted. In 1946 she was chosen to participate in a lecture tour of the United States, explaining what SOE and the French Resistance had done during the war. She married Henri Cornioley (Dédé acted as best man) and settled with him in France where they had a daughter. She now lives not far from Valençay where she was a major force in the F Section memorial project. The coming to fruition of the memorial, with the support given to it by the French authorities, helped soothe some of Pearl's criticism of the way in which the French government treated those who worked for the British during the war. She and Henri remained close to Dédé, who would meet up with them on his busi-ness trips to France and they once travelled to Mauritius as his guests. Henri died in 1999, but Pearl remains in the Loir-et-Cher, close to the Indre where she once operated, her love for France undiminished. In April 2004 she was presented with the CBE by Queen Elizabeth II during the latter's state visit to Paris to mark the centenary of the Entente Cordiale between Britain and France. The award was 'For services to UK-French relations and to the history of the Second World War'. Her Majesty rightly commented, 'You've waited a long time for this'; more overdue recognition came in 2006 when the Royal Air Force arranged a formal presentation of her parachute wings, there not having been an opportunity during the war.

Harry Rée, who parachuted into France with Dédé in April 1943, was one of SOE's most successful agents. Post-war, after his role with Jacqueline Nearne in the film *Now It Can Be Told*, he returned to teaching in England and became professor of education at York University. He became a leading advocate of comprehensive education and in 1974 he left York to return to classroom teaching in London until his retirement. He continued to campaign on educational issues, including the promotion of closer links between schools in the European Community. He died in 1991.

The French people who were recruited locally by SOE ran enormous risks in helping the British. Chief amongst these were Jacques (whom Dédé described as his 'right arm' during the war) and Pierre Hirsch who were of such importance that they were both brought back to England and thoroughly debriefed by SOE. They were keen that the British would speak up for them after the war, since they had not belonged to the Gaullist Resistance and Jacques, as a former French Army officer, wanted his service to be judged as a form of secondment from the Fighting French to the British. SOE and the British government subsequently confirmed their appreciation of the immense contribution of the two brothers by the award of an MBE (Military) to each. Both joined the French Army after their SOE service and after discharge, Jacques went on to become a senior civil servant, while Pierre became a successful businessman. Jacques died in 1984, Pierre in 2006. The Hirsch parents and Jeanne survived and each received a Mention in Dispatches from the British, but the Hirsch grandparents, arrested after Southgate's capture, were deported to their deaths.

Jacques Dufour, who had been fortunate to escape when the Germans captured Violette Szabo on 10 June 1944, survived the war and joined the French Army. Sent to Indo-China he was killed in 1946 in action against Viet Minh rebels.

Others who played an important part, but who could not travel to Britain, were invited to the Hôtel Cecil in Paris after the end of the war, where SOE debriefed and formally thanked them. Madame Gateau of the Poitiers *boîte aux lettres* was one such visitor in August 1945, lucky to have survived deportation to Germany, but reporting that her husband had been shot at Buchenwald concentration camp. Others who suffered a similar fate included the two courageous local mayors in the Châteauroux area who were both arrested. Auguste Chantraine was executed in Mauthausen concentration camp in March 1945 and is commemorated today in the Mairie of Tendu, where a room is named after him. On his farm, still owned by his son, a memorial marks its use by SOE for the dropping of arms and agents. A plaque in the Mairie of Dun-le-Poëlier and another in the Hôtel du Département in Châteauroux remembers Armand

Mardon, Mayor and local Conseiller Général, who died in Buchenwald in April 1945.

Among the other families who so bravely supported the 'Stationer' and 'Shipwright' circuits, Monsieur and Madame Bidet were arrested and deported to Germany; only Madame Bidet returned. Madame L'Hospitalier was freed by the FFI before she could be sent to Germany and her plucky mother, Madame Deriot, who was taken ill and sent to hospital immediately prior to Southgate's arrest on 1 May 1944, managed to escape on her own initiative. Robert and Pierrette L'Hospitalier successfully evaded the Germans looking for them and Robert was subsequently trained as an additional radio operator. They survived the war; Robert temporarily joined the French Army as a telegraphist and received an award from the British.

The immensely courageous Néraud family enjoyed no such good fortune. The young son, Jean, avoided arrest, but Madame Néraud and Colette were sent to Ravensbrück concentration camp. Madame Néraud died there in late 1944, but Colette, weak, very ill and heart-broken at the loss of her mother, was freed by the Russian Army at the end of April 1945 and put into the care of the Swedish Red Cross. After two months' recuperation in Sweden she returned to France, only to find there was no news of her father who had been deported to a different concentration camp in Germany. But even as she finished a letter to Dédé, in London, with this news, her tragedy deepened when confirmation arrived that her father had perished at Buchenwald in March 1945. It was almost too much for the brave Colette to bear, but in her letter to Dédé she pledged herself to be strong to care for her younger brother and this she did. She later married and raised a family of her own.

After Dédé's departure from France in September 1944, many of his FFI comrades-in-arms continued as part of the Free French Army pursuing the Germans. For Colonel Chêne in particular there was to be no respite from active service. On 10 September 1944 he was appointed commander of military region B2 and subsequently of region 9, and led the French forces surrounding the Germans in the La Rochelle 'pocket' which did not surrender until 8 May 1945. Post-war he kept in occasional touch with Dédé as he continued a career in the French Army, eventually retiring as a Brigadier General. He married a girl from Réunion who knew much of Mauritius.

One of the worst tragedies linked to Dédé's operations involved the fate of the SAS paratroopers captured by the Germans. In mid-December 1944 three mass graves were discovered in the Bois de Guron, part of the Forêt de Saint-Sauvant in the Deux-Sèvres region south-west of Poitiers. Exhumation revealed the decaying, yet still clothed, remains of thirty-one bodies, identified as those of the missing SAS troopers from 'Operation Bulbasket' and Lieutenant Lincoln Bundy, the shot-down USAAF pilot. All had been executed by the Germans. On 23 December 1944 the bodies were reburied with full military honours in the village graveyard of Rom. Three more of the SAS paratroopers remained unaccounted for, and it was later discovered that that they had received lethal injections while wounded and in the care of a German Army doctor in Poitiers. Their bodies remain undiscovered.

Of the SAS officers who survived, John Tonkin and David Surrey Dane corresponded with Dédé over the years. Tonkin settled in Australia where he worked as a mining engineer. He died in 1995. David Surrey Dane completed his studies to become a doctor and a highly-respected haematologist and microbiologist. The infectious 'Dane particle' in hepatitis B was named after him. In his later years he helped champion the cause of people who had received contaminated blood supplies, resulting in their being infected with HIV and hepatitis; he died in 1998.

The shot-down American flyers who had to thank SOE and the SAS for their return to England included Lieutenant Flamm 'Dee' Harper who had been so impressed with Dédé, considering him to be the epitome of a British officer and gentleman. Rejoining his fighter squadron in England, Harper returned safely to the United States in 1945 and elected to make a career of the air force. He was again shot down, evaded capture in Korea and retired as a Colonel in 1970. He today lives in Las Vegas and in recent years has revisited the Vienne to thank those who helped him when he was shot down.

Of Dédé's enemies in the German forces, those in the Châteauroux SD office fared worst. SS-Untersturmführer Metschler managed to slip out of the town just before its liberation, but 'Le grand Schmitt', the SD's brutal German-Czech who had lived in pre-war Châteauroux, was executed by maquisards as he lay in the town's hospital after a car accident. Metschler's detested French agent, Pierre Sutter, was eventually arrested and found guilty when tried by a court in Bourges. He was executed in May 1946.

In contrast, SS-Sturmbannführer Herold, SS-Haupsturmführer Linn and SS-Obersturmführer Hoffmann, together with their staff, managed to escape unscathed from the SD office in Poitiers before the Maquis could obtain revenge. Their luck continued to hold when, in 1946 and 1947, Herold and Linn were brought before a SHAEF inquiry and a subsequent war crime trial by the British into the executions of the 'Bulbasket' SAS men. Both were found blameless, while two of the German Army officers involved received the death sentence, later commuted to terms of imprisonment.

For the other Germans who had opposed Dédé and the Résistance, it was a perilous retreat across France. The Indian troops of the Indische Freiwilligen Legion der Waffen SS managed to reach Germany in late 1944, but in 1945, with the defeat of the Third Reich imminent, they attempted to seek sanctuary in neutral Switzerland. A desperate march along the shores of the Bodensee (Lake Constance) saw them try to enter Switzerland via one of the alpine passes. Intercepted and captured by Allied troops, they were turned over to the British who, mindful of the tinderbox nature of politics in India at the time, had no wish to conduct war crime investigations. Treated as ordinary prisoners of war, the Indians were soon shipped back to India with the minimum of publicity; they were dealt with leniently and soon released. For this tragic episode in Dédé's war, there was to be no justice in the villages of the Vienne.

# Chapter Eighteen

# Legacy

In assessing the wartime contribution of SOE and Dédé, the author has been helped by the gradual release in recent years of many of the remaining SOE records and files into the public domain at Britain's National Archives, formerly the Public Record Office, at Kew.

Until this relatively recent policy of openness, it was Britain's Secret Intelligence Service (SIS), also known as MI6, who were the guardians of the SOE records, ironically so in view of the fact that it was the wartime Head of the SIS, Sir Stewart Menzies, who repeatedly said that SOE were 'amateur, dangerous, and bogus'. But with Churchill as a guardian, SOE had survived its difficult gestation period. From its country sections only Yugoslavia received more arms than France, where F Section arranged the supply of some 10,000 tons of weapons (4,000 from 1941 to D-Day and 6,000 thereafter) to arm tens of thousands of *résistants*. Despite errors, betrayals and disasters, it organized almost 100 circuits, involving the despatch of 393 agents (including a peak total of forty-eight radio operators) to France. Of the men and women sent, 104 died, a sobering enough statistic, but better than the 50-50 chance of survival that recruits were warned to expect. It was later estimated that the Resistance, supported by SOE, succeeded in keeping five or six German divisions from the invasion areas and the Allied Supreme Commander, General Eisenhower, himself believed that this success shortened the war in Europe by nine months.

Of all F Section's circuits, Buckmaster recorded those of Dédé, Southgate and Pearl as having the highest percentage of successful drops in the whole of France, possibly in the whole of Europe. The 'Stationer' network was huge and to maintain security, compartmentalization was essential – to the extent, for example, that Pearl Witherington knew little or nothing of the work of Jacqueline Nearne and vice versa. In his debriefing in England, however, Jacques Hirsch recorded that the eventual arrests in the organization were, in many ways, inevitable. It had grown too big and in such circumstances it was impossible to maintain the separation of elements so essential to clandestine activity. The distances involved were enormous – to travel from Châteauroux to Pau, taking in Montluçon, Clermont-Ferrand and Toulouse, entailed a round trip of over 1,600 kilometres, no straightforward matter in the face of German controls and checks, Allied bombing and frequent sabotage.

The achievements of Dédé's own 'Shipwright' circuit were in a much shorter timescale than the activities of 'Stationer'. But given that they came mostly after D-Day and were in support of open, as opposed to clandestine, warfare, they were rather more dramatic. When the SAS arrived on the scene, they came with orders to arm and train the Resistance, but Captain Tonkin found that SOE, in the person of Dédé, had already laid much of the groundwork. As a consequence, many Maquis groups were quite capable of offensive operations without additional encouragement. A report by the British War Office later conceded that there was no evidence that 'Bulbasket' had taken part in arming or organizing the Maquis in the area, for the simple reason that Colonel Chêne's FFI head-quarters, with Dédé's SOE support, already had this task comfortably in hand. The mistakes of the planners were recognized in the very first discussions between Dédé and the SAS commander, and from the day of Tonkin's arrival, Dédé ensured that 'Bulbasket' received the best possible assistance, both from his own SOE network and from the local Resistance groups.

Of particular note was the joint SOE/SAS work with air support. The bombing raid on the fuel trains at Châtellerault was a particularly successful example of liaison between special forces behind the lines and conventional air forces. The gravity of the attack's results can be judged from the following Wehrmacht radio message, which was picked up and decoded by the 'Ultra' code experts in England: 'Urgent request for allocation of fuel for 2 Sugar Sugar [SS] Panzer Division from Army Fuel Depot, Châtellerault. Addressed to AOK 1 at 1100 hours, 13th June.' With their petrol stocks destroyed, the 2nd SS Das Reich Division was further delayed on its movement northwards to Normandy, and a journey which could have been made in three days ultimately took seventeen.

In addition, the three air attacks against enemy troop concentrations (at Bonneuil-Matours, the Château du Fou and the Caserne des Dunes) killed and wounded scores of the enemy and extensively damaged the targets. The air attack on the latter was another result of the excellent Dédé/Chêne/Tonkin (SOE/FFI/SAS) relationship and there was no doubt that it forestalled yet another large-scale German *ratissage*.

There was other intelligence reported that was never acted upon. The passage of Das Reich up the N147 was in itself a lucrative target and one that was radioed to England on 12 June 1944. It is interesting to speculate what havoc the medium bombers and fighter-bombers of the RAF or USAAF might have wrought against the slow-moving convoys of vehicles on the long straight road through largely open countryside. But the opportunity was missed. Other potential targets which were reported to London either by SOE or the SAS included: railway traffic through Parthenay, and the fact that the bridge there had been repaired following ineffective bombing; the discovery of two enemy-controlled crude alcohol factories; enemy units moving north on the Bellac–Lussac road; trapped loco-motives, a vital telephone exchange and an enemy headquarters in Poitiers; details of flying operations by Condor aircraft of the Luftwaffe from an airfield near Cognac; and enemy troop concentrations at Champagne-Mouton.

And what of Dédé, the individual, at war? In his book *Specially Employed*, Colonel Buckmaster wrote:

It has always seemed to me surprising that there were so many British or Dominion subjects, whose French was faultless, willing and anxious to undertake such supremely dangerous work. They were in no way conspicuous; the last thing we wanted in them was eccentricity. We denied them glamour, in their own interests; we made them look as homely and unremarkable as we could. In the words of one of them, they were 'just ordinary people, not particularly brave'.

With his innate modesty and reserve, Dédé matched this specification almost perfectly and was undoubtedly suited to the role of an agent. He was never garrulous or showy and his chosen profession and clandestine background as a sober accountant only added to his low profile. Describing Dédé's work prior to D-Day, Pearl Cornioley commented that his work 'was very stressful, yet Amédée did it for more than a year in Châteauroux. How he lasted, I don't know.' The answer lies in that, like Maurice Southgate his circuit organizer, Dédé made his own luck through his strong instinct for tight security. Southgate ultimately let his guard slip for just a few minutes, but Dédé never did. In the highly dangerous role of radio operator he continued to transmit until 19 April 1944, sending a staggering total of 248 messages without the Germans locating him. Buckmaster was later to write:

> Their [the Germans'] leave trains were derailed, their convoys ambushed, their communications cut, even their aircraft 'treated'. So that every now and then an 'accident' occurred in mid-air. These successes were laconically reported by Amédée's radio . . . They did not make any real difference to the conduct of the war at that time [1943] but, as earnest of what was in store for the German troops when the time came, these incidents were encouraging.

According to one note on his SOE file, Dédé received or organized fifty-five dropping operations, but other records, supported by Pierre Hirsch, suggest that Dédé was responsible for something like 125 landings or supply drops, involving over 4,000 containers and packages, with enough arms for 6,000 men. He also trained Pierre Hirsch as a radio operator for his own circuit and recruited another, Adrien Berge, for Pearl's 'Wrestler' network, both men capable enough that London accepted them for work in the field.

Once the invasion was under way, Dédé played a much more open and active role, but despite claims made by some of the more eloquent reports compiled by SOE headquarters, Dédé was not in command of the Maquis – his job was instead to provide arms, money and training. He was also an extremely successful peacemaker and there were several differences among the FFI leadership that were soothed by his intelligent diplomacy. General Chêne was later to write: 'I had complete confidence in him. His efficiency, the sureness of his judgement, the sang-froid that he displayed, his kindness and his natural elegance, won him all his interlocutors. He remains for me the perfect example of a comrade in arms.'

In his final F Section evaluation of Dédé, Colonel Buckmaster concluded:

A year's painstaking and patient W/T work (which was uncongenial to his temperament) proved an excellent foundation for his later work. When he became No.1 to Southgate, and, even more, when he succeeded the latter, he showed a grip of his job and a wise determination surprising in one so young and in many ways so temperamental. He behaved admirably and with immense bravery during the fighting and showed great tact in smoothing out problems between leaders. After his return to U.K. he felt the reaction more violently than most others, and experienced the need of living fast and dangerously and of proselytising. His choice for an object to champion fell on his native isle and he has shown more discretion in his attempts to throw all other commitments aside and work only for Mauritius. But what a grand lad.

And in the obituary that appeared in *The Times* of 7 February 1981, Maurice Southgate wrote: 'He was swift-moving and calm tempered, high spirited but never sudden, a splendid friend and a deadly enemy.'

That then was the straightforward summing up of Dédé the secret agent and war hero, but his later achievements as a businessman were no less impressive.

When Dédé died in 1981, his vision and guidance were greatly missed in the corridors of power of Rogers and Co. But the business foundations that Dédé had done so much to consolidate were far too firm to be upset by the death of one man. From 1984 Rogers followed a programme of decentralization and devolution to allow further expansion, making the most of the economic growth that prevailed into the next decade. The 1990s were also marked by the Rogers strategy to invest in the financial services sector. New activities included offshore services and the introduction of consumer credit facilities such as credit cards and hire purchase. In June 1990 the company was listed on the Stock Exchange of Mauritius and throughout the following years growth was particularly strong in the tourism and transportation sectors originally developed by Dédé. From its humble beginnings in 1899 Rogers celebrated its 100th anniversary in 1999 as one of the largest conglomerates in Mauritius.

Of Dédé's special business interests, both Air Mauritius and New Mauritius Hotels have continued to thrive. As Dédé had planned, the airline's route network continued to expand using Boeing 707 aircraft and in November 1984 another leap forward came when the airline's first Boeing 747 began operations with non-stop flights between Mauritius and Paris, Rome and Zurich.

To match the airline's development, the airport at Plaisance has also under-gone expansion. A major phase of this was already being mapped out when Dédé died and was completed from 1984 to 1986, including a new control tower. Now named the Sir Seewoosagur Ramgoolam International Airport, the site was further expanded in the late 1990s and is capable of handling 1.5 million passengers each year. It is certain that Dédé would have been delighted to see not only the modern airport named after his old friend, but Air Mauritius operating to, among other destinations, London and Paris with the Airbus A340 aircraft, as fine an example of Anglo-French co-operation as he could have wished for. Now a truly global airline, Air Mauritius currently serves twenty-one destinations in Europe, Asia, Africa and the Indian Ocean islands, with a fleet of twelve jet and turboprop aircraft and three helicopters.

Dédé's other driving ambition was to promote Mauritius as an exotic holiday destination. Helped by a cosmopolitan island population inclined by nature to be both welcoming and charming, New Mauritius Hotels have succeeded with a range of luxurious four and five-star hotel developments framed by dazzling white beaches and deep-blue lagoons. Under the brand name of Beachcomber Hotels (Rogers remain a major shareholder), in excess of 100,000 tourists are accommodated each year.

Hence, from being a faraway and little-known island associated with the unfortunate dodo, Mauritius, with its diverse mix of cultures, has become one of the most stable countries in the developing world. It has done so by diversifying from a fragile economy dependent upon one traditional crop industry, sugar, to one that is increasingly industrialized and which encompasses tourism, textiles and agriculture.

All this was the dream of Amédée Maingard de la Ville-ès-Offrans, a dream that came true.

# Notes

## Chapter 2

1 Ville-ès-Offrans, now a seventeenth-century manor house, still exists today in the village of Saint-Coulomb, close to the Pointe du Meinga.
2 There is a reference to him being on the Caribbean island of Martinique in 1789 as an officer in the Royal Corps of Artillery.
3 Records of Napoléon's Young Guard artillery also show a Capitaine Maingard, serving as an officer in the 1st Company of the 1st Battalion in 1813.
4 Appropriately for the Maingard family, in 1999 Saint-Malo was twinned with Port-Louis and projects shared by both towns have been promoted with the help of the Alliance Française in Mauritius.
5 Back in France, the other family branches were soon to die out, but not before Pope Pius IX conferred the hereditary title of Count on Arthur-Andre-Josselin Maingard, of Paris, in December 1873.

## Chapter 3

1 Colo had returned to Mauritius in May 1939 after completing his studies. In 1940 he responded to a call for volunteers by the RAF and returned to England to commence training as a pilot.
2 His letters home were sometimes in French, sometimes in English.
3 Colo subsequently flew as a Spitfire fighter pilot with 131 Squadron of the Royal Air Force in England.

## Chapter 4

1 Peter Churchill, *Of Their Own Choice*.
2 By late 1943, SOE headquarters were to decree that transmissions were not to exceed five minutes, and preferably much less, in order to avoid the Germans' detection services based in the Avenue Foch in Paris, where they monitored all possible frequencies.

## Chapter 5

1 It also came far too late for SOE's networks in Holland where the Germans were in control of almost all agents dropped up to the spring of 1943. There

was also some resistance from agents since the new unique code tables were printed on silk slips. If the enemy discovered them during a search, there was little chance of explaining them away.

2 This brother was almost certainly the Sergeant Rée, instructor and conducting member of staff, who penned the reports on Dédé's training at Wanborough Manor and Arisaig.

3 The aircrews of C Flight of 138 Squadron were exclusively Polish.

4 Halifax Mk II, BB330 NF-C.

5 The Halifax landed safely back at Tempsford at 0425 hours after a flight of seven hours.

6 In his own notes, written many years after the war, Dédé named the hotel as the Normandie, also situated in Tarbes. From official French records it is clear, however, that it was the Hôtel Family that was in Rue Victor Hugo and was requisitioned by the Gestapo in early 1943.

7 Coincidentally, Pilar Alvarez had also been a pre-war business contact of Southgate.

8 When Rée reached Clermont-Ferrand, Captain Rafferty was very concerned that the newcomer's French (it was said to have a strong Manchester accent) would arouse interest, if not suspicion. Rée was therefore sent on to the Franche-Comté region where his somewhat guttural accent might pass for that of Alsace. There he later set up his own, highly successful 'Stockbroker' circuit.

## Chapter 6

1 Eileen Nearne was later to survive capture courageously, ill treatment and long imprisonment by the Germans.

2 The willingness of the Hirsch family to help had also already extended to Monsieur Léon Hirsch lending 150,000 francs to Southgate until he could arrange for more funds to be delivered from England.

3 With his customary reserve, Dédé avoided calling this family by their name of Bidet. Instead, he referred to them as 'the Bids', but he could not help but smile over the fact that, appropriately, they lived in the rue des Bains des Soeurs in Montluçon.

4 Jones managed to escape on 3 September 1943 and returned to the UK via Spain. Rafferty had no such luck and was hanged by the Germans at Flossenbürg concentration camp on 29 March 1945 as the Russians approached.

5 Maigrot was, in reality, the name of a Franco-Mauritian family well known to Dédé.

6 A lurid description of this incident was written by Southgate in 1964 for the *Today* newspaper in Britain.

7 A note on Southgate's SOE personal file also suggests that the 'Stationer' circuit was responsible for the sabotage of a similar crane at Saint-Pierre-des-Corps, though this was some 120 kilometres north-west of Châteauroux.

8 Three months later, Eliane briefly returned to pick up a bag of clothes that she had left with Dédé. She had been in no hurry, she said, as she was now 'Queen of the black market' in Marseille and had everything she needed.

9 Henri Cornioley had joined the French Army in 1939 and was captured in June 1940. He had succeeded in escaping, was then demobilized and had been working with a group that helped former servicemen.

10 This would have been unusual since storage in large dumps was avoided as a rule, to prevent losing too much if the cache were found. Anything for an operation would soon be collected and used, otherwise supplies were dispersed.

## Chapter 7

1 Déricourt was arrested post-war and tried by the French. *L'affaire Déricourt* became sensational news in the French press and while there was no conclusive proof of his alleged complicity with the Germans, it is now generally accepted that Déricourt had been trading information to the enemy.

2 Unfortunately London did not finalize that operation and Major Antelme, his radio operator and a courier instead dropped on 28/29 February 1944 to a reception organized by another circuit that had been compromised. The Germans were waiting on the DZ; all three of the team were captured and subsequently executed.

3 Local French accounts describe Schwatschko as having served in an infantry unit of the French Army, but this does not match with SOE records.

4 In his post-war autobiography, *Rake's Progress*, Rake claimed a homosexual affair with Schwatschko while in France. Many of the details given by Rake are, however, clearly false – including a description of Schwatschko's death. Unfortunately some of these dramatic claims by Rake have been perpetuated in more recent publications.

5 Buckmaster himself was to concede in his other book, *Specially Employed*, that he could not claim that all the incidents he portrayed were factual. He describes a number of 'Stationer' activities in both books, but seems to have relied on his memory, or second-hand accounts of events, rather than contemporary notes or any methodical use of the surviving records.

6 The same night as the first Clermont-Ferrand raid, thirty Lancasters bombed the aircraft factory at Châteauroux airfield. This was almost certainly another target that had been reported by Dédé.

## Chapter 8

1 It was later discovered that Mattei had indeed been arrested on or about 2 April 1944, but he was of little use to the Germans as, being a new arrival, he knew practically nothing of the organization. He was imprisoned in Falkensee concentration camp near Berlin, and was fortunate to survive and be liberated by the Russians in April 1945.

2 The Office of Strategic Services (OSS) was the forerunner to the Central Intelligence Agency (CIA).

3 Wilen was eventually returned to England via Spain in August 1944, after Pearl had managed to keep her out of harm's way in safe houses.

4 When they eventually discovered his true identity, the Germans were overjoyed at the capture of Southgate, one of their most wanted men, with a price

of a million francs on his head. He passed through Fresnes prison in Paris before eventually being sent to Buchenwald concentration camp. Sentenced to death there, he was nevertheless one of a very small group of SOE prisoners who managed to survive and were liberated by the Americans in 1945.

## Chapter 9

1 Another possibility, stated in surviving SOE files, is that Southgate may have been given away by Audouard, who had been arrested in Ruffec shortly before Southgate. Audouard survived imprisonment, however, and subsequently returned to England in November 1944 when he was allowed to relinquish his commission. There was presumably therefore no evidence to support the theory that he had betrayed Southgate.

2 It was Dufour who was with Szabo when they were cornered by elements of the 2nd SS Panzer Division on 10 June 1944. Szabo was caught and ultimately executed, while Dufour succeeded in evading the Germans.

## Chapter 10

1 The D-Day messages were designed to trigger circuit action as soon as possible on or after the invasion, against a range of preselected targets (chiefly roads, railway lines and communications) as agreed between SOE and Supreme Headquarters Allied Expeditionary Force (SHAEF).

2 See Chapter 1.

3 From 1 July 1944 a Staff Headquarters for the FFI, known as the Etat-Major des Forces Francaises de l'Interieur (EMFFI), took over command of SOE's 'F' and 'RF' sections, the Jedburgh teams and the OSS French Section. The co-ordination staffs of 'F' and 'RF' sections were merged and, together with the Jedburgh Section, moved out of SOE's Baker Street premises into General Koenig's multi-national HQ in Bryanston Square, London.

4 Jedburgh 'Hamish' was dropped on the night of 12/13 June on a DZ near Bélâbre. The team consisted of: Lieutenant Anstett ('Alabama'), OSS, Lieutenant Schmitt (true name Blachere, 'Louisiana'), BCRA and Sergeant Watters ('Kansas'), OSS. Dropped too low, all three were very shaken and Watters twisted his ankle.

5 There is, however, no evidence of this on Schwatschko's personal file in Britain's National Archives.

6 The Détroit family received a personal letter of thanks from Buckmaster at the end of the war and are officially recorded in SOE's archives as having been helpers of Schwatschko.

7 Remarkably, in view of the potentially dire consequences had the equipment been captured, the SAS officers had come equipped with at least two cameras and film to record 'Operation Bulbasket'. Throughout their stay in France, Tonkin and his men therefore took a number of photographs, including several of their French helpers.

8 Wykeham-Barnes retired as Air Marshal Sir Peter Wykeham KCB DSO OBE DFC AFC, the family name having changed in 1955. He had joined the pre-war RAF as an apprentice and rose to become a Hurricane pilot in the Middle

East, with later Mosquito intruder operations from Malta. Taking over 140 Wing in 1944 at the age of twenty-nine, he had twenty-four confirmed enemy aircraft destroyed to his credit.

## Chapter 11

1 Gildee and Delorme continued to operate successfully throughout August and early September until the German retreat. They both returned safely to Britain on 17 September 1944.
2 Between April and September 1944 Groupement D received around twenty arms and supply drops from England.
3 Happily, and contrary to the fate I feared for him in my earlier book *Operation Bulbasket*, Trooper George Biffin avoided execution under the Kommandobefehl. Helped by a sympathetic Wehrmacht officer, he was sent to a normal POW camp and returned safely to Britain after the end of the war.
4 Before Tonkin's departure, and in contrast to the gravity of the meeting, Colonel Chêne used the SAS officer's camera to take a group photograph of Dédé, Jacques Hirsch, Lieutenant Colonel Blondel and Captain Tonkin, standing against a backdrop of the high country around the FFI headquarters.
5 Surviving SOE records confirm that in October 1944 SOE headquarters contacted their SIS (MI6) counterparts. They discovered that SIS had supposedly dropped this money on 3rd July to one of their agents south of Limoges. Clearly, the aircraft had been off track and had mistaken Dédé's reception lights for its target. On learning this, SOE swiftly repaid the sum to the SIS coffers.

## Chapter 12

1 See *Das Reich* by Max Hastings.
2 The short 35mm film of this attack is today held by the Imperial War Museum in London and is available for public viewing by prior appointment.
3 Later Air Vice-Marshal Sir Alan Boxer KCVO CB DSO DFC, died 1998.

## Chapter 13

1 Another airfield also then in use for regular Dakota flights was La Martinerie at Châteauroux, Dédé's former Priority A target. Occupied by the FFI on 20 August after the Germans had abandoned it, the airfield had been reported as ready for use four days later; the same day two USAAF aircraft landed to refuel.

## Chapter 14

1 A few pockets of isolated German resistance remained, some to the end of the war.
2 See Appendix 4.
3 National Archives, Kew, England ref: HS9/976/9.
4 SOE's recommendation for the award, nort entirely accurate, but erring in favour of Dédé's reputation, remains on his personal file at the National Archives, Kew, England ref: HS9/976/9.

## Chapter 15

1 From 1948 (until his death in 1961), the President of Air France was Max Hymans, an important SOE helper in the Châteauroux area from the very first operations in 1941.
2 In 1992 the island further developed its national identity by becoming an independent republic within the British Commonwealth.
3 Dédé also set up the Transcontinents travel agencies in Madagascar and Réunion.
4 Post-war, David Surrey Dane had shortened his family name to simply Dane.
5 See Chapters 16 and 17 for further details of the memorial and the SAS group.
6 It was later discovered that the mystery Belgian had 'borrowed' the identity of a brother officer he had known in Phantom. It must therefore be stressed that Sadoine was not the Belgian's real name and that the other Phantom officer, Captain John Sadoine, served loyally.
7 Colo was knighted as Sir Louis Pierre René Maingard in the Queen's New Year's Honours list of 1 January 1982, for services to shipping and industrial development.

## Chapter 16

1 Before being released by the War Office, Bellasis had become a German POW camp, from where, late in the war, SOE recruited anti-Nazi agents to operate in Germany.

## Chapter 17

1 See Chapter 16.
2 See Chapter 7.
3 Eliane Plewman was awarded a posthumous Croix de Guerre by the French government, but did not receive the MBE from the British, despite her file showing that she was recommended for such an award.
4 The George Cross ranks equal to the Victoria Cross. Violette did not qualify for the latter as she was deemed not to have been engaged in formal military action.

# Appendix 1

# Sources and Bibliography

## Sources

**GENERAL**

Correspondence with (the late) Gervase Cowell MBE, and Duncan Stuart CMG, successively former SOE Advisors to the British Government's Foreign and Commonwealth Office, London, England.

Personal interviews (conducted by the author, Tony Kemp or Alain Antelme):

Alain Antelme, UK and Mauritius, 2000–2004
Pearl Cornioley, France, 2003
Véronique Dalais and Louis-Réné Dalais, France, 2003
Jean-François Maurel, France, 2003
(The late) Jean Larcher, Mauritius 2001–2005
Sir Harry Tirvengadum, Mauritius 2001
(The late) Sir René Maingard, Mauritius 2001–2005
(The late) Pierre Hirsch, France 2003

*Business Magazine*, Mauritius, 23 July 2003.

www.intnet.mu – news and information service for Mauritius.

www.memorial-genweb.org – French genealogical and memorial website.

'The Jedburghs: A Short History' (unpublished) by Arthur Brown.

'The Geneology of the Maingard Family' (unpublished) by Veronique Dalais via Louis R. Dalais.

## ARCHIVES

Community Archives of Châteauroux, France (Archivist Jean-Louis Cirès): photographs; extracts from the book by Michel Jouhanneau, *Mémoire d'une époque. Indre 1940-1944*, published 1995; notes from Maurice Nicault, Resistance historian.

Archives Service, Tarbes, France (Archivist Sandrine Braun): extracts and photographs from *Résistance en Bigorre* by Maurice Bénézech; municipal records and documentation.

Musée d'Eguzon, Indre, France: photographs and conversations.

National Archives (Public Record Office), Kew, Surrey, England:

AIR 27/956 – Operations Record Book of 138 (Special Duties) Squadron
HS1/82 – interview of Major Maingard for Far East duties
HS6/515 – debriefing of Major Maingard by Major Angelo, 14 November
    1944, and final report of Major Maingard after second mission
HS6/526 – operational report of Jedburgh team HUGH
HS6/527 – operational report of Jedburgh team IAN
HS6/569 – report of Lieutenant Jacques Dufour to SOE F Section
HS 6/572 – debriefing of Jacques and Pierre Hirsch
HS6/579 – report by Squadron Leader Maurice Southgate
HS 6/587 and HS 6/568 – report by Flight Officer Pearl Witherington

SOE Personnel files:

HS9/976/9 Major Amédée Maingard
HS9/1395/3 Squadron Leader Maurice Southgate
HS9/1089/4 Lieutenant Jacqueline Nearne
HS9/293/5 Auguste Chantraine
HS9/1011/4 Lieutenant J. Andy Mayer
HS9/1195/1 Ensign Eliane Plewman
HS9/1238/1 Captain Charles Rechenmann
HS9/1240/3 Captain Harry Rée
HS9/1331/1 Lieutenant Alexandre Schwatschko (aka A. Shaw)
HS9/1568/1 Major Valentine Whitty

# Bibliography

FRENCH LANGUAGE

*Armée Secrète dans les F.F.I.* by Jacques Blanchard. Published F. Mathieu, France 1993. ISBN 2-9506436-1-2.

*Un Canadien Derrière Les Lignes Ennemies* by Judge Allyre L. Sirois. Les Éditions Louis Riel, Regina, Canada 1991. ISBN 2-921385-00-7; 0-920859-20-8.

*Hommes et Combats en Poitou 1939–1945* by Roger Picard. Éditions Martelle, Amiens, France 1994.

*Île Maurice, memoires de couleur* by Claude Pavard. Oasis Productions, Sèvres, France 1994. ISBN 2-9508687-0-3.

*L'Indre sous l'occupation allemande 1940–1944* by Sébastian Dallot. Éditions Gérard Tisserand, Clermont-Ferrand. 2001 ISBN 2-84494-058-7.

*Missions Secrètes et Déportations 1939–1945* by Bob Sheppard. Éditions Heimdal, Bayeux 1998. ISBN 2-84048-111-1.

*Pauline* by Pearl Cornioley. Éditions Par Exemple 1996.

*Résistance Indre et Vallée du Cher* by Georgette Guéguen-Dreyfus. Éditions Sociales, Paris 1970.

*La Vienne dans la Guerre 1939–1945* by Roger Picard. Éditions Gérard Tisserand, Clermont-Ferrand 2001. ISBN 2-84494-088-9

*La Vienne pendant la Seconde Guerre Mondiale 1944, Tome 3* by Gaston Racault. C.R.D.P. de Poitiers 1986.

ENGLISH LANGUAGE

*Accidental Agent* by John Goldsmith. Leo Cooper, London 1971. ISBN 0-85052-0371.

*Agents by Moonlight* by Freddie Clark. Tempus Publishing Ltd., Stroud, England 1999. ISBN 0-7524-1691-X.

*Amateur Agent* by E. Butler. Harrap and Co. Ltd., London 1963.

*Aristide – Warlord of the Resistance* by David Nicholson, Leo Cooper, London 1994. ISBN 0-85052-365-6.

*Beaulieu: The Finishing School for Secret Agents* by Cyril Cunningham. Leo Cooper, Barnsley, England 1998. ISBN 0-85052-598-5.

*Behind the Lines* by Russell Miller. Secker and Warburg, London 2002. ISBN 0-436-20534-3.

*Between Silk and Cyanide – a Codemaker's War 1941–1945* by Leo Marks. HarperCollins, London 1999. ISBN 0-00-653063-X.

*Das Reich* by Max Hastings. Papermac, London 1993. ISBN 0-333-59150-X.

*Das Reich* by Philip Vickers. Pen and Sword, Barnsley, England 2000. ISBN 0-82052-699-X.

*Dunsfold – Surrey's Most Secret Airfield* by Paul McCue. Air Research Publications, New Malden, England 1992. ISBN 1-871187-12-5.

*Flames in the Field* by Rita Kramer. Penguin Books, London 1996. ISBN 0-14-024423-9.

*Flight Most Secret* by Gibb McCall. William Kimber, London 1981. ISBN 0-7183-0038-6.

*F Section SOE* by Marcel Ruby. Grafton, London 1990. ISBN 0-586-20697-3.

*Gubbins and SOE* by Peter Wilkinson and Joan Bright Astley. Pen and Sword, Barnsley, England 1997. ISBN 0-85052-556-X.

*Hitler's Generals.* Edited by Correlli Barnett. George Weidenfeld & Nicolson Ltd, London 1990. ISBN 0-297-82054-0.

*In Search of the Maquis* by H.R. Kedward. Oxford University Press 1993. ISBN 0-19-820578-3.

*Inside SOE* by E.H. Cookridge. Arthur Baker Ltd, London 1966.

*Jacqueline* by Stella King. Arms and Armour Press, London 1989. ISBN 1-85409-009-7.

*Knights of the Floating Silk* by George Langelaan. Hutchinson, London 1959.

*Leaves of Buchenwald* (the poetry of Maurice Pertschuk). Editions Le Capuchin, Lectoure, 2003. ISBN 2-913493-45-9.

*A Life in Secrets* by Sarah Helm. Little, Brown, London 2005. ISBN 0-316-72497-1.

*Maquis* by George Millar. Cassell, London 2003. ISBN 0-304-36543-2.

*Mission Improbable* by Beryl E. Escott. Patrick Stephens Ltd., Sparkford, England 1991. ISBN 1-85260-289-9.

*Moondrop to Gascony* by Anne-Marie Walters. Pan Books Ltd., London 1955.

*Moon Squadron* by Jerrard Tickle. Wingate, London 1956.

*Nancy Wake* by Russell Braddon. Cassell and Co. Ltd., London 1956.

*Nancy Wake* by Peter Fitzsimmons. HarperCollins, London 2002. ISBN 0-00-714401-6.

*The Next Moon* by André Hue. Penguin Viking, London 2004. ISBN 0-670-91478-9.

*No Cloak, No Dagger* by Benjamin Cowburn. Jarrolds Publishers (London) Ltd., 1960.

*Odette* by Jerrard Tickle. Chapman and Hall, London 1949.

*Of Their Own Choice* by Peter Churchill. Hodder and Stoughton Ltd., London 1952.

*A Quiet Courage* by Liane Jones. Corgi Books, London 1990. ISBN 0-552-99435-9.

*Rake's Progress* by Dennis Rake. Leslie Frewin, London 1990. ISBN 09-087580-X.

*SAS Operation Bulbasket* by Paul McCue. Leo Cooper, London/Pen and Sword, Barnsley, England 1996. ISBN 0-85052-534-9.

*Secret Agent* by David Stafford. BBC Worldwide Ltd., London 2000. ISBN 0-563-48811-5.

*The Secret History of SOE 1940–1945* by W.J.M. Mackenzie. St. Ermin's Press 2000. ISBN 0-9536151-8-9.

*Secret War* by Nigel West. Coronet, London 1992. ISBN 0-340-58029-1.

*Secret War Heroes* by Marcus Binney. Hodder and Stoughton, London 2005. ISBN 0-340-82909-5.

*SOE 1940–1946* by M.R.D. Foot. BBC, London 1985. ISBN 0-563-20193-2.

*SOE in France* by M.R.D. Foot. HMSO, London 1966.

*SOE – Recollections and Reflections 1940–1945* by J.G. Beevor. Bodley Head, London 1981. ISBN 0-370-30414-4.

*SOE Syllabus* by the Public Record Office. Kew, London 2001. ISBN 1-903365-18-X.

*Specially Employed* by M.J. Buckmaster. The Batchworth Press, London 1952.

*They Came From the Sky* by E.H. Cookridge. Heinemann, London 1965.

*They Fought Alone* by M.J. Buckmaster. Odhams Press Ltd., London 1958.

*Undercover Operator* by Sydney Hudson. Pen and Sword, Barnsley, England 2003. ISBN 0-85052-947-6.

*Undercover. The Men and Women of the SOE* by Patrick Howarth. Phoenix Press, London 2000. ISBN 1-84212-240-1.

*Violette Szabo* by Susan Ottaway. Leo Cooper/Pen and Sword, Barnsley, England 2002. ISBN 0-85052-780-5.

*Von Rundstedt* by G. Blumentritt. Odhams Press Ltd, London 1952.

*We Landed by Moonlight* by Hugh Verity. Crecy Publishing, Manchester, England 1978. ISBN 0-947554-75-0.

*The White Rabbit* by Bruce Marshall. Cassell, London 2000. ISBN 0-304-35697-2.

*Who Lived to See the Day* by Pierre de Vomécourt. Hutchinson, London 1961.

*The Women Who Lived For Danger* by Marcus Binney. Hodder and Stoughton, London 2002. ISBN 0-340-81839-5.

*Xavier* by Richard Heslop. Hart-Davis Ltd., London 1970. ISBN 246-63989-X.

# Appendix 2

# Code Names and False Identities

## SOE British-trained Personnel

Lieutenant Elisée Allard (served as Lieutenant Charles Montaigne): *Henrique.*

Major John Farmer: *Hubert.*

Lieutenant Pierre Geelen (served as Lieutenant Pierre Garde): *Pierre, Pierre Grandjean.*

Captain Donovan Jones: *Lime, Isidore.*

Lieutenant Marcel Leccia (served as Lieutenant Georges Louis): *Baudouin.*

Major Philippe Liewer (served as Major Charles Staunton): *Hamlet, Salesman.*

Major Amédée Maingard: *Shipwright, Samuel/Sam, Guy Marguery, Amédée Maingrot.*

Sergeant René Mathieu: *Manufacturer, Aimée, Roger Milhaud, René Marie Millou.*

Lieutenant Pierre Mattei: *Huntsman, Gaetan.*

Lieutenant (James) Andrew Mayer: *Sexton, Franck, Jacques André Mallet.*

Lieutenant Jacqueline Nearne: *Designer, Jacqueline, Josette Norville.*

Captain Brian Rafferty: *Michel, Dominique.*

Captain Charles Rechenmann: *Julien, Rover, Charles Raymond, Claude Rolland.*

Captain Harry Rée: *César, Henri.*

Lieutenant Alexandre Schwatschko (served as Lieutenant Alexandre Shaw): *Olive.*

Lieutenant Allyre Sirois: *Gustave.*

Squadron Leader Maurice Southgate: *Stationer, Philippe, Hector, Maurice Leblanc, Robert Moulin.*

Ensign Nancy Wake: *Witch, Hélène.*

Ensign Odette Wilen: *Sophie.*

Flight Officer Pearl Witherington: *Wrestler, Marie, Pauline, Madame Cornioley.*

## SOE LOCALLY-RECRUITED HELPERS

Pilar Alvarez: *Irene.*
P.L. Bergé: *Tutur, Adrien.*
Jacques Dufour: *Anastasie.*
Jacques Hirsch: *Artur, Arthur, Jacques d'Allemand, François.*
Jeanne Hirsch: *Nenette.*
Pierre Hirsch: *Popaul, Pierrot, Pierre d'Allemand, Pierre d'Hamblemont.*

## RESISTANCE/MAQUIS/FFI

Auguste Chantraine: *Octave, Octraine.*
Colonel R.F. Chêne: *Cyclamen, Bernard, Commandant/Colonel Bernard.*
Armand Mardon: *Le Vigneron.*
Camille Olivet: *La Chouette.*

# Comparison of Military Ranks
## (Officers)

| British Army | Armée Française | Wehrmacht | Waffen SS |
|---|---|---|---|
| Field Marshal | Maréchal | Generalfeldmarschall | — |
| — | Général de Groupe d'Armées | Generaloberst | SS-Oberstgruppenführer |
| General | Général d'Armée | General | SS-Obergruppenführer |
| Lieutenant General | Général de Corps d'Armée | Generalleutnant | SS-Gruppenführer |
| Major General | Général de Division | Generalmajor | SS-Brigadeführer |
| Brigadier | Général de Brigade | — | SS-Oberführer |
| Colonel | Colonel | Oberst | SS-Standartenführer |
| Lieutenant Colonel | Lieutenant Colonel | Oberstleutnant | SS-Obersturmbannführer |
| Major | Commandant | Major | SS-Sturmbannführer |
| Captain | Capitaine | Hauptmann | SS-Hauptsturmführer |
| Lieutenant | Lieutenant | Oberleutnant | SS-Obersturmführer |
| Second Lieutenant | Sous Lieutenant | Leutnant | SS-Untersturmführer |

# Appendix 4

# Debriefing of Major Maingard by Major Angelo, 14 November 1944

[Author's note – some measure of Dédé's reticence to speak of his active service can already be gauged in late 1944 during this formal SOE debriefing. The record of the interview is to be found in Britain's National Archives, file reference HS6/515.]

Mission
W/T operator to Hector

## 1. A. CLANDESTINE ACTIVITY PRE D-DAY

1. Arrival.
I was parachuted with one other person, supposedly to a reception committee. We landed three kilometres away in a wood. We waited for three-quarters of an hour for the reception committee but nobody came so we decided to hide about five kilometres away. We stayed hidden here in a small wood for two days after which I decided to go to the contact address which had been given to me in London in case of emergency. All went well and I was put in touch with the organisation.

The following morning we went to fetch the agent dropped with me and brought him back to the town. The day after this we left as the Germans were looking for others. I went to Châteauroux where Hector came to see me four days later.

2. Cover.
The cover story given me in London was of use for the first two months after which I had to change it. As regards papers, I obtained the necessary papers for my new cover story from a contact I made on the spot. The papers I had were entirely false and were not registered, although in October 1943 I was able to

obtain an identity card which was registered. I was once questioned by the Gestapo on the train on this cover story and after half-an-hour it was accepted. (I think that one reason why this cover story was accepted was because my age was 33. Had I been 23 they would have gone into it more closely).

3. Situation in the area.

At the end of my arrival, the FTP were more willing than others to carry out *Résistance* work although later on, in September and October, a great improvement all round was noticed. The impression was that most people would have liked to have helped, but to start with they were too fearful.

4. Organisation.

The organisation had only been going for about two months before my arrival and nothing much had been done because we had very few contacts. For details of the set-up of the organisation when it had developed, see attached scheme.

5. Recruits.

We had two contacts from London and these two gave us names of others and thus helped to build up the organisation. If a man was not recommended to us in the first place and we particularly wanted him we would always make full enquiries about him and then would send someone else to recruit him. A person sent to recruit a man would know him beforehand. The recruiting for the sabotage troops was always done by the heads of the groups themselves. We frequently made use of messages over the BBC for convincing people of our bona fides.

6. Training.

Technical training in the use of arms and explosives would be given out in the country on farms. Usually the section leaders would read the instructions and, with the help of pamphlets sent out, the tutor would pass information on to their men. A certain amount of security training would also be given to a new recruit, usually in the form of an informal chat either at home or out for a walk.

7. Pay.

Agents received money for expenses and, where they had no other means of livelihood, some sort of wage. In the Maquis groups the men were paid either individually or to the chief for the upkeep of the men in order to avoid having to steal food. The family or dependents of an agent who had to leave the country or who was arrested, were always looked after.

8. Security rules for the organisation.

In the case of indiscretion an agent was either dropped altogether, told to leave the country or area or, if it was something more serious as happened in one case, orders were given to have him shot.

9. Premises.
I lived in the same house for 10 months under my cover and at the same time carried out my clandestine activity from this house, including W/T work. The address of this house was only known to five people. I always had a number of safe houses, farms etc, to which I could have gone in case of emergency.

10. Internal communications.
Post. Never once used it because I considered it dangerous owing to the possibility of censorship and the possibility of being linked up with another person.
Telegrams. Used frequently and without any trouble.
Telephone. Never used it, too dangerous.
Couriers. Used extensively, women especially, under cover of visiting friends or going for food.
Cut-outs. Not used.
Boites-aux-lettres. Dead ones never used. Live ones we used quite a lot (waiters, proprietors of cafes etc.).
Rendezvous. Cafes were usually avoided and people almost always met in houses or at pre-arranged places out in the street.
Meetings with unknown persons. Descriptions were used but no passwords. For meetings we always had a fixed danger signal. Time limits for waiting at rendezvous and alternative rendezvous were always arranged.

11. External communications.
For the first 10 months I worked from the house where I lived and then moved to another house from which I worked for a month when a new W/T operator came out to take over from me. I never had reason to use guards during transmissions. Although there was direction finding in the area they never got on to me. I had a contact in the police who would have warned me if there had been any danger.
Communication between myself and the organiser was always through direct contact, either he came to my house or I went to his.
We were put into contact with a man running a courier line through Spain to Portugal and through him a number of reports were sent to London.
No other methods of external communication were in use.

12. Enemy counter-intelligence in the area.
Regular controls were found at railway stations and on trains. At Toulouse there was a regular control and baggage was searched. Nothing had been heard of informers. I was followed for a day and a half but nothing serious resulted from it. This was probably due to my having been seen with a man who had been arrested in the town.

13. Casualties.
Various arrests took place in the organisation. In a lot of cases they seem to have been due to one person having been arrested in the first place and probably giving names of others, but it was never quite clear how the first person came to be

arrested. The W/T operator who took over from me was arrested after a fortnight and it was not clear how this was unless he had been direction found. This, in turn, led to Hector's arrest.

14. Interrogations.
Nothing to report.

15. Operations.
See previous reports.

16. Reception Committees.
A large number of reception committees were organised in our area all of which, whether receiving personnel or material, went off very successfully.

## 1.B. CLANDESTINE ACTIVITY POST D-DAY

From February/March onwards I was chiefly concerned with the formation of Maquis. From this time up to D-Day we were preparing to carry out our D-Day target attacks, having been forbidden to attack before D-Day.

## 2. A. MAQUIS PRE D-DAY

In February there were only two Maquis camps proper, one was 20 strong and the other 300 strong. Apart from these two camps there were 5,000/6,000 *sedentaires*.
Recruits for the Maquis were carefully vetted and questioned before they were allowed to join. In this way a number of recruits were found to be trying to penetrate Maquis groups. As a result of this there was no serious penetration of the Maquis in this area.
Up to D-Day the clandestine organisation was in close contact with the Maquis and was being prepared to join the Maquis on D-Day. Maquis groups in my area all under control and relations were excellent.
I dealt with the supplying of arms to the Maquis. They were paid so that they could buy food and they had to supply their own clothing. (They were later supplied with army boots).

## 2. B. MAQUIS POST D-DAY.

The German forces in the area consisted largely of garrisons though later, in the Vienne district, the Germans came up from the south and frequently attacked the Maquis.
D-Day targets consisted chiefly of railways, telephone and electricity supplies. We blew up the bridges over the Vienne and the Gartemps.
We received four Jedburgh teams, one of which was sent down to the Charente. Night receptions operations continued on a greater scale again very successfully. Not the contents of one container was lost.

# Index

208